Orange Proverbs and Purple Parables

Orange Proverbs

and

Purple Parables

The Enterprise of Reading the
Holy Scriptures as Scripture

W. R. Brookman

WIPF & STOCK · Eugene, Oregon

ORANGE PROVERBS AND PURPLE PARABLES
The Enterprise of Reading the Holy Scriptures as Scripture

Wipf & Stock
An Imprint of Wipf and Stock Publishers
199 W. 8th Ave., Suite 3
Eugene, OR 97401

www.wipfandstock.com

ISBN 13: 978-1-4982-0947-2

Manufactured in the U.S.A.   05/18/2015

Table of Contents

Preface

I APOLOGIZE. CONTRARY TO the impression you may have had as a result of reading the title, this book is not specifically about proverbs; nor is it precisely about parables. It is, rather, about how one might better read the Holy Scriptures. It introduces ways of thinking and reading that will transform you into a deep, thoughtful, and sensitive reader of the Bible. I hope you are not terribly disappointed upon hearing this news. The title was not designed as a bait and switch to lure you into thinking that new, witty, and remarkable explanations for selected proverbs and parables would be the center of attention within this work. Rather, this book considers a noble enterprise, namely, reading the Holy Scriptures as scripture. It is about how one ought to go about that endeavor.

Are you an avid reader of the Bible? That is, in all fairness, a genuinely subjective question. Yet, it is a purposeful question that you really should cognitively try to answer right now. Are you an everyday reader of the Bible, or are you a more sporadic reader? Do you sit down with Holy Scriptures quite routinely? Do you dust off your Bible about once a month and read a little bit? According to a study that is now two decades old, Americans exhibit a huge range of practice when it comes to reading the Holy Scriptures.[1] While the study is a bit outdated, I suspect that an up-to-the-minute research survey would essentially duplicate the findings.

This book tangles with a considerable mix of discrete elements, and for that reason, classifying it may be a little difficult. In that sense, it will be a bit of an interdisciplinary romp through the coming pages. You will read about the Bible from several different angles. However, this work will

---

1. Gallup, *Role of the Bible*.

primarily explore issues from the realm of reading. This book aims to be a catalyst in your development as a thoughtful reader of the Holy Scriptures as scripture. On top of that, this book will hopefully play with your imaginative and integrative sense of mind by challenging you to consider different aspects of reading the Bible. In the end, the goal is for you to read the Holy Scriptures as scripture. While that phrase will be unpacked and closely examined in the coming chapters, you will see how this new style of encounter with the Bible will, in all likelihood, invigorate your love, respect, and awe for the Holy Scriptures.

At this point, one may well remark, "Of course I read the Holy Scriptures as scripture. I read the Bible, and I know it is scripture." However, if I may, let me suggest that there is a broad spectrum of engagement involved in reading the Bible as scripture. This spectrum encompasses one's view of Holy Scriptures. What are the presuppositions you hold concerning the Bible? How do those assumptions play out as you read the Holy Scriptures? That is, what is the affective nature of the Holy Text for you? How do you understand what the Bible is saying, and given that, how do you interpret that understanding? And finally, there is the issue of the consequences of reading the Holy Scriptures as scripture. Once we understand the text, we can maneuver to comprehend its meaning. As a meaning for the text is determined, we are then able to commence the leap from meaning to application. That journey is an exhilarating one, and it will pay rich dividends for you.

Without a doubt, Christian identity has an integral connection to the Holy Scriptures. That means, as noted by Stephen Fowl, that "to identify oneself as a Christian is, at the same time, to bring oneself into a particular sort of relationship to the Bible in which the Bible functions as a normative standard for faith and practice."[2]

An interesting example of that phenomenon considered in this book can be demonstrated from the circumstances in which Jesus told the parable of Good Samaritan. The scene opens with a question from a lawyer who, we are told by Luke, was trying to put Jesus to the test. At this point, before the telling of the parable and its subsequent punch line, one might speculate about the intent of the lawyer.[3] Was he attempting to lay a trap for Jesus by asking the question (with a sinister motive), or was he (more innocently) trying to simply assess the competence of Jesus? The key term, used

2. Fowl, *Engaging Scripture*, 3.
3. Kilgallen, "NOMIKOS."

by Luke (*ekpeirazōn*–ἐκπειράζων) is usually translated in Luke 10:25 as "to test," but it can carry either nuance. It could have either the sense of merely trying to sound out someone on an issue, or the connotation of entrapment or testing in a negative way (more commonly used) could be present in the use of this word. Among commentators, opinion on this point is split. Some opt for the lawyer being hostile to Jesus in posing his question while others see no sinister agenda in the question at all, but rather they think the lawyer, having heard a lot about Jesus, was sincerely attempting to size up the fellow.

However, in trying to create a test for Jesus, whether in a hostile or simply in an inquisitive sense, the guy really did ask one of the all-time great questions. The sharp lawyer queried, "What must I do to inherit eternal life?" Jesus, in response, had two remarkable questions himself. "What is written, and how do you read it?" Perhaps a better rendering of that second question would be, "how do you interpret what is written?" Then Jesus told the parable of the Good Samaritan. When the story concluded, Jesus asked the baited question, "Who acted like a neighbor?" The lawyer really only had one option to answer, and he replied, "The one who demonstrated mercy." I suspect there was a bit of a dramatic pause, and then Jesus said to the fellow, "Go and do likewise." Of course, there is the rub.

The text of Luke 10:25–37 sets up what might be thought of as a paradigm. The picture is one of 1) discovering what is written 2) coming to an understanding of what it means, and 3) implementing the message of the text into your life—acting out the essence of the text. Jesus wanted the lawyer, and everybody else standing around, to actually enact certain behaviors toward other people, to all people, just as the Samaritan did in the story. In the simplest sense, that is largely to what this book points. Yet, in order to follow through on this paradigm of discovering, understanding, and implementing, one needs to read the Holy Scriptures as scripture. Reading the Bible as if one were reading just any old thing, be it the newspaper, a novel, or a letter simply will not produce a deep, penetrating, and transformational reading of the Holy Scriptures.

The sad state of affairs is that even "where the Bible's authority is acknowledged in principle, many seem to have lost the art of reading it attentively and imaginatively."[4] Davis and Hays note that "even in more Bible-oriented churches, there is little acknowledgment of the fact that making good sense of the Bible and applying that sense wisely to our lives is

4. Davis and Hays, *Art of Reading Scripture*, xv.

a hard thing to do. The disciplines of attentiveness to the word do not come easily to us, accustomed as we are to user-friendly interfaces and instant gratification."[5]

Therefore, it is the enterprise of reading the Holy Scriptures as scripture that is the focus of this book. At this point, before diving into chapter 1, you should be notified and assured about something. There is a particular danger for me as the writer of this book. I am an academician who teaches biblical studies as my profession. As such, I am quite aware of the danger. Do not fret, however. I have been warned and advised with some sobering words by Thomas Merton.

> Curiously, the most serious religious people, or the most concerned scholars, those who constantly read the Bible as a matter of professional or pious duty, can often manage to evade a radically involved dialogue with the book they are questioning . . . Any serious reading of the Bible means personal involvement in it, not simply mental agreement with abstract propositions. And involvement is dangerous, because it lays one open to unforeseen conclusions.[6]

I do, sincerely, want you to know that I resolutely want to continuously engage a radically involved dialogue with the Bible. As you will see, to truly read the Holy Scriptures as scripture is an enterprise that demands such involvement. Therefore, let us take the plunge together (metaphorically speaking) into the realm of being deep readers who are constantly in dialogue with the Holy Scriptures.

5. Ibid.
6. Merton, *Opening the Bible*, 24–25.

Acknowledgments

WORKING WITH GREAT COLLEAGUES is a genuine pleasure, and a number of my compatriots helped me along in the production of this project. I wish to thank Desirée Libengood for her careful and engaging feedback on an early version of this manuscript. Also, many thanks to Phil Mayo, Katy Wehr, Allen Tennison, and Glen Menzies for their comments, corrections, and suggestions on particular chapters. I am, indeed, very appreciative of the collegial atmosphere at North Central University that makes it a fun place to work. Being around creative and engaging people like those mentioned above certainly added an air of inspiration in the writing of this book.

Above all, I want to thank my wife, Patty, whose proofreading and impressive talent for playing with words and language enabled her to make a very significant contribution to this work. By means of suggestions, insightful grammatical analysis, and her usual witty perspective on things, she added considerably to the quality what you are about to read. While no one has, as of yet, found a grammar gene, I seriously suspect that my Patty may well have one.

Abbreviations

AugStud	*Augustinian Studies*
CJ	*Classical Journal*
FC	*Fathers of the Church*, Washington, DC
GRBS	*Greek, Roman and Byzantine Studies*
HE	*Historia ecclesiastica*
JPT	*Journal of Pentecostal Theology*
JRS	*Journal of Roman Studies*
NTS	*New Testament Studies*
PG	*Patrologia Graeca*, edited by J. P. Migne
PL	*Patrologia Latina*, edited by J. P. Migne
SC	*Sources Chrétiennes*
StPat	*Studia patristica*

1

What's in a Title?

Ah, Shakespeare and Wittgenstein!

YOU PROBABLY REMEMBER JULIET's lines as she waxed eloquent in one of the better-known scenes in *Romeo and Juliet*. From the balcony she crooned,

> What's in a name? That which we call a rose
> By any other word would smell as sweet,
> So Romeo would, were he not Romeo call'd,
> Retain that dear perfection which he owes
> Without that title. Romeo, doff thy name,
> and for thy name, which is no part of thee,
> Take all myself.
>
> Act 2, scene 2

We recognize that Shakespeare, as the author, had Miss Capulet ask the famous question, and one intriguing aspect of the scene is how he had Juliet dabble in the realm of the philosophy of language when she uttered those words, "What's in a name?" There is an entire academic field of study known as the philosophy of language in which the boundary lines of philosophy, linguistics, and cognitive studies meld interestingly together. One of the major players in that field was a fellow with a rather catchy name—Ludwig Wittgenstein (1889–1951). He made his mark in the philosophy of language as he wrestled with the relationship between statements and reality. The concept of a *name* was very important to Wittgenstein. He argued that a name is what he called a "simple sign."[1] The word *rose* would be what Wittgenstein would consider a simple sign. He would agree with

---

1. Frascolla, *Understanding*, 57–59.

Juliet. Were the object we name a rose be named otherwise, the object would remain the same. In this case, for instance, its alluring fragrance or its bedazzling beauty would, most certainly, not change.

There are not too many people around who would argue the point that Shakespeare's writings supply more well-known and widely quoted phrases than any other English language author. Yet, there is a great propensity for people who operate within American popular culture to misquote or merely paraphrase thoughts or texts—even those of Shakespeare. Naturally, the true purists see that as desecrating "The Bard." Not being a Shakespearean purist, I must admit that I have tainted the language of the man a few times myself. I think it irritates the socks off my daughter, who is somewhat of a Shakespearean devotee. Of course, it is usually not by design or with malice that I, or for that matter anyone, would twist or pervert the near-sacred syntax of the guy. But I do remember the reaction I once received from my daughter when I said, "Discretion is the better part of valor." You would have thought I got caught swearing a blue streak. She threw me a glare that could have sunk a battleship. (I can't remember if that is the proper idiom or if I just mangled someone else's great line too.) Yet, the true Shakespearean purist knows that the line properly quoted is, "The better part of valor is discretion." That is what I mean by near-sacred syntax. After all, I had the words right; only the order was somewhat skewed. I allude to Juliet's line "What's in a name?" because I wish to commence this book with a couple of comments about its title.

Shakespeare and Wittgenstein lead us to consider that the naming of a thing, in this case the naming of a book, is of some importance. In English, one might ask the question, "What is the name of the book?" That is exactly equivalent to asking, "What is the title of the book?" The title of a book oftentimes carries significant weight behind it. That is, any given book having a flashy or witty title would probably outsell the same book saddled with less than a catchy title. I suspect any publisher could verify that hypothesis.

Yet, it is true that even if the title of a book were different, the book would, itself, remain the same. Remember, the rose would still be the same thing even were it not called a rose. In antiquity, however, books did not have flashy, market-driven titles. In fact, in the ancient world, written works usually did not have titles at all. As it has been noted with regard to the naming of ancient works, the "situation is complicated by the fact that the concept of a book title was not as well established in antiquity as it is today: ancient titles often seem not to go back to the authors themselves, and particularly at early periods works might have had no title at all (being known by their opening words)."[2]

As you will see in the next few pages, the books of the Bible are good examples of this phenomenon of the title of a book being taken from the first word or first few words of the written work.

Naming the Books of the Bible

Quick, can you name the first five books of the Bible? Everyone probably knows the title of the first book of the Bible, and as you mentally tried to list the first five books just now, the first word out of your brain was Genesis, right? But, did you know that Genesis was not the original title of the book in its earliest form? That is because *all* of the commonly used English titles for the first set of books in the Bible, i.e., Genesis, Exodus, Leviticus, Numbers, and Deuteronomy have come to us through a historical process, and none of the titles by which we now know those books were original to the work.

. In the case of the first five books, all of them are from a section of the Bible known as the Pentateuch, a Greek term (*pentateuchos*) meaning, literally, five cases or implements or containers.[3] The word, Pentateuch, does not actually occur in the Bible. This term may have originally referred to five boxes or cases in which separate scrolls may have been kept, but it also may very well be connected in some way to the fivefold division of

---

2. Dickey, *Ancient Greek Scholarship*, 129–30. A number of works address the history of ancient books (especially Greek and Latin works) with regards to how titles began to be used. Examples include Nachmanson, *Buchtitel*; Schubart, *Das Buch*; Turner, *Greek Manuscripts*; and Schröder, *Titel und Text*. For the issue of titles in New Testament studies see Metzger, *Canon of the New Testament*. For an interesting work geared for a popular audience on the topic of ancient libraries in which the development of titles is discussed see Casson, *Libraries*, especially chapters 1 and 2.

3. The earliest attestation of the word, "Pentateuch," appears to be in a letter from Ptolemy, a Valentianian gnostic, addressed to Flora. The original letter can be dated to perhaps AD 150–75, but it is extant only as a copy in Epiphanius's *Adversus Haereses*, (Against Heresies) which dates to about AD 375. The intriguing portion of the word is the second element, *teuchos*–τεῦχος. It has a range of meaning in Homeric Greek including: implements of war, armor, arms, harness, the gear or tackle of a ship. In those cases, it is usually in the plural form. Later, in the classical period it is used in the singular to mean a vessel of just about any type. For example, it is used of various categories of urns, e.g., a balloting urn, a cinerary or funeral urn, or just a generic jar or pot. Aristotle even used the term to refer to the human body. Thus, the original connection to the Torah is a bit of a mystery.

the first section of the Hebrew Bible or Old Testament, namely, the Torah. In English, that collection of five books is oftentimes referred to as the
Law. Those books were originally composed in Hebrew,[4] but they were all
translated into Greek in the third century BC. That translation, known as
the Septuagint, became very widely used as the Greek language flourished
throughout the Near East in the Hellenistic Period (333–63 BC).[5] Indeed,
the Septuagint was the version of the Scriptures commonly used by the
first several generations of Christians as New Testament writers quoted and
paraphrased widely from that Greek translation. When it comes to tracing
the titles for the various biblical books, one needs to appreciate the pan-
oramic view of change that took place as the text moved from its original
language (Hebrew) into the Greek language and then into Latin.

Thus, while Genesis was originally written in Hebrew, the ancient
Israelites and later post-exilic Jews did not call the book Genesis. Rather,
what originally became the title or the name of the book was the first Hebrew word on the scroll of that book (*Bereshit*–בראשית)[6] which usually is

4. Not all of the Old Testament was composed in Hebrew. Portions of the books of
Ezra (4:8–6:18; 7:12–26) and Dan (2:4b—7:28) were composed in Aramaic.

5. The Hellenistic Period is usually defined roughly as the period from the death of
Alexander the Great (323 BC) until the dominance of the Romans in the Levant. However, it is a bit of a subjective thing, and I would argue for dating the Hellenistic Period
from 333–63 BC. It was in 333 BC that Alexander crossed through the Cilician Gates
and thereafter engaged the Persian army under Darius III in battle at Issus. Prior to that
time, Alexander had been liberating Greek cities in Asia Minor. I like 63 BC as the end
date of the Hellenistic Period, not because it marks, in any way, the end or demise of
Greek life and culture in the Near East, but it is more of a convenient political boundary
marker. The Roman General Pompey captured Jerusalem in that year, and it is definitely
a Roman-run operation in Palestine from that point onward. Demarcating the end of
Hellenistic culture and its influence upon non-Greeks is a little difficult to tightly define.
For that reason, there is not a universal consensus on what constitutes the Hellenistic
Period.

6. Transliteration is a method of writing a word from a non-Roman alphabet, in this
case Hebrew, in Roman characters so that one may read the word somewhat phonetically
without knowing the Hebrew alphabet. There are various systems for transliterating Hebrew, and I am using the very simplest system here. For example, the first word of Genesis could also be transliterated as *bĕrē'šit* rather than the simpler *bereshit* that I employ.
However, in the more complex systems, one needs to know a variety of diacritical marks
in order to use the system. For example, one would need to know that *š* is equivalent to
the /sh/ sound in English. Or, one would need to understand that *ĕ* and *ē* represent two
different Hebrew vowels. Thus, the simplest system is the best to use for someone who
has no knowledge of Hebrew. Also, I have transliterated the Hebrew words here with a
capital letter since they are the *incipit* words of the book and therefore function as the
title. In addition, I have used the simplest method of transliterating Greek words. Some

translated with the majestic English phrase "In the beginning." This was a very common practice in the ancient world, widely used far beyond the Hebrew cultural sphere.

Known by the Latin word, *incipit*, the first word or phrase of a book or manuscript was used as the normal way of referring to texts in antiquity. Thus, the practice far preceded the Latin term that was later used to label it. In fact, the tradition of titling or labeling a work by its first word or phrase goes all the way back to Sumerian scribes in the third millennium BC who oftentimes used an *incipit* on clay tablets.

In the case of the Bible, as with just about any book from antiquity, the use of an *incipit* was the usual way of referring to a written work. Thus, for example, in the book of Exodus, the *incipit* used was actually the second word of the book (*Shemot*–שמות). That word translated literally means "names" as the opening line of the text of Exodus begins, "These are the names . . ." (Exod 1:1). The book of Leviticus was originally known to the Hebrews as *Vayyiqra* (ויקרא) which is literally the verb for "and he called" (Lev 1:1), and that is the first word of the text. In the case of the book of Numbers, the original *incipit* was actually the fifth word of the opening line of the book in Hebrew. The book commences, "Yahweh spoke to Moses in the wilderness . . ." (Num 1:1a). The fifth word of that opening phrase is the Hebrew word *Bemidbar* (במדבר) meaning "in the wilderness," and that word originally functioned as the *incipit*, the ancient title of the book.

Finally, that brings us to the last book of the Torah, which is known to us as Deuteronomy. This is an interesting case. It is the second Hebrew word (*Devarim*–דברים) of the opening of the book that became the earliest *incipit* for this work. The book begins, "These are the words that Moses spoke to all of Israel . . ." (Deut 1:1a). *Devarim* is the Hebrew word for "words," and it is that catch word or *incipit* by which the Israelites knew that book. Thus, when translated into English, a title based on the original Hebrew *incipit* might simply be rendered as *Words*, but we know it instead as Deuteronomy because of the historical process alluded to earlier.

When the text of Deuteronomy was translated into Greek and became a part of the Septuagint version, it started to be called *Deuteronomion* (δευτερονόμιον) which means "second or repeated law." This Greek word

---

systems employ a macron over certain letters to designate the quality of a vowel. In that way, a distinction in the transliteration may be made between long and short vowels. Thus one may see the difference, for instance, between long ω (omega) transliterated *ō* and short o (omicron) transliterated *o*. However, in this book both long and short Greek vowels are transliterated with the same character; no macrons are used.

actually comes, not from the opening of the book, but rather, from Deut 17:18 ("When he takes the throne of his kingdom, he should, himself, write on a scroll a copy of this law . . ."). Thus, what became the *incipit* for the Greek form of the last book of the Torah was not taken from the opening of the work, but rather from a word embedded in the middle of the text that captured the essence of what the work was, namely, a repeated form of the law.

So it was with the Greek forms of Exodus, Leviticus, and Numbers. Whereas originally the *incipit* was drawn from the Hebrew opening word or phrase, as the text moved into Greek, the *incipits* (with the exception of Genesis) were based on a characterization of the book, as in the case of Deuteronomy. Remember that the title of Exodus was originally "Names" (*Shemot*-שמות). The title of Leviticus was originally "and he called" (*Vayyiqra*-ויקרא), and Numbers was first known as "in the wilderness" (*Bemidbar*-במדבר). All of those titles changed when the Greek text became commonly used. The second book of the Torah became known by the Greek term *Exodos*. That literally means, "(the) road/way out." This title, naturally, related to the point of the book. It is the story of Israel's going out from Egypt. Likewise, Leviticus, originally known as "and he called" (*Vayyiqra*-ויקרא) became known as *Leuitikos* taken from the Greek word *leuitikon* meaning "levitical" or "concerning the Levites." This, of course, alludes to the content of the book. Later, centuries after Jesus, rabbis started to call the book "Instruction of the Priests," which also gave an overall sense of its content. The Greek name of the book of Numbers became *Arithmoi*. That was clearly drawn from the several censuses presented in the book (Num 1:2–46; 26:2–50).

Quae convertit cum Hieronymus
(Things turn with Jerome)

When it comes to talking about the names of the books of the Bible, things do take a turn with Jerome (ca. AD 345–420). Latin came to the forefront of things when in 382 Pope Damasus I recruited Jerome as his personal secretary and asked him to revise and standardize some already existing Old Latin versions of the Bible. In fact, there were, at the time, many variations among the Old Latin texts that were in circulation, and this caused some confusion. Even beyond that, the Old Latin versions that were around were, frankly, not very well done. That is, the quality of the translation in these Old Latin versions was lacking in eloquence and literary artistry. There is a great story from Augustine that illustrates this very nicely. You will meet Augustine more in depth in chapter 3, but for now, suffice it to say, he tells a story in his work, *The Confessions* (bk 3, ch 5), in which he described his reaction to reading the Scriptures in one of those early Old Latin versions. He said, "When I studied the Bible and compared it with Cicero's dignified prose, it seemed to me unworthy."[7] It is important to know that this is Augustine looking back on his pre-conversion life. At that stage in his life he was a seeker, and he took up reading the Bible simply to find out what the Scriptures were like. As a scholar who deeply admired the craft of using language eloquently and as one who was highly influenced by the artistry of Cicero's use of the Latin language, he was quite disappointed in the quality of the literary form of the Bible. The good news is that some years later he was dramatically converted, incidentally and somewhat ironically, by means of his reading the Bible. You will actually read a portion of Augustine's account of his conversion in chapter 3. So, in the end, things do turn out. Yet, at his first inquisitive look at the Scriptures, he was not impressed. Looking back after a number of years on that event, with the hindsight of a believer, he remarked that,

> At that time, though, I was in no state to enter, nor prepared to bow my head and accommodate myself to its ways. My approach then was quite different from the one I am suggesting now . . . My swollen pride recoiled from its style and my intelligence failed to penetrate to its inner meaning. Scripture is a reality that grows along with little children, but I disdained to be a little child and in my high and mighty arrogance regarded myself as grown up.[8]

Thus, Augustine essentially says, "Look, I was an arrogant, snot-nosed punk when I first read the Bible, and I didn't know the first thing about spiritual things at the time." Well anyway, that is my paraphrase of his sentiment. But things were about to change in regards to the Latin Bible as Jerome came on the scene.

Pope Damasus I desired a unified and updated Latin text to become the standard. He consequently drafted Jerome, a scholar's scholar, for the task of revising the text. Jerome was spectacularly well versed in the classics, and he had great breadth of learning. Yet, what Jerome started to produce was not simply a revision of the Old Latin text. Rather, as his work developed and evolved, Jerome commenced an essentially new translation in

7. Augustine, *Confessions*, 47.
8. Ibid.

Latin. For the Old Testament, his translation was drawn from the Hebrew texts rather than from the Greek Septuagint. That was a novel approach at the time, and it was not without controversy. Interestingly, some scholars hold that Jerome was not the only individual involved in the production of this new translation. Portions of the New Testament seem to have been the translation work of others.[9] Yet, this version became the standard form of the Bible for well over a thousand years, and Jerome was the only name associated with its creation. By about the year 1200 Jerome's translation had become known as the *versio vulgate* meaning the "universal or common translation." Subsequently, this version became known simply as the Vulgate. The influence of this translation is difficult to overvalue. This was *the* version of the Bible throughout the entire Middle Ages, and prior to the nineteenth century it was the basis for most modern Bible translations. Things did, indeed, turn with Jerome.

From the Vulgate version, the titles of some of the books of the Bible changed. Our commonly used titles in English are generally drawn from the Latin titles that became vogue as the influence of the Vulgate grew. Thus, our English spelling of Exodus and Leviticus is taken directly from Latin without any change. Numbers is taken from the Latin, *Numeri*. Remember that the Greek form of that book had been *Arithmoi*. The Vulgate used *Psalmi* in translating the Greek *Psalterion*, and of course, we get our English title, *Psalms*, from that. However, some English speakers still use the title, *The Psalter*, for this collection.

Therefore, it can be said that the naming of the books of the Bible was, indeed, a long historical process as the Old Testament was translated from Hebrew to Greek to Latin. Add to that the manner in which books came to be known in antiquity through the use of the *incipit*, and one can begin to appreciate more fully how the titles of the books yield a very interesting story. The titles, as we have come to know them in English, are originally drawn from the text itself, and it is, naturally, the various texts that come to be known to us as books.

There Is No End to the Making of Books

It is, of course, books we are talking about when we speak of the various compositions that became a part of the Bible. In antiquity, a book generally

---

9. See, for example, Metzger, *Text of the New Testament*, 76; Aland and Aland, *Text of the New Testament*, 188; Wegner, *Journey from Texts*, 252.

took the form of scrolls that had been attached end to end. Later, in the Roman period, wooden tablets that had been laced together also came into use. Known as a *codex*, this proved to be easier to use than a long scroll. Whereas scrolls were generally written on only one side, a codex was usually written on two sides. By the early Christian era, sheets of papyrus or leather parchment began to replace the wooden tablets. Such papyri and parchments were bound together, making a collection of writings much lighter and more manageable. Most of the early Christian documents surviving from the second and third centuries were constructed in the form of a codex.

In the Old Testament, the semantic range of the word for "book" (*sefer*–ספר) was quite broad. As stated by Solomon[10] (Eccl 12:12), there does not seem to be any end to the making of books, and the content of what was labeled as a book varied considerably. The Hebrew term was a borrowed cognate from the earlier Akkadian word, *sipru*, which may be regarded as any sort of written document, and it is best to think of the Hebrew term in that respect. In Gen 5:1 and Neh 7:5 a genealogical record is referred to as a book. Royal archives are called "the book of records, the annals" in Esth 6:2. The term can also designate such things as a letter (Jer 29:1), a legal document (Deut 44:1), a collection of law (Deut 28:1; Josh 1:8), or a royal decree (Esth 8:10). Thus in the Old Testament, there is great diversity in the content of what is called a book.

In the New Testament, the term *biblion* (βιβλίον) is used to refer to any scroll or book. Eventually, the plural, *biblia* (βιβλία), was used by Greek speaking Christians to stipulate the entire collection of books that became the Old and New Testaments, and the word *Bible* ultimately derives from this term through Latin. Paul asked Timothy (2 Tim 4:13) to bring him "the books" (τὰ βιβλία). He also asked him to fetch "the parchments" (*tas membranas*–τὰς μεμβράνας). This latter term is borrowed from Latin and can only have the meaning of parchment made from animal skin.

---

10. The traditional view of the rabbis was that Solomon was the author of Ecclesiastes. However, since about the time of Luther, many Protestant scholars have tended to date the book to a period considerably later than the time of King Solomon (tenth century BC). The title of the book, Ecclesiastes, is a Greek translation of the Hebrew *qohelet*–קהלת. The name of book (*the incipit*), in Hebrew is *Qohelet*, and that is oftentimes translated into English as "Preacher." While Solomon is not named in the text as the author, the rabbis' view was based on a straightforward reading of 1:1 where *qohelet* is in apposition to "son of David, king in Jerusalem."

Consequently, there is disagreement among commentators whether these two terms are synonymously used to refer to the Scriptures in this context.

Jerome referred to his Latin translation as the *biblioteca divina* which means the "divine library." Remember that it became known as the Vulgate much later, long after the time of Jerome. This would seem to be evidence of the Holy Scriptures having a sense of a collection of individual books at the time of Jerome (fifth century AD). Latin subsequently borrowed the Greek term, *biblia* (βιβλία) for "books." However, our understanding of the Bible as a single book takes shape in the 1200s when a subtle linguistic change in Latin had the singular feminine form (*biblia -ae*) being more and more commonly substituted for the plural neuter which happened also to be formed exactly the same in the nominative case (*biblia -orum*). Over time the plural form, "the books," was replaced with the "the Book" as the singular form became more commonplace within various European vernacular languages which borrowed the Latin form.[11] So it is that we have the "Bible."

Judging a Book by Its Cover

You have heard the old adage, "Don't judge a book by its cover." Yet, I am a person who has actually purchased a number of books after simply being attracted by the title on the cover. I like catchy titles, and a witty name for a book can go a long way toward endearing a reader to the work before even a word of chapter 1 has been read. Of course, a great title for a book by no means guarantees that it will be a great read. That is, while a title may be influential, it does not necessarily guarantee that a wonderful title will be followed by inspiring, artistic pages that weave a brilliant story or create a vivid, memorable experience in the mind of the reader.

Naturally, a common objective of a writer is to combine the title of the book and the body of work into an effective whole. Since a book is never separate from its title, the two are forever entwined. A piece of great literature is bound to its title—of course, so is lousy literature. In fact, I recently came across an interesting, little book with the title *Bizarre Books: A Compendium of Classic Oddities*. The back cover lauds it as "The most hilarious, off-the-wall collection of the wildest, weirdest real book titles, subtitles, and author names ever compiled." It is essentially a listing of books with weird, exotic, humorous, or ironic titles. For example, consider

11. Williams. "The Bible," 169.

the following authors' names and the double entendres created by the title they selected for their book:

Jane Arbor, *The Cypress Garden*, 1969

Aaron H. Axelrod, *Machine Tool Operation*, 1941

Geoff Carless, *Motorcycling for Beginners*, 1980

Raymond W. Dull, *Mathematics for Engineers*, 1926

Roger Grounds, *The Perfect Lawn*, 1974

Louis Lasagna, *Obesity: Causes, Consequences, and Treatment*, 1974

William W. Looney, *Anatomy of the Brain*, 1932

Anna Mews, *Care for Your Kitten*, 1986

Rev. E. E. D. Pepper, *Spices from the Lord's Garden*, 1895[12]

Also within this work is a compilation of titles from a wide array of books in various categories. For example, the authors cite a novel penned by George Hughes Hepworth published in 1881 by Harper & Bros. with the title, *!!!*. That is it; the title is three exclamation marks.[13] How does one even say that? I'm not quite sure how to cite it. Should those exclamation marks be in italics? That looks a little strange. Should there be a period after the three marks when I have that title at the end my sentence? That looks just plain wrong.

In the category of language learning books, they draw attention to *The New Guide of the Conversation in Portuguese and English in Two Parts* by Pedro Carolino, published in 1869. While the title is a little awkward, it is not outlandish. In this case, however, it is the material between the covers that is outlandish. Clearly, Pedro did not have a measure of fluency in English. In the preface to the second edition one finds the following (warning—you must read the next two paragraphs closely because, as a native English speaker, your eyes will play tricks on you).

> We were increasing this second edition with a phraseology, in the first part, and some familiar letters, anecdotes, idiotisms, proverbs, and to second a coin's index.

12. Ash and Lake, *Bizarre Books*, 24–36.
13. Ibid., 37.

The *Works* which we were conferring for this labour, found use us for nothing; but those what were publishing to Portugal, or out, they were almost all composed for some foreign, or for some national little aquainted in the spirit of both languages. It was resulting from that corelessness to rest these *Works* fill of imperfections, and anomalies of style; in spite of the infinite typographical faults which some times, invert the sense of the periods. It increase not to contain any of those *Works* the figured pronunciation of the English words, nor the prosodical accent in the portuguese: indispensable object whom wish to speak the English and Portuguese languages correctly.[14]

Well, that was a little difficult and frustrating to read, wasn't it? Can you imagine trying to learn English from that? As if that were not enough, below are some of the "familiar phrases" listed in Carolino's *Guide.*

Let us go on ours feet.

At which is this hat?

Dress your hairs.

Tell that do you will do.

It not rains. It thinders. It lightens.

I have trinked too much.

I have mind to vomit.[15]

Of course, a very common feature of language learning books is the dialogue where one encounters a typical conversation and one can practice a natural sounding conversation. Following is a portion of a dialogue in Carolino's book.

Dialogue #35—With a Bookseller

What is there in new's literature?

Little or almost nothing, it not appears any thing of note.

And yet one imprint many deal.

That is true; but what it is imprinted. Some new papers, pamphlets, and other ephemeral pieces; here is.

14. Ibid., 53–54.
15. Ibid., 55–56.

But why, you and another book seller, you does not to imprint some good works?[16]

One finds essentially the same thing with within the pages of Min
Hou and Lin Yutong's 1934 edition of *Correctly English in Hundred Days*.
Beyond that, one can even find the answer to those daunting theological
issues in works such as Richard Jack's *Mathematical Principle of Theology;
or, the Existence of God Geometrically Demonstrated* (1745), or R. L. Dione's
*God drives a Flying Saucer: Astounding Biblical Revelation that prove the
existence of UFOs and explain their spiritual significance to mankind* (1973),
or perhaps William Henry Henslowe's classic, *Beard Shaving, and the Common Use of the Razor, and Unnatural, Irrational, Unmanly, Ungodly and
Fatal Fashion Among Christians* (1847).[17]

What's in a Title?

Have you noticed after reading some of the titles above that all of a sudden
the title of the book you are holding in your hand does not seem all that
strange? Yet, the title of this book, *Orange Proverbs and Purple Parables*,
may still present itself as a bit of a mystery to you. True, it is a catchy title,
but what in the world is meant by those words? I suspect that you have never
heard of an orange proverb. Nor have you, in all likelihood, ever heard of a
purple parable. The meaning behind this rather enigmatic title will be carefully explained in chapter 2. First, however, I wish to draw attention to the
subtitle of this book, *The Enterprise of Reading the Holy Scriptures as Scripture*. This may, perhaps, also seem to be a bit of a curious phrase to you. At
the outset, I must admit, I did not coin the phrase, "reading the Scriptures
as Scripture." I wish I had. It is a great phrase that cleverly captures the essence of much of what this book is about. Rather, I have merely borrowed
this particular expression as a part of the subtitle. Gavin D'Costa in his
book *Theology in the Public Square* used the exact phrase.[18] Yet, D'Costa and
a few others who have employed the phrase generally use it in a different
sense than that which I am going to develop. I will, however, take credit for

16. Ibid., 56.

17. Ibid., 184–87.

18. D'Costa, *Theology*, 134. A few others using the phrase include: Paddison, *Scripture*, 135 and Möller, "Renewing," 166; John Barton, in his *Reading the Old Testament*,
also used the phrase but merely as a section heading when he discusses the work of
Brevard S. Childs and the issues of canon criticism.

adding the adjective "holy." Of course, I do not mean that in the sense of my being the first to employ the adjective holy in describing the Scriptures; most certainly, that is not the case. Rather, what it means is that I am not sure one can find elsewhere in English the exact phrase, "reading the Holy Scriptures as scripture," particularly as a part of a title. Yet, the word "holy," it would seem to me, is important, if not crucial, to communicating the fullest measure of how Christians ought to conceptualize the Scriptures.

It appears that the earliest uses of the word "holy" to describe the Scriptures are those instances by three contemporaries: Philo (20 BC—AD 50), Paul (died ca. AD 65), and Josephus (AD 37–100). Philo was a Hellenistic Jewish philosopher who used the phrase "The Holy Scriptures" (*ta hiera grammata*–τὰ ἱερὰ γράμματα)[19] which is exactly the same phrase used by Paul in 2 Tim 3:15 where he writes to his young coworker Timothy, "you have been acquainted with the holy writings which are able to instruct you for salvation through faith in Christ Jesus." Josephus, who wrote slightly after the others, used the phrase "holy books" (*hierōn bibliōn*–ἱερῶν βίβλων)[20] in referring to the Hebrew Scriptures.

While others have used the phrase, "reading the Scriptures as scripture," in a fleeting moment, I will use the phrase as a thematic contour throughout this book. That is, by the end of the book, I want that phrase to have some substantive meaning for you and actually function in your life. I want the phrase to work in such a way that your reading of the Holy Scriptures will be changed, transformed, altered because of the fact that you are reading the Bible as scripture. This book aims at a cognitive and spiritual reorientation from your present mode of reading. This book is for those who conscientiously read the Scriptures, but the design is to have you, in the end, not to be a mere reader of the texts. The goal is for you to read the Holy Scriptures as though they were scripture. It will be a new way of reading for you, and the practical working out of how one develops this new way of reading is what this book is really about.

Furthermore, with respect to the subtitle of this book, yet another question may arise. One might well inquire, what is meant by referring to the "enterprise" of reading the Scriptures? That particular word certainly conjures up the notion of a formidable undertaking. That is true because, after all, you are reading the Holy Scriptures! That *is* a formidable undertaking. Yet, the focus will not be merely reading the Bible, but rather, the thrust

---

19. In Philo's *De specialibus legibus* 2.159, 238 and *De vita contemplative* 28, 75, 78.

20. Josephus, *Contra Apionem* 1.1.

bad reputation—in some cases deservedly so. Too often Paul's comments on submission are taken out of context and portrayed as dominance of one person over the other. This common misconception ignores his original call to mutual submission (5:21) and becomes a one-sided discussion of male authority. This distorted definition misses the point of the Ephesians passage and makes a mockery of Lordship altogether.

The New Testament concept of submission is difficult for couples to grasp, because it flies in the face of contemporary insistence on privacy and individuality. Couples have become so engrossed in the pursuit of their own "rights" that it's difficult or impossible for them to think in terms of *us* in the relationship. Too many married individuals are interested in finding personal fulfillment, feeding individual needs, and maintaining self identity. They often see anything that forces them to give up personal rights and privileges as the enemy of their happiness. They monitor the value of their relationships by asking such questions as "What can the other person do to make me happy?" or "What am I getting out of this relationship?" The focus is on the individual and not the marriage partnership.

However, under the Lordship of Christ, each person is called to be other-focused. The apostle Paul does this in Eph. 5 by calling for mutual submission. Mutual submission means that both husband and wife must look at the relationship through the thoughts, values, needs, and desires of the other person. In speaking to the husband, Paul says that he should consider his wife's needs and desires as being the same as if they were his own. The wife is to submit in the same way to the needs of her husband, learning what he desires and needs and doing her best to fulfill them as allowed under the Lordship of Christ.

In this attitude of mutual submission, each spouse shows ultimate respect and love for the other. Each knows that he or she is valued, loved, and cared for by his or her spouse. Mutual submission also brings a couple into obedience to the Word of God, a crucial step toward bringing their marriage under the Lordship of Christ.

Mutual submission changes the way we relate to each other as children of God and shows the world that our relationship is truly different. When our relationship is brought into obedience to God, and the Holy Spirit fills us with all the fullness of God, we'll see significant changes in how we talk with each other, how we react toward each other, how we seek to understand each other, and how we live in an attitude of forgiveness toward each other. None of these can be done consistently without a holy submission to God and each other.

VITAL AREAS OF MUTUAL SUBMISSION

Conversation

When we submit to the Lordship of Christ, we must also bring conversation under His guidance. According to Paul, God would have us speak to each other in loving truthfulness. In Eph. 4:15 we are told to "[speak] the truth in love." Under the Lordship of Christ, couples would never intentionally and deliberately hurt the other with words.

Hurting his wife was clearly the motive of the young man who sat across from Jeanette and me in an evening counseling session. Both husband and wife were hurting from years of arguments and marital difficulties. Tearfully, the young woman shared some of the pain she had suffered in the relationship, some of which he was not even aware. As she spoke, we could see the red rising in his face until he looked as if he might explode, which he did. For the next several minutes he filled the room with accusations, vilifications, insults, with some curse words thrown in for good measure. At the end of his tirade, he topped it off with the statement "I'm just telling the truth."

In fact, he *was* telling the truth. Over the preceding several will be upon a way of reading the Holy Scriptures that is widely known as the spiritual reading of the text. Whereas Eugene Peterson speaks of this as an "art,"[21] I have selected to label it as an enterprise. I think we are both correct, and both terms aptly apply.

So why even use such a subtitle if it needs so much explanation? I use it because it is a very important concept, and the distinguishing features of *how* one reads the Scriptures is central to what this book is all about. This book examines some aspects of a very noble enterprise, namely, reading the Holy Scriptures as scripture. Note that this book is not meant to be a comprehensive look at the topic. Rather, this is an introductory sort of book that is designed for the relative novice and, perhaps, the veteran who needs a bit of a renewal or shakeup in their pattern of reading the Holy Scriptures. It is hoped that this book will get you thinking about some things that you have not thought about before. Hopefully, there will be a fair measure of enjoyment for you as you make your way through the following chapters and experiment with some of the new thoughts and perspectives you may encounter along the way. The life of the mind and the life of the spirit are exciting domains, and my prayer is that you will fitfully challenge both your mind and your spirit as you explore and work your way through the pages to come.

So it is that we Christian readers of the Bible have a task before us. We are to engage in this great enterprise of reading the Holy Scriptures with a certain sense about us, and that sense is carried on through a realization that "the term 'Holy Scripture' is to indicate the place occupied by the biblical texts in the revealing, sanctifying and inspiring acts of the triune God."[22]

Just What You Don't Want to Hear at this Point

At this point, you probably do not want to hear about a certain grammatical issue. I am sorry. I apologize, but I am not able to empathize with you on this point because I love it—grammar, that is. However, I am aware that many people do not like grammar. In fact, I get a sense from some of my students that they particularly loathe it—grammar that is, not me. Yet, I can understand loathing; after all, I rather loathe Brussels sprouts. Perhaps it is because many people have nightmarish recollections of an old, grade-school teacher, and that sets off memories of torturous grammar lessons.

21. Peterson, *Eat This Book*.
22. Webster, *Holy Scripture*, 8.

When I say old grade-school teacher, I mean *old*. I remember, Mrs. Weaver, my first-grade teacher. She was about eighty when I had her, and I think she taught about another twenty years after I passed through first grade. At least, that is *my* recollection. I know a school was named for her years after I entered adulthood. Okay, I may be in a minority when it comes to grammar, but it may be a large minority. It seems that people either love it, or hate it.

With that in mind, I think it is worth the moment to explain something you will be seeing throughout this book. You may have already noticed, as you were reading along, some aspects of capitalization that may be a bit confusing. This particularly involves the words: biblical, Bible, Scripture, and scripture. Being a bit of a grammarian at heart, I provided for you here a brief quotation from *The Society of Biblical Literature Handbook of Style*, which is used as a guide for publication in the professional field of biblical studies.

> In general, a word or phrase used as a title of the whole or a specific part of the Bible is capitalized: the name of a genre is not capitalized. Thus, any ancient and modern designation for the Bible, a book of the Bible, a division of the biblical canon (e.g., Pentateuch), or a discrete section of a biblical book (e.g., Primeval History) may be a proper noun and so capitalized.[23]

Note that when used as an adjective, biblical is not a proper noun, and it is not capitalized. The capitalization rule for Scripture/scripture also depends on the use of the word. When it clearly refers to the entire corpus, synonymous with Bible, the word is capitalized. I have used the phrase, reading the Holy Scriptures as scripture, a number of times, and you may have noticed the word is capitalized in the first instance but not in the second. The first use of the word points to the collection of texts, i.e., the Bible; it is, therefore, capitalized. The second use points to what that collection is—it is scripture. That is a descriptor of the collection, not the collection itself, and it is, therefore, not a proper noun. Yet, when used as the subtitle of the book, both words are capitalized (*The Enterprise of Reading the Holy Scriptures as Scripture*). Now, of course, the meaning of the word "scripture" as it is employed requires some explanation as that is the last piece of the puzzle to catching the full sense of the subtitle of this book. After all, everything hinges on our having a meeting of the minds concerning what is meant by that, and, of course, it is a little more complex than what you may initially think. Therefore, our unpacking of what it actually means that the

23. Alexander, *SBL Handbook*, 19.

Holy Scriptures are to be read as scripture will be more fully examined in chapter 4. See, that grammar point was not so painful, was it?

So, what's in a title, or in the case thus far, a subtitle? Plenty! This subtitle (*The Enterprise of Reading the Holy Scriptures as Scripture*) is packed with a composite of words and phrases that, as you read along in this book, should combine to generate a deep-seated desire within you to fulfill the primary reason for reading the Bible, namely to encounter God.

2

Orange and Purple Texts

Orange and Purple Where They Shouldn't Be

WHO EVER HEARD OF an orange proverb, and what is meant by a purple parable? These two phrases unveil a somewhat strange juxtaposition of words by the unusual linking of color and genre. A concept that is not demonstrated by these phrases is what is known as *collocation*. Collocation is the term used to label the result of linguistic forces at work in languages whereby words tend to occur in conjunction with other particular words. For example, take the phrase *green grass*. The words *green* and *grass* form a rather natural collocation since green is the semantic indicator of the natural color of grass. In that sense, it is a lexical pattern, and one expects to see certain words in close proximity to each other due to this phenomenon. This linguistic feature of collocation is present in all languages, and it is an aid in vocabulary learning if the learner is able to discern these natural lexical links. Thus, there is a well-known quote among linguists that comes from J. R. Firth. He was a famous professor at the University of London's School of African and Oriental Studies who, in the 1940s and 1950s, studied how the context of a word impacts its meaning. Firth's catchy saying is, "You shall know a word by the company it keeps."[1] This quip captures the notion of collocation in a wonderful way.

However, language is extremely complex. As one might expect, for the new language learner, it is not as simple as just mastering such natural collocations as a means for easily building a massive vocabulary in a target language. Consider, for example, the following sentence. John heard

---

1. Firth, *Papers*, 11.

nothing but white noise in the background. White noise is an example of what is known as a restricted collocation where, in a two-word phrase, the meaning of one of the words is restricted or unique to that particular phrase. If you do not know what white noise is, then you did not get this, but the gist is that white does not mean white in this restricted collocation. Think about meaning in the following sentence. Harold is a true blue blood. You would look quite in vain in a dictionary for the meaning of blue that it has in this phrase. Imagine a learner of English coming across this phrase for the first time. Yes, there is a bit of a blurring here between a phrase that is a restricted collocation and an idiom. However, here, the point is simply that certain words tend to cluster with certain other words.

Here is where orange proverbs and purple parables come into play. While the previous sentence is grammatically correct, it probably sounds a bit awkward to you. It just seems intuitively unnatural to a native English speaker. That is because the words, orange and purple, are violating their usual collocational preferences. Clearly, the adjective *orange* does not normally bind itself to the noun *proverbs*. In fact, this is, in all likelihood, the first time you have ever seen those two words together. The word *orange* teams much more naturally with pumpkin or sunset. Nowadays, it also links with the word *crush* because of the soft drink. If you are a Broncos fan, *orange crush* is also a natural collocation because of the Denver football team. The Orange Crush Company goes back to 1911, and the orange crush defense of the Denver Broncos dates back to the early 1970s. However, before the early twentieth century, one would probably not find any examples of the phrase *orange crush* in English.

Likewise, *purple* is not generally linked to the word *parables* as a collocation in English. *Purple parables*—it is a weird sounding phrase to a native speaker. Can you think of an English noun that would form a more natural collocation with purple? How about *purple prose*? Have you ever heard that expression? It is a fairly well-known phrase in literary studies.[2] *Purple prose* refers to language which is so over-the-top it draws undue attention to itself because of its extreme ornate, flowery, or embellished wording. A commonly cited example of *purple prose* is the first sentence penned by Edward Bulwer-Lytton in his 1830 novel entitled *Paul Clifford*. The famous sentence reads as follows. "It was a dark and stormy night; the rain fell in torrents—except at occasional intervals, when it was checked by a violent

2. The phrase, purple prose, seems to have originated with the Latin poet Horace (65–8 BC) in his work *Ars Poetica* (line 15).

gust of wind which swept up the streets (for it is in London that our scene lies), rattling along the housetops, and fiercely agitating the scanty flame of the lamps that struggled against the darkness."[3]

Purple flower would also be another good example of a natural collocation using purple. Or, how about *purple haze*? The example of purple haze is interesting. If you recognize the phrase as the title of a Jimi Hendrix song from 1967, you are probably about my age. If you recognize it from Dickens' *Great Expectations*, you are really good. I would say that you know your literature. Try this one—*purple rain*. Most people would connect that phrase in their mind with Prince's album by that title or with the 1984 movie in which the pop rocker starred. However, if you are a little older, you might recall a classic song entitled "Ventura Highway" by the group called America. That song has the phrase *purple rain* in the lyrics. The meaning of the phrase in the context of "Ventura Highway" referred to a restless feeling of boredom and irresponsibility.

Pondering Proverbs, Parables, and More

Hopefully, in the coming pages and chapters, this rather unusual teaming of words, *orange proverbs* and *purple parables*, will take on new significance for you. This strange framing of words should prove to spark for you some new ways of reading, thinking about, and enacting the Holy Scriptures. Such changes in the way you conceptualize and actualize the Scriptures will greatly enhance a lifestyle that is focused upon following the ways of Jesus. The notion of proverbs and parables would seem to be clear enough, at least for the moment, as even the novice in reading the Bible has heard of these terms and probably has a basic sense of their distinctive features.

Proverbs, of course, are very powerful cultural elements. They are short, oftentimes witty, sayings that encapsulate in a concise way a piece of moral or societal wisdom. Proverbs are commonly learned at an early age within each distinctive cultural milieu. That is, for the most part, American kids learn American proverbs, Somali kids learn Somali proverbs, and kids from China learn Chinese proverbs. You most likely heard, as a youngster, proverbs like, "God helps those who help themselves," or "A penny saved is a penny earned." These are classic American proverbs credited to Benjamin Franklin. Many people will probably think of the book of Proverbs in the Old Testament when someone mentions the word, and to be sure, that is

3. Bulwer-Lytton, *Paul Clifford*, 17.

the quintessential collection within the Scriptures of this very important genre of wisdom. Ah, wisdom! Now there is a thing worth seeking. This notion was captured well by Hugh of Saint Victor who, in the twelfth century, penned a work called the *Didascalicon*. It was designed by Hugh to function as an elementary introduction to the Christian life, and the opening line reads in part, *Omnium expetendorun prima est sapientia*—"Of all things to be sought, the first is Wisdom."[4]

The Bible paints a crystal clear picture of the value of wisdom. It is more precious than rubies. Nothing you can think of can compare to it (Prov 8:11). The astounding thing is, "God possesses it and, we are taught, it can be ours as well."[5] Therefore, at least as a starting place, let us agree that there may be something very worthwhile in experimenting with ways in which we can better conceptualize and apply to our life the nuggets of wisdom found in biblical proverbs.

The same may well be said of parables. I would hazard to say that the vast majority of the general public knows what a parable is. I would also think that the majority has heard of the parable of the Good Samaritan. Yet that parable, while widely known and broadly understood, is way too rarely practiced in the lives of people. While many have heard of the parable and may even understand the teaching point Jesus made about it, they oftentimes do not live out or actualize the essence of the parable. In the world of everyday human relations, the parable of the Good Samaritan is often perceived as good theory, but it is not commonly a realized practice.

There you have it—proverbs and parables. They are a couple of the basic building blocks in the collective structure known as the Bible. Granted, you may already understand the distinctive nature of proverbs. You may even truly get the idea of parables. Yet, I wonder if there is not some way that you and I could more effectively take what we have in the Bible and put it into practice as the people of God. Moving from theory to practice in anything is a challenge, but isn't it a grand experiment to ingest what we are given in God's Word and actually be transformed as a result of that nourishment? That is one of the goals here. It is in that direction that this book will attempt to nudge you.

First, however, there is a need to set the stage for the coming chapters by bringing into focus the metaphor that is the very foundation of this book. Our two unusual phrases, orange proverbs and purple parables,

4. Taylor, *Didascalicon*, 46. See also Illich, *Vineyard*, 7.

5. Fox, *Proverbs*, 3.

may suggest that an investigation of those two biblical genres will form the framework of this project. However, that is not the case. Those two genres merely set up the metaphor that will lead us down a path to reading the Holy Scriptures differently than we have done in the past. Rather than just considering some proverbs and a few parables, the discussion in this book will be of some larger issues. The focus will be on how one might better read the Bible in order to comprehend more fully and accurately the disclosures about himself that God is, most assuredly, giving us in the Holy Scriptures.

However, because the unique juxtaposition of color and genre produces an almost unsettling uncertainty of what is actually meant, the initial task at hand is to explore the concept underlying this strange pairing of words (orange proverbs and purple parables) as a means of thinking about and processing the words of the Holy Scriptures.

Adele or Chomsky?

As we know, language is unbelievably complex. Yet, the paradox is that language is child's play. Kids learn language naturally and easily. Yet, language is much more complex than rocket science. Just think of it, kids, when they create a sentence, are doing higher level cognitive things than the scientist who calculates what the escape velocity from the Earth is for a given rocket. First of all, language is truly infinite, for, as a fellow by the name of Noam Chomsky pointed out, it is generative. That is, we can generate, or create, new phrases or sentences that have never before been uttered by any human being, and they will be understandable. Consider the following sentence. "Daniel Boone decided to become a pioneer because he dreamed of pigeon-toed giraffes and cross-eyed elephants dancing in pink skirts and green berets on the wind-swept plains of the Midwest."[6] While it is a strange sentence, it is grammatically correct and understandable. That is why it is a fairly well-known example of Chomsky's point about language being generative. But, who is this guy Chomsky, and what in the world is that stupid sentence about Daniel Boone doing in this book?

If you are not familiar with Chomsky, you should be. Why? Simply put, he may well be the most famous person you have never heard of. Now, to be sure, there are different ways of measuring fame. I confess that there are many famous people with whom I am not familiar. Many of the famous people I don't know happen to come from the entertainment world. Thus,

6. Fromkin and Rodman, *Language*, 4.

while millions of Americans knew the name, I must confess, I really did not know who Lady Gaga was for the longest time. However, I have been enlightened, and I can now regrettably say that, as of the writing of this chapter, I do know who Lady Gaga is. Another example of my ignorance of famous people could be drawn from the popular television series *Dancing with the Stars*. I do not think I have ever endured a complete episode, but I have seen their promotional ads when they announce who the stars will be for the next season. Generally, I end up mouthing, with a pained expression on my face, "Who are those people?" I usually do not know the stars; I have never heard of those people. Thus, were there one, I would undoubtedly flunk the test on American popular culture.

I had somewhat the same thing going on in a class a few years ago. A student was listening to some music before class one day, and as I walked into the room, I asked him about it.

I queried, "What are you listening to?" (Yes, I know I dangled my preposition.)

"Adele," he replied—seemingly without missing a beat as his left arm was swaying to some rhythm heard only in his headphones. I put my hands up in the air in a clear gesture of total ignorance. I had no idea if Adele were a band, a woman, or the name of a song. I mouthed the words, "I've never heard of Adele." The student read my lips perfectly.

"Are you kidding me?" He was clearly taken aback by this professor's blatant cultural gaffe of not knowing Adele. Since it is difficult to express tone in the written word, let me just flat out tell you. It was a very sarcastic sounding, "Are you kidding me?" He clearly was startled and somewhat insulted, I think, that there was someone on the planet who did not know about Adele.

"No, tell me about Adele." I thought I would try to take on the role of an inquisitive crosscultural learner rather than that of an ignorant buffoon. So it was that I learned a little about Adele that day.

Now, I am not going to get into a debate here over who is more famous, Chomsky or Adele. After all, Adele is an entertainment star who evidently has sold a bazillion copies of her songs. It would be tough to argue against that. And then there is Chomsky, a linguist. It would seem to be, clearly, a mismatch in a "Who is more famous?" contest. In light of all this, why would I even suggest that Chomsky may be the most famous person you have never heard of before? Believe it or not, there is a rationale to offering up a linguist as the most famous person you have never heard of in your life.

A few years ago, the Institute of Scientific Information completed an interesting study in which they calculated the most often cited or quoted people in all of literature throughout history. As you might expect, all the big names were on the top-ten list. Shakespeare, Aristotle, Marx, the Bible, and Plato were all listed among the top-ten most-cited authors or sources. But then, there at number eight, was Noam Chomsky, the linguist. He is the most-quoted living person on the list, and he is in his early 80s as of the writing of this chapter.

I actually attended a lecture given by Chomsky once. In early 1991, I was teaching as an Andrew W. Mellon Faculty Fellow at Harvard University, and the First Gulf War had just started. Chomsky was a longtime social/political activist who widely and loudly criticized American foreign policy. I certainly was aware of his reputation in that arena in addition to his fame as a linguist. I saw on a flyer that he was going to speak at a Unitarian church in Boston one evening shortly after the outbreak of the war. I went to hear him—not so much to hear his message but simply to hear how he spoke in public. He was okay, but it was nothing flashy. He reminded me of Woody Allen except that he was not funny.

So it is that Chomsky's role in my writing this book is that of providing some grist for the mill. As you will see, this work will end up touching on a number of arenas, fields, and disciplines as we explore the world of reading the Holy Scriptures as scripture. Language plays a huge role in this enterprise, and my interest in language has been bolstered by some very influential linguists over the years.[7] Of course, the Holy Scriptures employ language; hence, the nature and use of language is a key element in any discussion on the reading of the Bible.

When 5 + 2 = Yellow

Naturally, one normally thinks that the title of a book might offer some sort of clue to its contents. However, the title of this book might still be a bit of

7. Noam Chomsky, Steven Pinker, and George Lakoff have certainly influenced the way I think about language generally. John Searle (Speech-Acts), Benjamin Whorf and Edward Sapir (language relativity), and Harvey Sarles (language and human nature) have added greatly to the way I conceptualize certain aspects of language. I actually took my first anthropological linguistics class as a first-year graduate student from Sarles way back in 1976, and he certainly piqued my interest and curiosity in all things language related.

a mystery for you. Actually, the framing of the title for this project was inspired by the existence of a very peculiar neurological condition about which I have, of late, become quite intrigued. However, I want to be clear from the outset that I do not have this condition. Rather, I am merely appropriating it as a metaphor within this book because of its extreme novelty and vivid imagery. First, let me describe a little about this rather curious neurological phenomenon called synesthesia, and then I will explain how the condition provides the metaphor behind the title and premise of this book.

In his startling work, *Wednesday is Indigo Blue: Discovering the Brain of Synesthesia*, Richard E. Cytowic presents an intoxicating look at an incredibly fascinating condition known as synesthesia. This very bizarre, neurologically based condition is one in which two or more senses in the afflicted individual, who is called a synesthete, are triggered or linked together. The word *synesthesia* is derived from the Greek words *syn* (σύν) meaning "together," and *aisthēsis* (αἴσθησις) meaning "sensation." Synesthesia is, thus, a bringing together or blending of senses. Of course, the better-known, related word is anesthesia, meaning "no sensation." Anyone who has ever been to the dentist fully appreciates that word and the concept (being without sensation) that is behind it. But what is meant by the blending or linking of senses that one finds in synesthesia? Strange as it may sound, there are some people (synesthetes) who experience musical notes as color or who may taste sounds. Some experience sounds as smells, and others may know days of the weeks as colors. While there are many documented variations of how synesthesia may be manifested, I am sure that just a couple of examples will suffice to grab your attention.[8]

What would you think of the following equation: $5 + 2 = 7$? Well, you would probably think nothing of it, right? That is the normal way you experience numbers, and $5 + 2 = 7$ is nothing out of the ordinary for you. There is nothing unusual or peculiar about it. However, what if you saw the equation as $5 + 2 =$ yellow? That does not quite make sense to you, does it? Yet, some synesthetes perceive numbers as colors, and for them, there is no escaping the link.

---

8. Campen, *Hidden Sense*, 131. For example, at least forty-five variations of types of synesthesia have been documented including: grapheme (letters, numbers, syllables, or words)/colors, time unit/colors, vision/taste, smells/sound, musical notes/colors, musical notes/taste, lexeme/taste, and many more. The most commonly reported types are: letters/colors, time units/colors, musical sounds/colors, general sounds/colors.

A recent experiment at the University of Waterloo in Ontario, Canada, indicates that for colored-number synesthetes, there is no thinking about numbers without perceiving their colors. In the experiment, Professors Michael Dixon and Philip Merikle, assisted by their graduate student Daniel Smilek, found that just presenting an equation such as 5 + 2 = was enough to evoke an experience of yellow for their subject, C., a colored-number synesthete whose synesthetic response for 7 is yellow. She did not first have to see the number 7 written out or hear it spoken in order to have her colored-number response. Rather, simply being presented with something that would induce the thought of the number, such as an arithmetical equation, was sufficient to induce the synesthetic response.[9]

While many synesthetes perceive numbers as colors, the fact is, they all see those numbers as different colors. That is, not all synesthetes see 7 as yellow like the subject in the experiment described above did. They may see 7 as light green or camel brown or vivid purple. There does not seem to be any rhyme or reason for why they see the color they do. However, whatever the color they do experience as 7, it will remain with them for a lifetime. If 7 is mauve for the individual as a child, it will be mauve for that person the remainder of her or his life. In this bizarre world of synesthesia, females dominate. A Cambridge University study put the ratio of female to male synesthetes at 6:1 as it seems most likely that the trait is passed from father to daughter through the X chromosome.[10]

As you read along, you will discover that the word *disorder* is probably not the proper word for this condition. Neither, I think, is malady, illness, or disease the correct way to label it. Researchers have found that the most common variant of the condition is individuals who perceive colored days. For instance, Thursday may be perceived by the individual as light green.[11]

Patricia Lynne Duffy is a synesthete who wrote a wonderful book entitled, *Blue Cats and Chartreuse Kittens: How Synesthetes Color Their Worlds*. In it, she tells about her experience of growing up with synesthesia and how she and her father finally discovered that something was amiss. One day in the kitchen, she was learning how to write the letters of the alphabet, and she realized all she had to do to change a "P" to an "R" was to draw a line down from its loop. As she recalled,

9. Duffy, *Blue Cats*, 71.

10. Ibid., 26.

11 Simner et al., "Synaesthesia," 1024–33.

And I was so surprised that I could turn a yellow letter into an orange letter just by adding a line.

"Yellow letter? Orange letter?" my father said. "What do you mean?"

"Well, you know," I said. "P is a yellow letter, but R is an orange letter. You know—the colors of the letter."

"The color of letters?" My father said.

It had never come up in any conversation before. I had never thought to mention it to anyone. For as long as I could remember, each letter of the alphabet had a different color. Each word had a different color, too (generally, the same color as its first letter), and so did each number. The colors of letters, words, and numbers were as intrinsic a part of them as their shapes, and like the shapes, the colors never changed. They appeared automatically whenever I saw or thought about the letters or words, and I couldn't alter them.[12]

For those synesthetes who manifest grapheme/color links, Cytowic notes that it "now seems clear that for the majority of synesthetes it is the concept inherent in a grapheme that induces color—not the visual shape itself. To demonstrate this, note that capitalization and font style generally do not change an induced color: j, J and 𝒥 all evoke the same synesthetic color."[13]

Another interesting book written by a synesthete is Jamie Ward's *The Frog who Croaked Blue: Synesthesia and the Mixing of the Senses*. I highly recommend those books by Duffy and Ward for getting an insider's perspective on synesthesia. It is truly an amazing condition that, I think, may invite some comparison to ways in which we could be reading the Holy Scriptures. Just think about your senses being blended. Wouldn't you think that it would undermine or distract your attention or focus? To the contrary, synesthetes do not think so. In fact, Cytowic, possibly the world's greatest authority on synesthesia, states that synesthesia is "a rich way of feeling, highly enjoyable for those who possess it. To lose it would be a catastrophe, an odious state . . . Synesthetes have a well-developed innate memory that is amplified by use of the parallel sense as a mnemonic device."[14]

Cytowic thinks that the "visualized system created by synesthesia may also sometimes serve to reveal some new properties of knowledge."[15] He

12. Duffy, *Blue Cats*, 1–2.

13. Cytowic, *Wednesday*, 75.

14. Cytowic, *Synesthesia*, 46.

15. Ibid.

notes how, when one considers the world of the synesthete, "the function of seeing is not limited to vision."[16]

Seeing and Reality

There are different ways of perceiving reality, and one might ask oneself, should Christians have a different interpretive view and means of reading the Holy Scriptures? That is, should we "see" things differently? This brings me to one of my favorite examples of this issue, one I have used elsewhere.[17] In a book entitled *Patterns of Discovery*, Norwood Russell Hanson put forth a very interesting and quite famous question drawn from the following scenario.

> Let us consider Johannes Kepler: imagine him on a hill watching the dawn. With him is Tycho Brahe. Kepler regarded the sun as fixed: it was the earth that moved. But Tycho followed Ptolemy and Aristotle: the earth was fixed and all the other celestial bodies moved around it. Do Kepler and Tycho see the same thing in the east at dawn?[18]

Of course, the answer from Hanson's position would be, "No, they do not see the same thing." To appreciate fully the wit and the profundity of this scenario, one must recognize the utter separation of understanding between the two gifted astronomers. There they are upon the hill. Kepler sees heliocentrically; Brahe sees geocentrically. Yes, of course, they have received the same retinal image through their eyeballs as they looked out at the scene. But as Hanson noted, "eyeballs are blind."[19] The difference between the two observers, Kepler and Brahe, is interpretive; they both have the same visual data, yet they saw things very differently.

The Kepler/Brahe story was originally set in the context of Hanson discussing the notion of observation. He would, later in his book, develop an argument against the idea of what is called theory-free observation. Hanson's point was that there are no theory-neutral observations. We all come to our observations with the baggage of experience, belief, and presupposition. While Kepler and Brahe were looking at the same object, they each came to that experience with their own baggage. For Kepler, the sun

---

16. Ibid., 321.

17. Brookman, *Global Scenes*, xix–xx.

18. Hanson, *Patterns*, 5.

19. Ibid., 6.

was coming into view as Earth was turning on its axis. Contrarily, Brahe saw the sun as it was starting to make its daily trip around a stationary planet. Thus, for Hanson, "Seeing is not only the having of a visual experience; it is also the way in which the visual experience is had."[20]

In his book, Hanson was attacking a two-staged model of seeing. This Two-Staged Theory presumes that seeing involves two distinct things. First, there is the raw perception or data, i.e., photons hitting rods and cones in the retina. Second, it also involves the *interpretation* of that physical perception. Hanson goes on to argue that there is no seeing apart from interpretation.

Just as Kepler and Brahe saw things differently in Hanson's little story, so also should Christians see things differently from nonbelievers. While Christians have the same retinal images as everybody else, we had better see things differently. For as Hanson so cleverly put it, "There is more to seeing than meets the eyeball."[21] It is the lens of the Holy Scriptures that enables us to see in such a way that we not only perceive the photons of the historical, resurrected Christ event upon our retinas (faith), but we are also able to render that sight in such a way as to initiate cognition and behavior formulated upon an interpretive model of Christ's gospel.

The Synesthetic Analogy for Reading the Holy Scriptures

The thematic analogy I would like to suggest runs something like this. Just as synesthetes have clearly been found to have an unusually high propensity for creative thought, highly unusual modes of perception, and just plain "seeing" things differently, so ought the Christian reader of the Holy Scriptures who authentically desires to follow the way of Jesus have different perceptual and interpretive senses that will be continually blended in new ways. The blending of these senses will result in a wildly creative desire and ability to draw upon the holy texts in such a way that new paradigms of thought and praxis will result. This entails a reading of the Holy Scriptures that is not normal, not ordinary. It requires a reading of God's Word quite beyond the usual way of reading, that is, as if one were merely reading a newspaper or a James Michener novel. No, this profound enterprise of reading the Holy Scriptures as scripture is an extra-ordinary way of approaching the Bible. Yet, this is not some new-fangled methodology. To the

20. Ibid.
21. Ibid., 7.

contrary, only the analogy of synesthesia is new. The actual theories, traditions, and methods behind reading the Holy Scriptures as scripture have a very rich history. One particular tradition, historically known as *lectio divina*, or sacred reading (also widely known as spiritual or contemplative reading) will be the focus of attention in chapter 6.

This mode of spiritual reading has been described as "a reading that honors words as holy, words as basic means of forming an intricate web of relationship between God and human."[22] I think that, perhaps, synesthesia provides a great analogy for thinking about the spiritual reading of the Bible, this enterprise of reading the Holy Scriptures as scripture in which we wish to engage. For, as it has been noted, "the capacity of thinking by analogy has been one of the fundamental examples of transformation. This juxtaposition of two concepts to encourage greater understanding of one (or both) can be directly paralleled to the spontaneous, neutrally driven acceptance that the letter P is also 'dark green' . . ."[23]

In the same way that the synthesete may discern a day of the week to be a particular color, so also the spiritual reader of the Holy Scriptures (by analogy) discerns new juxtapositions. In turn, that produces transformation. Thus, in a metaphorical sense, the spiritual reader is a synthesete who sees connections and networks that are not apparent to the one who reads the Bible in a normative mode of reading, as if one were reading, for example, Gibbon's *The Decline and Fall of the Roman Empire*. There is, to be sure, a dual sense in what happens. It is a combination of the uniqueness of Scripture (remember, it is like nothing else being read) and the dynamic rendering of what is being read by the individual in a cognitively, spiritually, and emotively peculiar process. Under these conditions, there *are* orange proverbs, and there *are* purple parables! There is an unheard of, unprecedented apprehension of thought by the reader. As I have mentioned, this is not a normal, everyday mode of reading. Rather, this *is* the enterprise of reading the Holy Scriptures as scripture.

A couple of years ago, there was a wildly popular book by Donald Miller entitled *Blue Like Jazz*. At first glance, one might think that his title had some sort of synesthetic link behind it. However, the fact is that Miller's book title was not drawn from the world of synesthesia. Rather, the title came from, as Miller wrote about it, a metaphor of the stars in the heavens. "There is something beautiful about a billion stars held steady by a God who

22. Peterson, *Eat This Book*, 4.
23. Mulvenna, "Synaesthesia," 218.

knows what He is doing. (They hang there, the stars, like notes on a page of music, free-form verse, silent mysteries swirling in the blue like jazz.)"[24] But a point must be made. There is power in a connection of things that ordinarily are not connected in one's mind. I use the synesthesia example to highlight a memorable context in which that happens. There are people (synesthetes) who make connections between colors and days of the week all the time. In the same way, a spiritual reading of the Bible opens up connections, associations, and insights about God the likes of which would not normally be made if one were not reading the Holy Scriptures as scripture.

A Kaleidoscope Effect

Much of this book centers on our ways of reading of the Bible. As you will see in the coming chapters, there are many elements and aspects to consider as one reads the Holy Scriptures as scripture. Additionally, to be sure, those Scriptures present us with a montage of texts. There are varieties of genres and texts that originate in wide-ranging historical periods. Yet, when one reads those sacred texts as scripture, when one reads the Holy Scriptures, if you will, as a synesthete (for that is the metaphor) an added dynamic will manifest itself. Could it possibly be described as a kaleidoscope effect?

Did you have a kaleidoscope as a kid? Do you remember how you saw those beautiful images of bedazzling geometric shapes in vivid colors as you looked through the scope? Then, by simply rotating the scope ever so slightly an entirely new panorama of colorful shapes appeared in unique configurations. It was mesmerizing to say the least. The kaleidoscope effect yields a *fractal* experience. If you are not familiar with fractals, you will be after you read chapter 7 where a metaphor of the fractal nature of the Holy Scriptures will be developed as we consider the world of exegesis and hermeneutical interpretation.

What Kind of Book Is This?

One of the questions that may well have arisen in your mind after reading the first two chapters is, what kind of book is this? Is it a book about theology, or is it about spiritual life? Is it about hermeneutics, or is it about philosophy, or linguistics, or cognitive science or even the mathematics of

24. Miller, *Blue Like Jazz*, 100.

fractals? The fact of the matter is that I am not sure how to best answer that question. Perhaps one should just reserve judgment on this particular question and simply plow ahead into the unknown. Yet, what you can know for sure is that I give you my assurance that this book follows a path, albeit a winding one, that is designed to get you thinking about how *you* read the Holy Scriptures. Along the way, many avenues of consideration will be introduced, played with, and assessed. After all, you have already been introduced to Shakespeare, Wittgenstein, and Chomsky. You have learned that 5 + 2 can equal yellow, and you have seen that two people (Kepler and Brahe) observed the same sight in the sky but saw that event in remarkably different ways. In the end, you will, hopefully, be reading the Holy Scriptures as scripture, but you will not be too concerned about how this little book will be classified in the Dewey Decimal System. Rather, you will be experiencing a new sense of joy and fulfillment in how the Bible has become a more powerful resource in your life.

3

Orienting Oneself

The Place-Setting Episode

SUPPOSE YOU WERE SITTING down to dinner with some strangers, and a question arose on proper place-setting etiquette. On which side of the plate is the fork to be placed? You feel at ease, even though you are surrounded by strangers, because your mother taught you many years ago how to set a table properly. On top of that, you worked in a rather swanky restaurant for a couple of years, and you think you may be able to impress the other guests with your knowledge and experience on the topic.

Then suppose the person next to you said, "The fork should be on the south side of the plate." Immediately, the person across the table from you remarked, "Yes, the fork should be on the north side of the plate." What would you think? Your first thought might be something like, "Wait a second, I learned that the fork should be on the left side of the plate." This talk about the north and the south side of the plate does not make any sense to you, and you probably would have a confused look on your face. After all, that is not the way we think. On top of that, one person said it should be south, and the other person said it should be north of the plate. Would you say anything, or would you simply start on your salad and see how the conversation continues? When in doubt, wisdom might suggest that you keep quiet and start in on the meal until you can make some sense of what is happening.

Wouldn't that be an uncomfortable and disorienting situation? You prudently decide to wait and hear what some of the other guests have to say on the topic. Unfortunately, your cognitive dissonance grows as the guy on the end of the table suddenly says, "Indeed, while the dinner fork should be east of the plate, the shellfish fork should properly be placed on the west side of the plate." Everybody at the table nods in agreement, and the topic of conversation suddenly shifts to the wonderful smelling bouillabaisse being served. It is as if you were in the Twilight Zone. The conversation made no sense whatsoever. Who talks like that? What is going on here? Why were they using directions like that? We don't think like that! You find yourself completely disoriented.

The importance of being properly oriented, as opposed to being disoriented, is exactly the point I want to explore here. For as one considers the call we are under to follow the way of Jesus, it quickly becomes very clear that one needs a proper view of God, self, and a whole host of elements like servanthood, grace, relationships, and humility in order to live a righteous, holy life. That is, one needs a proper orientation toward God and the things of his kingdom in order to follow the true way of Jesus. A person who is disoriented toward God and the things of God will not generally find it possible to pursue the way of life to which Jesus calls us. Of course, one's orientation can change. The disoriented person can, indeed, become properly oriented. But even once a person is properly oriented, the need exists to maintain a proper understanding and sense of God's way.

Now, back to your surreal dinner experience in which forks were spoken of as being on the north, south, west, and east side of the plate. If anything is clear, it is that you were disoriented by what the others were saying about the placement of the fork. As it turns out, there is a very interesting explanation to what was said at that peculiar dinner. The strange conversation serves as an example of orientation, in this particular case spatial orientation. However, I think it may well serve as a terrific analogy to that sense of spiritual orientation so necessary in the quest for what I want to call the Scripture-filled life. This is a life in which one cultivates a sense of reading the Holy Scriptures as scripture, and that, in turn, empowers one to maintain and enhance one's proper orientation toward God. I will develop the notion of the Scripture-filled life in more detail in chapter 4, but for now, suffice it to represent a life that is fully lived as a true follower of Jesus as one gleans spiritual wisdom, understanding, and insight from a proper reading of the Bible.

Those Wiley Pormpuraawans

What is the answer to what seems to be a riddle? How can one speak of forks on the east side of a plate? Enter Lera Boroditsky.[1] I suspect you have not heard of her. I hadn't either until I picked up a recent copy of *Scientific American*. Paging through it, I came across an article entitled, "How Language Shapes Thought."[2] I've always had an interest in languages, so when I saw the title of the piece, I was immediately drawn to it. Within a few sentences I realized this was a very interesting person doing some captivating research that I should read.

Here is a fast overview of her findings that will fully explain the bizarre fork incident. It seems that on the west coast of Cape York Peninsula in Australia there is an aboriginal community in an area call Pormpuraaw. One of the languages spoken in that region is Kuuk Thaayorre. As Boroditsky explains the language:

> Unlike English, the Kuuk Thaayorre language spoken in Pormpuraaw does not use relative spatial terms such as left and right. Rather Kuuk Thaayorre speakers talk in terms of absolute cardinal directions (north, south, east, west, and so forth). Of course, in English we also use cardinal direction terms but only for large

1. Lera Boroditsky is an Associate Professor of Cognitive Psychology at the University of California San Diego where she heads a very cool research lab in which she and her colleagues study the relationship of cognition and language.

2. Boroditsky, "How Language Shapes," 63–65.

spatial scales. We would not say, for example, "They set the salad forks southeast of the dinner forks."[3]

Think about it for a moment. In order to speak this language a person has to be acutely aware of which direction she or he is facing at *all times*. Impossible? Actually, as Boroditsky describes it, it is child's play. She writes,

> I am standing next to a five-year-old girl in Pormpuraaw. When I ask her to point north, she points precisely and without hesitation. My compass says she is right. Later, back in a lecture hall at Stanford University, I made the same request of an audience of distinguished scholars—winners of science medals and genius prizes. I ask them to close their eyes (so they don't cheat) and point north. Many refuse; they do not know the answer. Those who do point take a while to think about it and then aim in all possible directions. . . .
>
> A five-year old in one culture can do something with ease that eminent scientists in another culture struggle with. This is a big difference in cognitive ability. What could explain it?[4]

Boroditsky describes a series of experiments that linked the absolute spatial representations present in Pormpuraawan culture (east, west, north, south) with how they also represented time. Whereas Americans will set out time sequences (based on pictorial representations, for instance of a boy growing into a man) in a left to right fashion, the Pormpuraawans did it quite differently. The results of her tests were fascinating.

> Unlike the Americans, who laid out time from left to right regardless of their cardinal facing direction, the Pormpuraawans spontaneously took their facing direction into account when making their arrangements. When facing south, they were likely to lay out time from left to right; when facing north, they were likely to lay out time from right to left; when facing east they were likely to lay out time as coming toward them; and when facing west, they were likely to lay out time as moving away from them. This was true even though the participants were never told which way they were facing.[5]

Boroditsky's research is truly intriguing. She is broadly interested in the intersection of language and cognition, and she employs an impressive

3. Ibid., 64.

4. Ibid., 63.

5. Boroditsky and Gaby, "Remembrances," 3.

interdisciplinary approach by bringing together aspects from a variety of disciplines (anthropology, neuroscience, linguistics, and psychology) in her quest to better understand thought and language. I found her particular case of the Pormpuraawans to be so interesting that I wanted to utilize it as an analogy in some way, and I think I've got it.

Just as the five-year-old Pormpuraawan girl instinctively knew which direction was north, so also our orientation toward the Holy Scriptures should be instinctive to the point that the Word of God serves as an orienting beacon for our thoughts, speech, and actions. As Pormpuraawans can speak their language correctly only by being properly oriented, so we are able to live correctly only through a proper orientation toward God and his Scriptures. In that sense, we are just like the Pormpuraawans—we need to be properly oriented.

How Are You Oriented?

Of course, there are many ways of thinking about being properly oriented in life. What are some of the central things in your life around which you orient yourself? Family? The pursuit of a great paying job? Relationships with people? Facebook? Ministry? Your local sports team? Everybody orients himself or herself as they cognitively arrange priorities for how they will live. Another factor is the reality that those priorities may, and oftentimes do, change over time. Some things in life are seemingly more important than other things at any given time. Everyone decides on their own which things are higher in importance, and no two people are exactly the same in how the prioritizing plays out over the course of a lifetime.

Indeed, there are a lot of things in life that can work to disorient you. However, the person who is living a Scripture-filled life will be so oriented by God's Word that any life situation is sustainable. Yes, horrendous things can happen. Yes, bad things can happen to good people.[6] Yet, when your life is oriented and fixed on the Scriptures, you have an ultimate anchor. But what exactly are these Holy Scriptures that they command so much power?

My premise is, of course, that our orientation for life is to be founded upon the Word of God. It is through this elemental orientation to the Holy Scriptures that one is better able to discern and love God. It is through the regimen of immersing ourselves in the Holy Scriptures, of absolutely loving those sacred texts, that we become better able to fathom the transcendent

6. See especially, Kushner, *When Bad Things Happen.*

God who has revealed himself through his Word, the Bible. As you read this book and seriously contemplate the enterprise of reading the Holy Scriptures as scripture, I fully expect the Holy Spirit to be at work in you, in your mind and in your heart, to rekindle or, perhaps, to ignite for the first time within you a flame of passion for consuming the Holy Scriptures in a new way.

The great Reformer, John Calvin (1509–1564), developed a very interesting doctrine of the Holy Scriptures during the Reformation. Yet, his doctrine deals not so much with the nature of the biblical texts or their origin, but rather it deals with *reading* them. Indeed, power is at the very center of the theory of reading the Bible held by Calvin. As Wesley Kort has noted, "While one normally reads a text for knowledge and meaning, Calvin sees those as secondary to Scripture's power."[7] Kort cites a famous passage from Calvin's *Institutes* (1.8.2) as follows:

> But it is only in reading Scripture that its power can fully and beneficially be experienced. "Then in spite of yourself, so deeply will it affect you, so penetrate your heart, so fix itself in your very marrow, that, compared with its deep impress, such vigor as orators and philosophers have will nearly vanish." . . . Power for Calvin is both personal, the power to penetrate the reader's heart, and cultural, the power of the text to endure and to influence diverse cultures.[8]

It will "fix itself in your very marrow!" This is how Calvin described the power of the Holy Scriptures to penetrate your heart. What is the Bible that it wields such awesome power? How ought one to think about or describe what it is we have in the Holy Scriptures?

It's a Strange New World

It was 1917. In the middle of one of the most horrendous wars in history, a relatively unknown Reformed pastor from the little municipality of Safenwil in Switzerland presented a lecture to a small congregation in the nearby town of Leutwil. Then only thirty years old, Karl Barth (pronounced Bart) had been invited to deliver a lecture as part of a series that Pastor Eduard

7. Kort, *Take, Read*, 26.
8. Ibid., 27.

Thurneysen had planned for his congregation.[9] Barth entitled his presentation, "The new world within the Bible." It seems Barth's lecture resonated particularly well with the host pastor and with his congregation. A few days after the conference, Thurneysen wrote a letter to Barth in which he heartily congratulated him for connecting so well with his parishioners.[10]

Of course, it was this same Karl Barth who went on to become one of the most famous theologians of the twentieth century. Best known for his massive, thirteen-volume work, *Church Dogmatics*, Barth's legacy is certainly cemented as one of the great theological thinkers of the past century. Indeed, *Church Dogmatics* is legendary in theological circles. Yet, it is his now-storied lecture from that very modest conference in the backwoods of Switzerland in 1917 that has challenged many to reassess their view of the Bible. For in that little church, Barth began by presenting an intriguing question when he queried, "What sort of house is it to which the Bible is the door?" This little inquiry was followed up immediately with another. "What sort of land is spread before our eyes when we throw open the Bible?" Naturally, the questions were rhetorical; Barth did not expect an on-the-spot answer from anyone within that little gathering of parishioners. Rather, in his lecture, he was going to lay out the answers as he stood there before the congregants.

The lecture Barth presented was later published in a collection of his earliest essays culled together into a book called, *Das Wort Gottes und die Theologie* (*The Word of God and Theology*). In a subsequent translation into English by Douglas Horton, the title of the book shifted slightly to *The Word of God and the Word of Man*. The translator also took a small liberty with the title of the now-famous lecture. The original German title was simply "*Die neue Welt in der Bibel*" ("The New World Within the Bible"), and that is how it first appeared in print in German. However, as he translated it, Horton added the word "strange." This was a subtle but intriguing nuance. Thus, Barth's famous lecture/essay has hence become widely known in the English speaking world as, "The Strange New World within the Bible."[11] The addition of the word "strange" by Horton actually seems quite appropriate once one has read the essay, even though a German equivalent word was

---

9. Barth, *Theology*, 15. Thurneysen, himself is best known for his work in pastoral care (*A Theology of Pastoral Care*), also invited Emile Brunner and Gottlob Wieser each to deliver a lecture during the three-day conference.

10. Ibid.

11. Barth, *Word of Man*, 28.

not used by Barth. This is so because, within the essay, Barth described what one may label as a largely unknown and unexplored terrain that exists between the covers of your Bible.

Throughout the lecture and the subsequent published form of it, Barth kept asking, "What is there within the Bible?" He itemized some of the self-evident answers. There is history in it. There is morality; there is religion in it. But he reduced these sorts of things to mere dross, peripheral issues and concerns. For Barth, it was not the inclusion of these things that makes the Holy Scriptures such a wonder.

> In fact, the chief consideration of the Bible is not the activities of humans but the activity of God—not the various paths we could take if we had the good will to do so, but the powers from which a good will is first created. Its chief concern is not the way in which love unfolds and proves itself as we understand it, but with the existence and outpouring of an eternal love, love as God understands it. Its chief interest is not our capability to function in our ordinary old world, hard-working, honest, and helpful way, but in the establishment and growth of a new world, in the world in which God rules, and in which *his* morality rules.[12]

Then he surprised his listeners/readers with this shocking tidbit:

> Can you guess what is coming next? It is precisely not the right human thoughts about God that form the content of the Bible, but rather the right thoughts of God about humans. The Bible does not tell us how we are supposed to talk with God, but rather what God says to us. It does not say how we are to find our way to him, but how God has sought and found the way to us. It does not show the right relationship into which we must place ourselves with him, but the covenant which God has made with all those who are the children of Abraham in faith, and which God has sealed in Jesus Christ once and for all. This is what stands in the Bible. The Word of God stands in the Bible.[13]

Aha! That is the point for Barth. The Bible surprises us because it pulls us into its reality. It is not our thoughts about God, but rather, God's thoughts about us that inhabit the Bible. The Holy Scriptures do not cater to our petty aims and agendas. Reading the Bible demands a new orientation through which we discover God on his terms. Barth challenges us with

12. Barth, *Theology*, 23.
13. Ibid., 25.

the available option, the freedom of choice we have to reject this strange new world of the Bible. Yes, of course, we can be quite comfortable within the Christianity we know. The Bible that is already comfortable for us can merely be maintained. That would certainly be the easy route. Barth exhorts us toward a new way as he says, "Once more, we have the freedom of choice. We could certainly declare: 'I cannot get anywhere with this. The concept 'Word of God' is not a part of my world view. I will stand by that old 'pious' Christianity that I am used to, with its particular viewpoints of this or that stripe.' Or, we could open our ears to what 'passes all understanding.'"[14]

For Barth, the Holy Scriptures opened an entirely new landscape. He wrote, "A new world stands in the Bible. God! God's lordship! God's honor! God's inconceivable love!"[15] Barth argued that the Bible is not about "the virtues of humanity but the virtues of God, who has called us out of the darkness to his wonderful light!"[16]

Therefore, let it be known that an aim of this book is one of exploring this newfound terrain, this strange new world within the Text, the Word of God, the Holy Scriptures. That is a fairly sobering enterprise. Thus, it is good to remember always that prayer before, during, and after the reading of the Holy Scriptures is a fundamental element which strengthens and invigorates the modes of reading and apprehending that will be further explored in chapter 4.

What Sort of House Is It?

When we talk of the Holy Scriptures, it is no surprise that questions oftentimes arise which involve presuppositions and definitions. A common issue at hand concerns the quest for a meeting of the minds in constructing a conversation about the Holy Scriptures. In that wonderfully titled chapter, "The Strange New World within the Bible," Barth coyly asked, "What is it that we actually have in the Bible? What sort of house is it to which the Bible is the door?"[17] Barth certainly stressed that there is, indeed, a strange new world within the Bible. In fact, it is so strange it can almost be a somewhat haunting thing. Consider Søren Kierkegaard's anguished lament:

14. Ibid.
15. Ibid., 26
16. Ibid.
17. Ibid., 28.

To be alone with the Bible! I dare not! If I read it—the first passage I come upon is the best—I am bound immediately. It asks me (yes, it is just as if God Himself asked me): have you done what you read? And then, then—yes, then I am caught, then it is either to act at once or immediately make a humiliating admission . . . and this book, God's Word, is an extremely dangerous book for me. It is a domineering book. If one gives it a finger, it takes the whole hand. If one gives it the whole hand, it takes the whole man and then, perhaps, suddenly alters my whole life according to a gigantic measure. I will not be alone with it.[18]

That quirky old Dane seemed also to know that the Bible was not just any old book. An eccentric, but brilliant, Christian philosopher, Kierkegaard (1813–1855) knew there was something different about that book.

Then there is the case of Augustine (AD 354–430). He is one of my favorites. Augustine was an incredibly prolific and profound Christian writer. His literary output was so vast, in fact, that it has been said in an early ditty written in honor of Augustine that, "He lies who says that he has read all of you [Augustine]."[19] A decent paraphrase of that saying might be something like this: "You're a liar if you say that you have read everything Augustine has written." That is probably quite true. Yet, while you, in all likelihood, will never read anywhere near everything that Augustine has written, I might point you, in particular, to one especially powerful work of his that everyone should read. It is on my top-ten list of books that I would recommend every Christian to read. That work is known as *The Confessions*. It is a classic tale that is very readable. It is an enrapturing story with a surplus of meaning that is essentially Augustine's autobiography.[20] Within it, he relates the captivating story of his dramatic conversion by reading the Holy Scriptures.

---

18. Kierkegaard, *Self Examination*, 32–33.

19. *Mentitur qui se totum legisse fatetur* is the first line of a little poem attributed to Isidore of Seville (ca. AD 560–636). In its entirety, it reads: "He lies, who avers that he has read all of you. In fact, what reader can even have all your works? For you shine, Augustine, in the glory of a thousand volumes: your books themselves bear witness to what I say. However much one may like to have volumes of book of many authors, if you have Augustine [O reader], he is enough for you." This translation is from Newton, *Scriptorium and Library*, 80.

20. Autobiography may not technically be the correct terminology to use. See, for example, Misch, *History of Autobiography in Antiquity*.

If you have never read the story of Augustine's conversion, you are in for a treat right now. Settle back comfortably in your chair, and ponder his story. As Augustine later described it:

> In some way, I'm not just sure how, I threw myself down under a fig tree and let the tears gush freely. These were the streams that proved a sacrifice acceptable to you, my Lord. Not in the exact words of Scripture but in some similar vein I talked with you for a long time. I asked, "And thou, Lord, how long wilt thou be roused to such fury? Do not remember the sins of former times"—for I felt they were still holding me. I ended on a dismal note: "How long, how long? Tomorrow and tomorrow? Why not now? Why not put an end to my sin right this hour?"
>
> I was going on like this, weeping in bitter dejection of spirit, when I heard a voice coming from the house next door. Whether it was a boy's or a girl's I don't know, but it was singing over and over in a kind of chant, "Take up and read, take up and read." Immediately my demeanor changed. I thought back over the children's games I know, trying to recall wither I had ever heard such an expression used. I knew of no such game. Stanching the flow of tears, I stood up for I could only interpret the words as a kind of divine command to open the Scripture and read the first passage I came across. I had heard how Anthony once dropped in unexpectedly at a church service during a reading of the gospel, and was inspired by what he heard as if it were addressed to him personally: "Go and sell what you have and give it to the poor, and you shall have treasure in heaven; and come and follow me." By this word from the Lord he was converted to you right on the spot. So I returned quickly to the bench where Alypius was sitting. When I had moved from there I'd left behind the copy of the letters of the Apostle. Now I grabbed up the book, opened it, and read silently the first portion of Scripture on which my eyes lighted: "Not in reveling and drunkenness, not in debauchery and licentiousness, not in quarreling and jealousy. But put on the Lord Jesus Christ, and make no provision for the flesh, to gratify its desires." I had no need or wish to read further, for when I came to the end of the sentence, instantly, it seemed, a light of certainty turned on in my heart and all the fog of doubt disappeared.[21]

---

21. Wirt, *Confessions of Augustine*, 117–18. Another excellent English version which I would recommend to you is that of Maria Boulding, *The Confessions* published by New City Press. New City Press is engaged in publishing a large-scale project as a series entitled *The Works of Saint Augustine: A Translation for the 21st Century*.

It was the mysterious and alluring voice of a child telling Augustine to "Take and read!" the Scriptures. The phrase is a famous one in theological circles. *Tolle, Lege* (Take! Read!) is the Latin used by Augustine, himself, as he recalled the event. To his credit, he obeyed the strange, childlike voice. He read Romans 13:13–14, and as he later wrote, "a light of certainty turned on in my heart."[22]

Augustine then went and told his friend, Alypius, what had just happened to him. As it turns out, Alypius had just read the start of Romans 14, and he, likewise, was encouraged and strengthened by the words of the text and had decided to change his life also. Augustine was not surprised by this. He figured Alypius might do something like this because, as Augustine noted, "he was of a higher moral fiber than I for a long, long time."[23] Immediately the two fellows went off to tell Augustine's mother what had happened, and she, of course, was thrilled. God, through his Holy Scriptures, had spoken to Augustine and Alypius, and they both dedicated their lives to serving him as a result. Again, what are these Holy Scriptures that they have such power?

What is Scripture?

Karl Barth knew there was some sort of a strange new world within the Bible. Yet, there is a great, true story, with almost an apocryphal sounding air to it, which captures Barth's view of the Bible's character in a wonderful way. In 1962 Barth was on a tour of the United States. This renowned theologian, who had penned the immense and influential *Church Dogmatics*, was asked by a student at Princeton University, "what had been the most momentous theological discovery of his long life."[24] One surely would have expected an answer of proportional profundity to come out of the mouth of this larger than life figure in theology. However, after pausing a moment to gather his thoughts, Barth replied in the words of the children's song, "Jesus loves me this I know, for the Bible tells me so."[25]

---

22. Ibid., 118.

23. Ibid.

24. Mangina, *Karl Barth*, 9.

25. Widely known today as a children's chorus, the music was composed by William Batchelder Bradbuy (1862) using the words of a poem he had found in Susan Warner's 1860 novel, *Say and Seal*.

Kierkegaard had a sense of fear and trembling about the Bible, and he was afraid to be alone with it.[26] Augustine, by obeying the voice speaking to him, took and read the Scriptures. As a result, he was converted. Indeed, what are these Holy Scriptures such that they have the power to do these and similar things in the minds and hearts of human beings?

To be sure, there are many opinions, even within the church, about what the Scriptures actually are. To simplify things, I will set out just a few of the general ideas held in this book concerning the nature of the Holy Scriptures. I hope that you agree with all these notions. However, even if you do not agree, perhaps we can come to an understanding that Barth, Kierkegaard, and Augustine were on to something, and the Holy Scriptures present us with something that is strangely different, a little haunting, and can elicit changes in one's heart and mind. Those are not very theological ways of talking about the Holy Scriptures, but those points may be a good first step for us in apprehending what it is we actually have in the Bible.

Thus, it is not my intent here to restate or summarize an entire dogma of the Sacred Scriptures. There are many good works that do that quite well. If you are interested, a book that I highly recommend is John Webster's *Holy Scripture: A Dogmatic Sketch*.[27] It is a little book, only 137 pages, but it is densely packed and very rewarding. It is challenging to read, but it really packs a punch for the reader as Webster engagingly weaves together a "sketch" of what we have in the Bible. Yet, tastes differ, and Webster's book does not strike a chord with everyone. N.T. Wright seemed a little disappointed in Webster's book since it didn't address "what the text actually says." Wright noted that "one would never have known, from reading this book, anything at all about what the Bible contains."[28] Yet, quite beyond Webster's book, there are, of course, many theological surveys that include doctrinal statements on what the Holy Scriptures actually are.[29]

Again, rather than delve into the labyrinth of this topic, I want to merely present several foundational concepts from which I work within this book. I think you will, most certainly, get the message that a very high view of Scripture is held by this writer. I believe the limited number of

26. *Fear and Trembling* is, in fact, the title of a work by Kierkegaard that was published in 1843. In it, he deals with the vexing episode of Abraham's sacrifice of his son Isaac in Gen 22. It is a short work that you may find to be a page turner.

27 Webster, *Holy Scripture*.

28. Wright, *Scripture*, 12.

29. For good examples, see Berkhof, *Systematic Theology*, 144–69 and Berkouwer, *Holy Scripture*.

generalizations I make in the following few pages about the nature of the Holy Scriptures will function just fine for you to take on this enterprise of reading the Holy Scriptures as scripture. After all, there are, to be sure, some nit-picking differences between some in the church with regards to certain detailed aspects of how one ought to define the nature of the Bible. For example, there are various theories and nuances of inspiration and revelation. There are different ways of talking about inerrancy, and there are multiple opinions on the language that should be used in speaking about any such notions. Most Protestant denominations have developed their own doctrinal statements regarding the Holy Scriptures. Roman Catholicism and Eastern Orthodoxy (in its various forms) have refined their particular language for addressing what the Holy Scriptures are. As N. T. Wright comments:

> The sixteenth-century Reformers appealed to scripture over against the traditions which had grown up in the church during the Middle Ages; the churches which stem from the Reformation all emphasize (as the early fathers had done) the central importance of the Bible. Whether Lutheran or Reformed, whether Anglican, Presbyterian, Baptist or Methodist, or whether the newer Pentecostal churches, all officially accord scripture the central place in their faith, life and theology. This has marked out the post-Reformation churches from the Eastern Orthodox and Roman Catholic churches, which give a more complex and interwoven account of how scripture operates within the life of the church.[30]

Authentic Christians, generally, I think, come to the table with at least a basic sense, in their own mind, of what the Bible is. To be sure, however, there can still be differences between believers' understanding of what the Holy Scriptures are. Yet, most of those differences should not impede using this book as a means for thinking about how *you* read the Holy Scriptures. If you belong to one of the previously mentioned Christian traditions, you, in all likelihood, have the necessary grist we need for the mill in order to talk about how we read the Bible. Yet, there are a few points that should be made at the outset in order that you clearly understand some of the premises behind what is said in forthcoming chapters.

Let us start with a basic notion, central to an understanding of scripture that has been termed the "Scripture Principle."[31] As Vanhoozer notes,

---

30. Wright, *Scripture*, 2.

31. See, for example, Pinnock and Callen, *Scripture Principle*.

this "principle represents the historical orthodox view that the Bible is to be identified with the Word of God."[32] That is the primary starting presupposition for all that gets said in this book. If you do not share that as your own deeply-held presupposition, this book probably is not going to make a lot of sense to you.

Can you say *Viva Vox Dei*?

Agreeing then, as we do, that the Holy Scriptures are, in some way, the Word of God, we can consider a corollary to that notion that is also behind some of the things I write concerning the Holy Scriptures. I would like to introduce you to the concept that the Bible is *viva vox Dei*—"the living voice of God." This may be a phrase you have not heard before, but it is an interesting and key concept. The reason for this is the fact that what *does* divide a good many Christians on the issue of the Holy Scriptures is the concept of authority. There is quite a range of opinion out there about the authority of the Bible. As van den Belt writes, "The authority of Scripture has become problematic in modern times. The historical-critical approach to the Bible, modern cosmology, and the violence in the Bible—to name just a few issues—have made it difficult to accept Scripture unconditionally as the source and norm for faith and life. The shift towards a postmodern context makes the issue even more complicated."[33]

The notion of the Holy Scriptures being the very living voice of God (*viva vox Dei*) certainly should impact one's view concerning the authority wielded by the Bible. By means of the living voice of God, the "church not only reads about but is confronted by God himself in communicative presence and action."[34] But what effect does the living voice of God have on us; what is the impact of reading/hearing the living voice of God? John Webster adroitly speaks to this when he addresses what he says is "most interesting about what happens when Christians read the Bible."[35] His view is that the *viva vox Dei* actually creates faith and obedience within the life of the reader. This is an important point for us to get. When you read the Holy Scriptures as scripture, the living voice of God is speaking to you, and that, in turn, *will* bolster your faith and obedience. Perceiving the Holy

32. Vanhoozer, *First Theology*, 128.

33. Belt, "Scripture as the Voice of God," 434.

34. Vanhoozer, *Drama of Doctrine*, 229.

35. Webster, *Word and Church*, 58.

Scriptures as *viva vox Dei* endows an authority upon the Bible. As Pinnock notes, "The real authority of the Bible is not the scholarly exegesis of the text, open only to the elite scholar, but the Word that issues forth when the Spirit takes the text and renders it the living voice of the Lord. Therefore, it is not a text we can master through techniques but a text that wants to master us."[36]

Another important theological term oftentimes associated with the authority of the Bible is the Greek word *autopistia*.[37] The horse sense of this word is that the Holy Scriptures, in being *autopistos*, are, in and of themselves, altogether trustworthy and as an extension, authoritative. The word, *autopistos*, is not actually used in the Holy Scriptures. That is, the Bible does not define itself as being *autopistos*. Rather, the word comes to be popularly used in the Reformation and post-Reformation periods in speaking of the nature of the Holy Scriptures largely because John Calvin (1509–1564) used it in his famous *Institutes of the Christian Religion* (1.7.5). "Let this therefore stand: those whom the Holy Spirit has inwardly taught, truly finding rest in Scripture; it is indeed *autopistos*—it should not be submitted to demonstration by proofs—while it still owes the certainty that it deserves among us to the testimony of the Spirit."[38]

This is where there is quite a proliferation of opinions on the authority of the Holy Scriptures because some modern biblical scholars who engage in a certain type of historical criticism don't buy into the notion of *autopistia*.[39] Consequently, Green notes that the "result of such an agenda is less a reading of the scriptural narratives and more a reconstruction of the histories to which those scriptural texts presume to bear witness."[40] Green does not have any time for that particular type of historical criticism (i.e., what he calls Historical Criticism), and it seems to me that his concerns as a theological interpreter of the Bible regarding such methodology and its presuppositions are quite well founded.

36. Pinnock and Callen, *Scripture Principle*, 182.

37. *Autopistia* is variously translated but has the idea of something that is credible in itself—something that is self-authenticating. The prefix *auto* means "of itself" or "by itself." *Pistia* is from the Greek word *pistis* (πίστις) meaning "faith." Used together, *autopistia* has the sense of something that is to be believed in and of itself.

38. Translation by Belt, "Scripture as the Voice of God," 438.

39. See Green, *Practicing*, 44–45. Green speaks of three categories of historical criticism (Historical Criticism1, Historical Criticism2, and Historical Criticism3).

40. Ibid., 45.

In his magisterial study of *autopistia*, the concluding sentences of van den Belt's book offer up a worthy sentiment in which the concepts of the Holy Scriptures being the living voice of God and being altogether authoritative because they are self-authenticating are stated quite eloquently.[41] He writes, "A Reformed Christian can only give one answer to the question why he believes the Bible: because the Holy Spirit convinces him in Scripture that he hears the living voice of God and therefore he finds rest in it. The sheep recognize the voice of the Shepherd and follow him, trusting him as the Truth."[42]

I am not sure that the adjective, Reformed, is needed in the previous quotation. I know plenty of Christians not in a Reformed tradition who would enthusiastically endorse the sentiment of the statement van den Belt makes above. Further, the notion that it is the Holy Spirit convincing us of the reality and truth behind our perception of the Bible is, I believe, important. This particular work of the Spirit is known as the *testimonium* of the Holy Spirit. A powerful aspect of how we combine these elements is due to the fact "that the *testimonium* of the Spirit also governs the *autopistia* of Scripture; the Spirit not only gives testimony in the hearts of the divine origin of Scriptures, but also of their *autopistia*." [43] In other words, we see these traits in the Bible, i.e., it is the living voice of God and is self-authenticating, because the Holy Spirit is testifying to that in our hearts.

Thus, so far, we carry with us in this book the fundamental presupposition that the Holy Scriptures are, in some way, the Word of God. Next, we have joined with that the notion of the Bible actually being the living Word of God (*viva vox Dei*) and the idea that the Holy Scriptures are to be believed, and in that way, they are self-authenticating (*autopistia*). Beyond that, there is one more basic and well-known point to be mentioned; namely, the Holy Scriptures are inspired.

Self-Descriptive Language within Scripture

One of the first verses many new Christians learn is 2 Tim 3:16 ("All scripture is inspired by God and profitable for teaching, for reproof, for correction, and for training in righteousness."). The broader context is, of course,

41. Belt, *Authority of Scripture.*

42. Ibid., 336.

43. Calvin used the phrase, *testimonium Spiritus Sancti Internum* to refer to the inner testimony of the Holy Spirit.

the missive of Paul to his kindred spirit and helper, Timothy, in which he encourages his younger compatriot concerning living a Christian life given the pressures and persecutions one continually faces. The key concept for the discussion here is, naturally, Paul's use of the word, which is most often translated into English as "inspired," to talk about the Holy Scriptures. Once again, Jerome's Latin Vulgate version influenced what happened as early English translators drew on the Vulgate's use of *inspirata* in the text of 2 Tim 3:16.

However, the original Greek word used here by Paul is *theopneustos*– θεόπνευστος, and that, quite literally, is rendered as "God-breathed." This is the most often cited source in discussions about the doctrine of inspiration. As with most theological doctrines, it is a more complex labyrinth than might appear at first glance. There have been a number of books (or chapters within books) on the topic, all of which address different nuances and issues regarding the concept of inspiration.[44] For example, it has been argued that the English word, "inspiration," is, perhaps, not the best rendering of the Greek word. Indeed, the NIV (New International Version) employs the phrase "God-breathed" to translate *theopneustos*.

When it comes to this concept of inspiration, Webster is careful to note, and rightfully so, that "Theological talk of the inspiration of Scripture needs to be strictly subordinate to and dependent upon the broader concept of revelation. Disorder threatens a theology of Scripture if the notion of inspiration is allowed to aggrandize itself and usurp the central place in bibliology."[45]

That is, 2 Tim 3:16 is not to be seen as the be all and end all prooftext upon which one's entire understanding of the Holy Scriptures is cast. Webster points to the broader issue of revelation, under which inspiration should be subsumed. Thus, one might properly reckon inspiration as following from the fact "that through Holy Scripture God addresses the church with the gospel of salvation."[46] Thus, we need to recognize that "Faith's certainty is grounded in God alone, not in inspiration; faith is 'founded' on Scripture, not because of its formal property as inspired but because Scripture is the instrument of divine teaching which proceeds from God."[47]

---

44. See, for example: Law, *Inspiration*; Fackre, *Doctrine*; Abraham, *Divine Inspiration*; Achtemeier, *Inspiration of Scripture*.

45. Webster, *Holy Scripture*, 31.

46. Ibid., 32.

47. Ibid., 33.

Another biblical text which is intriguing when considering doctrinal points of the Holy Scriptures is that of 2 Pet 1:21. This text reads in part, "Those moved by the Holy Spirit spoke from God." As Briggs notes, "despite the prominence given to 2 Tim 3:16 in discussions of inspiration," the passage of 2 Pet 1:21 "is actually more helpful for understanding what is at stake in the idea."[48]

Inspired and Inspiring

While the notion of inspiration is important within any conversation of what the Bible actually is, our holistic view of what the Holy Scriptures are is not solely dependent on the concept of inspiration. To be sure, there is more than meets the eye. For the Holy Scriptures are not only inspired (*theopneustos*), they also inspire. By the fact that your faith and obedience are bolstered by reading the Holy Scriptures, you are inspired *by* the living voice of God.

As already noted, it is definitely not my intent to summarize or critique the wide spectrum within which one finds all the doctrinal fine points to address the question, "What really are the Holy Scriptures?" Not because it is not important, but rather, the true thrust of this book builds upon bringing to the table a very basic sense of what the Bible is, and then reading those sacred texts in such a way that the power of the Holy Scriptures that Calvin talked about will be manifested in your life. The next chapter will delve more into that, but for now, the purpose of this chapter was simply to solidify a basic orientation for you.

Which Way is Up?

The points that have been under discussion so far, that is, the Bible as the Word of God (the Scripture Principle), the living voice of God (*viva vox Dei*), self-authenticated (*autopistia*), and inspired (*theopneustos*), all relate to this question of "What really are the Holy Scriptures?" Yet, as I have attempted to make clear, nothing near a full discussion of those topics is even going to be attempted here. In my opinion, a full discussion and crystal clear understanding of all those fine points is not absolutely necessary at

48. Briggs, *Reading the Bible Wisely*, 73.

this stage in order to actualize the goal of this book, which is to get you reading the Holy Scriptures as scripture.

Remember that at the end of the day, it is your orientation toward things that will keep you grounded. On those days when you seemingly don't know which way is up (and those days do come along once in a while) it is your orientation to the Holy Scriptures which will enable you to gain, once again, your footing and to know exactly where you are. For it is in the Holy Scriptures that we hear God. We hear the very living voice of the divine. As we read, we listen with an expectancy and openness. But, beyond even that, we seek to understand the things of God on deeper levels and to be transformed through the process of encountering God in the Holy Scriptures. The next chapter begins to explore some of the elemental considerations and strategies for developing a new and fruitful way of reading the Bible. Keep in mind, just as the Pormpuraawans orient everything spatially to the cardinal directions, so ought we be oriented to God's Word in order that we hear and things make sense.

4

Reading as One Ought

The Scripture-Filled Life

I BELIEVE THAT I first came across the phrase, "the Scripture-filled life," in a little book entitled *Scripture by Heart*.[1] I really like that phrase—the Scripture-filled life. It captures a great notion or concept in a very pithy way. Of course, many people are familiar with Rick Warren's best-selling book, *The Purpose-Driven Life*. Those two phrases ("the Scripture-filled life" and "the purpose-driven life") not only have similar grammatical structures and phonetic rings to them, but they also have in common the aim to describe a life of worth in which God is manifest and glorified by the way an individual lives.

A very lamentable characteristic of our modern American Christian culture, particularly since the advent of television (early 1950s) and especially since the appearance of the Internet (1990s), is a general decline of biblical literacy within the church. That is to say, people within a believing community, generally speaking, know less about the content within the Holy Scriptures than was ordinarily the case in previous generations. One of the overriding objectives of this book is to function as a catalyst in nudging you toward a deeper relationship with God by making some changes in the way you read the Bible. The natural result of such a deepened relationship is the desire to spend time with the Holy Scriptures, listening to the *viva vox Dei*. Whatever the amount of time you currently spend reading the Bible, whatever your habits or practices of devotion are presently, you can build on that to expand the role of the Holy Scriptures in your life. It is not

---

1. Kang, *Scripture by Heart*, 29.

merely a quantitative change in time spent reading, but more importantly, it will be making some qualitative changes in the *way* you read the Holy Scriptures that is the real objective. For as you will see, contrary to the usual mode of thinking predominant within the American cultural sphere, there is no fast way to cultivate an intimate relationship with the Holy Scriptures other than spending quality time in a deep, focused reading of God's Word. Naturally, the investment of time and effort in reading the Holy Scriptures will pay rich dividends in cultivating a more grounded and effective relationship with God. A further consequence will be a Christian lifestyle that is more in step with the call that, as a believer, Jesus has on your life.

As a starting point, might we not admit that we presently do not fully read the Holy Scriptures as we might? Could you not admit, along with me, that in the scheme of really important things, we have lagged in cultivating a discipline and a way of reading the Holy Scriptures in which we are intently listening to the *viva vox Dei*? All of us could probably make some headway if we were to be honest with ourselves. Remember our friend Ludwig Wittgenstein? He aptly noted that, "Nothing is so difficult as not deceiving oneself."[2] In truth, haven't we deceived ourselves by thinking that our casual, periodic perusing of the Holy Scriptures is perfectly adequate for us in our Christian life?

Rather than continuing along in your current pattern of glibly reading the Bible without actively listening to the living voice of God, without experiencing the transformative power of God's Word, wouldn't you like to commence a great enterprise of reading the Holy Scriptures as scripture? That is the task at hand. A reading of the Holy Scriptures as scripture will lead you in a direction and along a path that, hopefully, you truly wish to go. The sad state of our biblical literacy and our ineffectual habits of how we read the Holy Scriptures inhibit us in so many ways. There is a very sobering sentiment captured in a famous quote by Jerome. His thought might be paraphrased as "Not knowing the Scriptures is akin to not knowing Christ."[3] Yet, a simple awareness of the fact that it is through the reading of the Holy Scriptures that one is able to hear and encounter God can propel you into new patterns and habits of how you read the Bible. It can start you on a journey into living a Scripture-filled life.

In order to actualize a Scripture-filled life, a person most certainly needs an orientation toward God that is the foundation of all that one

2. Wittgenstein, *Culture and Value*, 34e.

3. Jerome, *Isaiam prophetam*, PL 24, col. 17.

does. This orientation toward God serves to ground one's reality properly and to enable the follower of Christ to pursue faithfully the ideals of the kingdom of God. Beyond that, there needs to be a practical understanding of what a sustained, serious, sacred reading of the Holy Scriptures can, indeed, accomplish. Augustine is a great example of one who recognized the transformative power of reading God's Word. The serious reader, the one who embraces this enterprise of reading the Holy Scriptures as scripture, in today's colloquial nomenclature, "reinvents herself or himself." As a result of reading the Holy Scriptures as scripture, Augustine came "to read himself differently; he reedits the narrative of his own history and redirects his life."[4] That is, Augustine was truly transformed by his reading of the Holy Scriptures. As Studzinski put it, "Reading the Scriptures was, as Augustine came to see, truly a transformative experience; a reader, through a contemplation of the scriptural text, moves inward and upward to a higher understanding and then to an ethically informed life. Augustine's own experience of personal reform through reading as presented in the *Confessions* grounded his vision of what the practice of reading the Scriptures could do."[5]

The amazing thing is, Augustine was not different from you or me. Oh, maybe he was considerably smarter than I am, but I mean in the sense of his humanity. He was as each of us is—a fallen sinner who has been rescued by Christ. Yet, Augustine recognized that in reading the Holy Scriptures, he was able to make contact with the mind of God.[6] So it may be with you. That is, there is nothing unique or extra ordinary about Augustine's experience that you cannot experience. The movement inward and upward that Augustine came to know through his reading of the Bible is not counterintuitive. It is, in reality, the transformative power that a believer naturally, quite naturally, gleans from a thoughtful, prayerful, and sustained reading of the Holy Scriptures as scripture. That is a Scripture-filled life.

Such is the case that as you begin to build a Scripture-filled life, you will commence to unleash a transformative process in your very own life. By engaging the enterprise of reading the Holy Scriptures as scripture, a lá Augustine, you can formulate a "rereading and a reediting"[7] of your own life.

4. Studzinski, *Reading*, 76. Studzinski alludes here to Stock, *Augustine the Reader*, 14.
5. Studzinski, *Reading*, 77.
6. Ibid., 79.
7. Ibid., 83.

A Decision to Upgrade

Perhaps, at this point, you have already mentally assented to the idea that upgrading your commitment to reading the Holy Scriptures would be a good thing. You fully buy into the premise that, indeed, a Scripture-filled life is a noble endeavor. You cognitively assent to the notion that reading the Holy Scriptures with a different sense than what you have done in the past, most assuredly, would be an uplifting and edifying thing as a part of your spiritual growth and development. That is fantastic; but again, let it be said that simply diving, helter-skelter, headlong into the Bible without some fundamental changes in your reading habits will not automatically produce the kind of long-range, sustained, and serious engagement with the Holy Scriptures that is being advocated in this book.

It must also be made crystal clear that this is not a "how to" book, listing the simple and straightforward steps one must take to succeed in the task at hand. It is not a recipe card that you can take in hand and just mix the ingredients in the correct proportion, as if one were in quest of the perfect cake. No, you will need to move, thoughtfully and prayerfully, i.e., with your amazing mind and by the work of the Holy Spirit, inward and upward. As Casey remarks, "Experts in various fields are lured onto television talk shows and required to reduce their life's labor into five minutes of moronic simplicity. Like children who need their food cut up for them, we prefer to deal with little pieces rather than to chew over complex issues for ourselves. If we wish to be nourished directly by the Scriptures without seeking a pre-digested substitute, then we will probably need to develop new skills."[8]

Indeed, a conscious effort needs to be made in amending some existing patterns of how you have read the Bible in the past. Along with that, changing some of your set ways of viewing the text need to be addressed before our enterprise of reading the Holy Scriptures as scripture may effectively begin.

Old Habits Die Hard

To be straightforward, there are a few rather large and looming impediments to overcome in one's quest of reading the Bible in a new way, to read it, truly, as scripture. An initial hurdle for most readers will be the already established patterns of how one has read the Holy Scriptures in the past.

8. Casey, *Sacred Reading*, 8–9.

You cannot simply be reading the Bible in the very same way you have in the past; you will need to make some changes. As Casey has put it, many people have convinced "themselves that the Bible thinks as they do."[9] That, unfortunately, is a debilitating mindset that will seriously retard a proper reading of the Holy Scriptures as scripture.

A related barrier is that of pure habit. That is, certain habitual attitudes and behaviors that you have maintained can easily derail your decision to upgrade your reading of the Holy Scriptures. These habitual attitudes and behaviors are very likely to impinge upon our noble enterprise. What can be done about that?[10]

Habit formation is an intriguing aspect of the human mind. For example, we may easily identify something like conspicuous consumption as a habit we might wish to abandon, or at least diminish. Yet, the reality still exists that it is difficult for us to break habits of behavior, even if we are keenly aware of their existence. Habits are tough to shed. As one study notes, an "explanation for this failure to change behavior is that many aspects of unwanted lifestyle habits are immediately gratifying. That is, habits are maintained by incentives (e.g., the convenience of taking the car), biological factors (e.g., addiction to nicotine in cigarettes, metabolism in obesity), or the psychological needs they serve (e.g., self-esteem boost from shopping)."[11]

While shopping is not really the issue at hand, it serves to illustrate the point that there are some fascinating aspects of human cognition that impact our behavior, even the habitual patterns of how one has been reading the Bible. It is easy to have good intentions, but it is difficult to break behavioral habits. Thus, "when a behavior is new, untried, and unlearned, the intention of the individual will be primarily responsible for the behavior. However, that fact changes over time, and intention become less of a factor, and circumstances of environment become a very strong force. This grows to the point that, as behavior repeatedly takes place, habit increases and becomes a better predictor of behavior than behavioral intentions."[12]

Thus, the research shows that it will not be your good intentions that will carry you through on the noble quest to become an effective reader of

9. Ibid., 7.

10. Some material in this section appeared previously in Brookman, *Global Scenes*, 137–40.

11. Verplanken and Wood, "Interventions," 92.

12. Triandis, *Interpersonal Behavior*, 205.

the Holy Scriptures. Rather, you will need to establish patterns of practice that will, in the long run, establish you as a reader, hopefully, in a style somewhat akin to Augustine.

Why does the research demonstrate that good intentions are not enough? It seems that our brains work in such a way that habit formation is a very natural thing. The major mechanism in how we tend to establish habits is found in a part of the brain known as the basal ganglia. When it comes to the basal ganglia, one of the leading researchers is Dr. Ann M. Graybiel. She is the Walter A. Rosenblith Professor of Neuroscience in the Department of Brain and Cognitive Sciences at MIT. Graybiel was a 2002 recipient of the National Medal of Science, and she has written extensively about this fascinating bundle of nerves that is largely responsible for the neural patterns we know as habits.[13]

"Use doth breed a habit"

You and I both know that there are good habits, and then there are bad habits. While the assumption might be made that habits cannot be broken, the fact seems to be that there is a certain plasticity of the brain that allows for changes in habitual behavior.[14] Of course, we all know that changing or breaking a habit is difficult to do. Anyone who has tried to quit smoking, change eating habits, or quit watching TV knows that changing habitual patterns of behavior is a challenge. That is because several factors are in play, consistently favoring habit over intent. For instance, given that strong habits are "cued relatively directly by the environment with minimal decision making, the practiced response is likely to be more immediately available than thoughtfully generated alternatives."[15] A second factor is that "habits require minimal regulatory control."[16] That is, a "greater capacity is required to suppress habits than to carry out alternative behaviors that require conscious guidance and deliberation."[17] This is where the basal ganglia come into play. That wonderful and complex structure of the brain,

---

13. Graybiel, "Guide to the Anatomy"; Graybiel and Grillner, *Microcircuits*; Graybiel and Saka, "Basal Ganglia."

14. Graybiel and Grillner, *Microcircuits*, 31.

15. Verplanken and Wood, "Interventions," 93.

16. Ibid., 93.

17. Ibid.

according to Graybiel's research, is crucial in the circuitry and processing of behavior that becomes habit.

Research demonstrates that habits are very easily affected by the environment or circumstances into which we place ourselves.[18] In fact, putting yourself into familiar circumstances, whether that is location, friends, mood, etc., can trigger habitual behavior totally aside from your intentions or decisions; that is your basal ganglia at work.[19] On the other hand, changing a habit is very achievable, and oftentimes it is accomplished through changing one's circumstances.[20] That is to say, habitual gambling can more easily be thwarted by not going to casinos rather than by mere good intentions not to gamble. Fascinating as this brief exposé into the neuroscience behind some of our human behavior has been, one might be asking, "What is the point of this?" You may be wondering something like this—"I thought we were exploring aspects of reading the Holy Scriptures as scripture. What does the basal ganglia have to do with that?" Actually, I would say, it has plenty to do with that.

In our effort to become effective, new-style readers of the Holy Scriptures, establishing new habitual behaviors will be very desirable. The good news is that this is very doable. What would it take to get our basal ganglia to drive us to prayer in the same manner that it drives an addictive gambler to gamble? What would it take for us to read the Holy Text as scripture in such a way that we are hearing the living voice of God in newfound ways? Actually, simple repetition goes a long way to establishing and conditioning the sort of neuro-firing circuitry within the basal ganglia that will make desirable behavior habitual. Chapter 5 will deal with some specific ways of reading that will act as a catalyst in our enterprise. That is, based on the cognitive and neuro-scientific research that is available, you can learn and firmly establish habits of things like praying and reading.

Aesop May Have Had it Right

Perhaps today is the day that you wish to begin a conscious, rational, and prayerful movement toward a Scripture-filled life. However, within our culture of instant gratification and fast results, the novice reader needs to have realistic expectations. If you are currently in a pattern of reading the

18. Ibid., 91.

19. Ouellette and Wood, "Habit and Intention," 54–74.

20. Wood et al., "Changing Circumstances," 918–33.

Bible sporadically, be reasonable. Do not light out on an immediate quest to read the Bible for two hours a day, every day. That is, probably, a formula for failure. Remember that it is going to be the qualitative method of reading, not the sheer number of minutes you spend with the Holy Scriptures open on your lap that will determine your movement into a Scripture-filled life.

Remember Aesop? Do you remember the fable of the tortoise and the hare? Do you remember the moral of that particular story? If not, let me jog your memory. Aesop was a Greek who, it is generally thought, may have lived about 620–564 BC. There are a few references to his life in some of the ancient sources including Aristotle, Herodotus, and Plutarch, but generally speaking, he is a character shrouded in mystery. We do not factually know very much about the man. Yet, you hopefully had a childhood that included at least of few of his fables. The one about the tortoise and the hare has particularly wide appeal and is generally one of the better-known of Aesop's stories. The gist of the tale has the slow but persistent tortoise winning a race against the blazing fast but rather over-confident hare.

In a sense, we need to "slow down our intellectual metabolism and not expect to find quick and easy solutions."[21] In a word, we need some patience in this enterprise of reading the Holy Scriptures as scripture. Pawing at the entirety of the Bible in order to gobble it all in is not the way to approach a Scripture-filled life. Rather, when it comes to a deep and sustained reading of the Holy Scriptures, it would be good for us to develop a rational addiction. That is, a theory of rational addiction is one in which "rational means a consistent plan to maximize utility over time. Strong addiction to a good requires a big effect of past consumption of the good on current consumption."[22] In other words, the enterprise is long and slow as one continually builds upon good habitual behavior. How you read the Holy Scriptures now will dramatically impact how you will read them in fifteen years.

The Potency of God's Word

The kingdom principle of sowing and reaping will be at work in our enterprise. A strong case may, most certainly, be made that when communities of faith are moved to renewal, the "rediscovery of Scripture" tends to

---

21. Casey, *Sacred Reading*, 8.
22. Becker and Murphy, "A Theory of Rational Addiction," 675–700.

be linked to the change.[23] "It was an encounter with the Holy Scriptures that decisively influenced Augustine, Martin Luther, John Wesley, and the movements they led."[24] In such cases we see examples of the potency of the living voice of God. It elicits in individuals and in communities of faith a transformational strengthening of faith and yields amazing consequences as a result of those transformations.

The benefits of inculcating one's life with the Holy Scriptures are immeasurable. If one were looking for a specific text to latch onto in this regard, Romans 15:4 speaks very pointedly to some very specific outcomes from the study of the Scriptures. Paul says, "For whatever was written in the former days was written for our instruction, so that by steadfastness and by the encouragement of the scriptures we might have hope." Therefore, our present hope in God and the righteousness of his kingdom is bolstered by our building a Scripture-filled life in which we are reading the Holy Scriptures as scripture. One could go on and on, but of course, an apologetic presentation for the potency of the Bible in one's life may hardly be needed at this juncture. I suspect that you and I are literally on the same page at this point. We probably agree in heart and mind with the premises thus far. The problem is usually not so much discounting the transformative power of God's Word so much as simply not engaging the Holy Scriptures systematically as scripture in our reading. But, how does one do that? Where does one begin? In what manner does one proceed in such a daunting enterprise? The coming chapters will consider these questions and reflect on some interesting aspects of reading the Holy Scriptures as we ought.

There is a very apt thought by Richard Foster, who wrote, "When we come to the Scripture we come to be changed, not to amass information."[25] That ought to be our mindset. Unfortunately, many people typically read the Bible with what might be called secondary motives. It is not that these secondary motives are necessarily bad in any sense, but oftentimes the primary reason for reading the Holy Scriptures is lost in the shuffle of secondary motivations. For example, it is a common case that the Bible is read with an intellectual frame of reference or mindset. Perhaps one wants to gain a better grasp of the history or better appreciate the artistry of the great literary work resident within the pages of the Bible. As noted, these aims are not bad or sinister. Such aims are very legitimate. They are just

23. Burgess, *Why Scripture Matters*, 19.

24. Ibid.

25. Foster, *Celebration*, 60.

not meant to be the primary aim. They are ancillary and ought to be very consciously secondary in our reading of the Bible. God is self-manifested and self-revealing in the Holy Scriptures. An encounter with God, an encounter with the actual, living voice of God (*viva vox Dei*) should always be our primary motivation in reading the Holy Scriptures. It is with that motivation in the forefront of our hearts and minds that we are fully reading the Holy Scriptures as scripture. Unless that core motivation and recognition is present in the heart and mind of the reader, the activity of reading the Holy Scriptures will drift to the left or to the right into a potential sea of secondary concerns.

As we engage the enterprise of reading the Holy Scriptures as scripture, we need to eagerly anticipate and forthrightly expect that the Holy Spirit will let loose that power of which Augustine spoke—that power of the Bible to transform a life. With the presupposition firmly in mind that in the act of reading the Holy Scriptures God is speaking, we are opened up to a realm of unparalleled perception. Of course, just because God is speaking does not mean that we are listening, understanding, or in any way internalizing the revelatory disclosure that the Lord makes. The Scriptures require a *way* of reading.

As Wittgenstein famously noted, "You cannot hear God speaking to someone else, you can only hear Him if you are being addressed."[26] While Wittgenstein meant this in a grammatical, not a theological sense, it is very true in either sense. Thus, if the reader does not have an awareness that God speaks to individuals and that he speaks to individuals through the Holy Scriptures, then one might well read and read and read from the scriptural texts without ever having a sense of being the addressee to whom God is speaking. Unfortunately, this is oftentimes the case with readers of the Bible, even those within a community of faith. That is where this book comes into focus. The goal, the design, the prompting of this work is to get you reading the Holy Scriptures in a new way so that you come to the text of the Bible with an anticipation that God will be speaking directly to you.

The Ought Factor of Reading

So what ought we be doing when we read the Bible? We modern readers tend to read in a given slot on the spectrum of ways of reading that is quite distant from the early church fathers. To those patristic readers,

26. Wittgenstein, *Zettel*, section 717.

Scripture was the magnetic pole of their thought. In this way, the fathers differ from modern readers, not in any particular assumption about a verse or episode, or in any specific method, but in their overall assumptions. Modern readers assume what the Bible means by accurately referring to an *x*, whether event, mode of consciousness, or theological truth. For the fathers, the Bible is the array of words, sentences, laws, images, episodes, and narrative that does not acquire meaning because of its connection to an *x*; it confers meaning because it *is* divine revelation. Scripture is ordained by God to edify, and that power of edification is intrinsic to scripture.[27]

I am not suggesting, although it may initially sound so, that the church fathers had it exactly right and that we should follow precisely in their footsteps. I am suggesting that we moderns, in all likelihood, miss some crucial dimensions of reading the Holy Scriptures that earlier generations of readers picked up on as they read.

Reading the Holy Scriptures as Scripture

Reading the Holy Scriptures is like no other enterprise. It is like no other reading we do in that nothing else being read is like the Holy Scriptures. The Bible is different from any other type of text you may read. This is a crucial presupposition I make in this book. More will be said about the nature of this enterprise of reading the Holy Scriptures in subsequent chapters, but for now, the notion of the Bible being different is an underpinning element of the argument I wish to make. As a result of the Bible being different, you are engaged in an entirely different sort of enterprise when you read the Holy Scriptures as scripture.

Joel B. Green, in his book, *Seized by Truth: Reading the Bible as Scripture*, has nicely captured an important aspect of this notion. He writes,

> In short, "the Bible is Scripture" is first and foremost a theological statement. It draws attention to the origin, role, and aim of these texts in God's self-communication. It locates persons and a community of people, those who read the Bible as Scripture, on a particular textual map, a location possessing its own assumptions, values, and norms for guiding and animating particular beliefs, dispositions, and practices that together constitute that people.[28]

27. O'Keefe and Reno, *Sanctified Vision*, 11–12.
28. Green, *Seized by Truth*, 5.

The fact of the matter is, a person can simply and unassumingly read the Bible and, in the process, miss the pungent reality of reading it as scripture. That is, there is something crucial that is missing in this too commonly employed type of reading. Reading the Bible as scripture involves something more. That "something more" must include, at a very basic level, an understanding that the Holy Scriptures are addressed to us. In that sense, Green makes mention of the idea that the Bible has, somewhat, the nature of mail addressed to us, namely believing individuals and the church.[29] This nifty and oft alluded to idea comes originally from Paul Van Buren's portrayal of the church as, essentially, "reading someone else's mail."[30] Yet Van Buren's ultimate argument is quite disappointing in that he would seemingly have Christians "forfeit our claim to a stake in the texts."[31] That, we most certainly do not want to do! After all, it is addressed to *us*.

Reading the Holy Scriptures as scripture also entails certain attitudes we carry into the text. Consider the following snippet taken from Cosgrove's *The Meaning We Choose*. "Hence, reading the Bible as scripture calls for certain attitudes toward the text, among them a predisposition to read for elegance, nuance, weightiness and depth."[32]

While I agree with the proposition as it is stated, there is clearly much more to attitude than the few examples he lists. In fairness to Cosgrove, his intent here was not to provide a full list or discussion of those attitudes that are needful in order to properly read the Bible as scripture. Rather, this quotation is in the context of his making a point that depth and profundity are what he calls correlational criteria; they are related aspects of how one reads/interprets the Holy Scriptures. He says, "these ancient hermeneutical principles of relevance and profundity are closely related since attributing profundity to an interpretation of scripture is a perspectival judgment dependent on the identity and situation of the interpreters. What one community greets as profound, another may object to as merely abstruse.

---

29. Ibid., 50. In addition to Green, see also Davis, "Teaching the Bible Confessionally," 25, and Seitz, *Word Without End*, 4. Van Buren, himself, summarizes some of his points concerning this idea in his *According to the Scriptures*, 93.

30. Van Buren, "On Reading Someone Else's Mail," 595–606.

31. Davis, "Teaching the Bible Confessionally," 25. See also Van Buren, "On Reading Someone Else's Mail," where he intimates, quite incorrectly I believe, that Christians should give up their rights to the interpretation of the Hebrew Bible since it is, really, someone else's mail, namely the Jews'.

32. Cosgrove, "*Hermeneutica Sacra*," 55.

'Relevance,' then is a necessary condition of profundity, for when we say that something is profound we mean that it touches us deeply."[33]

At this point, one might well pause and resolve to reflect very conscientiously upon the sorts of attitudes we typically carry into our reading of the Holy Scriptures. In the next chapter, we will investigate some of the ways and means that will likely elicit a better reading of the Bible by us. One aspect that will be considered in more detail is the powerful linking of prayer to reading. As an integral prelude, a prayer of entrance into the very act of reading the Holy Scriptures offers a perfect setting in which one may introspectively consider one's attitudes. Such attitudes may well fluctuate from day to day. That fact alone would seem to reinforce the importance and the prudence of making prayer a consistent element in our practice of reading the Holy Scriptures as scripture.

33. Ibid., 54.

5

Methods of Reading

How We Think

HAVE YOU GIVEN MUCH thought to how you think? Naturally, how you think tremendously impacts how you read. I recently read a very fascinating book on the topic. It is called, *Thinking, Fast and Slow*.[1] Not only was it a very interesting read, I also learned a lot about how we think. As it turns out, you and I do some pretty fascinating things within the recesses of our minds. Thinking is very complicated, yet in this delightful romp through the human brain, Daniel Kahneman weaves together a number of wonderful stories and vignettes from our cognitive worlds as he convincingly builds a case for two general modes of thinking: fast and slow.

Kahneman, winner of the 2002 Nobel Prize in Economics, describes these two main manners of thinking, and he simply names them System 1 and System 2. System 1 is a fast, almost automatic and unconscious way of thinking. It is the system that operates all the time, and we are able to complete a large range of activities using System 1. For example, Kahneman cites some representative activities of System 1 thinking as:

Detect that one object is more distant than another.

Complete the phrase "bread and . . ."

Detect hostility in a voice.

Answer to 2 + 2

Understand simple sentences.

1. Kahneman, *Thinking*.

Read words on a large billboard.[2]

System 2, on the other hand, is slow. It proceeds deliberately with analytic and conscious effort in steps to reason out a thing. The sort of activities dealt with by System 2 "have one feature in common: they require attention and are disrupted when attention is drawn away."[3] In addition, System 2, while it is deliberate and rational, is also noticeably lazy. It seems that it tires quite easily. As Kahneman puts it, System 2 has "a reluctance to invest more effort than is strictly necessary."[4] Filling out a tax form or parking a car in a small spot, those are examples Kahneman gives as activities in which System 2 kicks into action. Then he gives the following example about System 2.

> One of the main functions of System 2 is to monitor and control thoughts and actions "suggested" by System 1, allowing some to be expressed directly in behavior and suppressing or modifying others. For an example, here is a simple puzzle. Do not try to solve it but listen to your intuition:
>
> A bat and ball cost $1.10.
>
> The bat costs one dollar more than the ball.
>
> How much does the ball cost?
>
> A number came to your mind. The number, of course, is ten—10¢. The distinctive mark of this easy puzzle is that it evokes an answer that is intuitive, appealing, and wrong. Do the math, and you will see. If the ball costs 10¢, then the total cost will be $1.20 (10¢ for the ball and $1.10 for the bat), not $1.10. The correct answer is 5¢.[5]

Most people reading that little puzzle will respond, as Kahneman says, with the answer of 10¢. In fact, "more than 50% of students at Harvard, MIT, and Princeton gave the intuitive—incorrect—answer. At less selective universities, the rate of demonstrable failure to check was in excess of 80%."[6] It seems that System 1 provides a very quick, intuitive suggestion and System 2 lazily "endorsed an intuitive answer that it could have rejected

2. Ibid., 21.
3. Ibid., 22.
4. Ibid., 31.
5. Ibid., 44.
6. Ibid., 45.

with a small investment of effort."[7] Remember, System 2 is generally lazy. Think of it; one of the earmarks of System 1 is that of understanding a simple sentence. How might that impact your reading of something that demands deliberate concentration? If you are casually reading something, your thinking is most likely System 1 thinking, and you are missing the sort of deliberate and focused aspects of thought that System 2 delivers.

The good news is that the extent of the careful and deliberate checking that is characteristic of System 2 actually varies among individuals.[8] You can consciously improve your attention and concerted effort when reading a text. You can develop a slow and deliberate style of reading the Holy Scriptures that will enhance the work of System 2 as you engage the text. Another piece of good news is that "very little repetition is needed for a new experience to feel normal."[9] Thus, System 2 thinking is desirable for critical, attentive reading, but it is lazy. However, with practice and conscious effort, you are able to become a more attentive reader.[10] As it turns out, you can hone your attention.

> In everyday language, the term "attention" also refers to an aspect of amount and intensity. The dictionary tells us that to attend is to apply oneself presumably to some task or activity. Selection is implied, because there are always alternative activities in which one could engage, but any schoolboy knows that applying oneself is a matter of degree. Lulled into a pleasant state of drowsiness by his teacher's voice, the schoolboy does not merely fail to pay attention to what the teacher says; he actually has less attention to pay.[11]

Another pretty fascinating aspect in all of this is the finding that when we are focused and attentive, engaged in System 2 thinking, our pupils dilate—always. That is, the pupils of our eyes are "sensitive indicators of mental effort."[12] Eckhard Hess provided much of the ground-breaking study on what is called pupillary responses, and a large literature on this specific subject has subsequently developed.[13] Hess described "the pupil of the eye

---

7. Ibid., 44.

8. Ibid., 46.

9. Ibid., 78.

10. See especially, Kahneman, *Attention and Effort*.

11. Ibid., 3.

12. Kahneman, *Thinking*, 32.

13. See, for example: Hess, *The Tell-Tale Eye*; Hess and Polt, "Pupil Size," 192; Kahneman and Peavler, "Incentive Effects," 312–18; Kahneman and Wright, "Changes of Pupil

as a window to the soul" because of this phenomenon.[14] Think of it; when you are concentrating, your pupils *will* dilate. This is a failsafe indicator that something very interesting is happening in your brain.

Getting Into the Flow of Things

Have you ever found yourself so enraptured in an activity that you completely lost a sense of time? Have you had the experience of not hearing someone talking to you because you were totally fixated on something you were doing? In such cases you were focused and concentrating at such a high level that the rest of the world was, in a sense, shut out. You were enjoying yourself while performing whatever task it was you were doing at the moment. Your pupils were, indeed, dilated. In such a case, you are said to be in a state of *flow*. The elite research guru of what is known as flow theory is Mihaly Csikszentmihalyi. While this formidable Hungarian name (pronounced something like–*cheek-sent-mə-hy-ee*) is certainly not a household name, he is the widely recognized premier scholar on this fascinating topic.[15]

Flow is a mental state, a phenomenology of the inner state of a person who is fully immersed in an activity. Csikszentmihalyi has described flow as completely focused motivation. How does one know when one is in the flow? Indeed, there are indicators, and you can be self-aware of being in the flow. In their research, Nakamura and Csikszentmihalyi identified six factors as encompassing an experience of flow.[16]

- intense and focused concentration on the present moment
- merging of action and awareness
- a loss of reflective self-consciousness (i.e., loss of awareness of oneself as a social actor)

Size," 187–96; White and Maltzman, "Pupillary Activity," 361–69; Ahem and Beatty, "Pupillary Responses," 1289–92.

14. Kahneman, *Thinking*, 32.

15. See, for example: Csikszentmihalyi, *Beyond Boredom*; Csikszentmihalyi, *Finding Flow*; Csikszentmihalyi, *Flow*; Csikszentmihalyi, *Creativity*; Massimini and Carli, "Systematic Assessment."

16. Nakamura and Csikszentmihalyi, "Flow Theory," 195–206.

- a sense that one can control one's actions; that is, a sense that one can in principle deal with the situation because one knows how to respond to whatever happens next

- a distortion of temporal experience (typically, a sense that time has passed faster than normal)

- experience of the activity as intrinsically rewarding, also referred to as autotelic experience

Those aspects above can appear independently of each other, but it is in combination that they constitute a so-called flow experience. While it seems that anyone can enter a flow state, it also appears to be the case that some personality types are more naturally fit to experience flow. Csikszentmihalyi postulated the "autotelic personality."[17] This is the type of person who enjoys life and tends to do things for their own sake as opposed to trying to achieve some external goal. "This kind of personality is distinguished by 'meta-skills,' which enable the individual to enter the flow and stay in it. These meta-skills include a general curiosity and interest in life, persistence, and low self-centeredness, which result in the ability to be motivated by intrinsic rewards."[18]

How about you? Do you exhibit any of those meta-skills? Are you naturally curious about things? Are you persistent? Are you excited about life? Where are you on the scale of self-centeredness? If you do exude some of these traits, if you are not a self-centered individual, then you are well on your way to being the sort of autotelic individual that Csikszentmihalyi describes below.

> An autotelic person needs few material possessions and little entertainment, comfort, power, or fame because so much of what he or she does is already rewarding. Because such persons experience flow in work, in family life, when interacting with people, when eating, even when alone with nothing to do, they are less dependent on the external rewards that keep others motivated to go on with a life composed of routines. They are more autonomous and independent because they cannot be as easily manipulated with threats or rewards from the outside. At the same time, they are

---

17. See Csikszentmihalyi, *Finding Flow*, 116–30 and also Csikszentmihalyi, *Beyond Boredom*, 112.

18. Nakamura and Csikszentmihalyi, "Flow Theory," 197.

more involved with everything around them because they are fully immersed in the current of life.[19]

Flow takes attention. Yet, there are definite limits to our attention. While there is a huge amount of information (input) that is available to a person at any time, there are limits to what the brain can process at any given moment. Csikszentmihalyi notes that we can process about 126 bits of information a second, and just to have a normal conversation with somebody requires about 40 bits of information per second.[20] This means that you are using about one-third of your capacity for processing information when engaged in a conversation with one person, if you are truly listening to what they have to say. Have you ever tried to listen closely to what two people are saying at the same time? It is extremely difficult. Try concentrating on what three people are saying at the same time; you cannot do it. All of your attention is taken, and there is no more available room for more input. This is what happens when you are in a state of flow. Virtually all of your attention is given over to the task; there simply is no more attention that can be allocated to other input. When you are in the state of flow, you are giving close attention to whatever is enrapturing you.

> The limit on attentional capacity appears to be a general limit on resources. . . . The completion of a mental activity requires two types of input to the corresponding structure: an information input specific to that structure, and a non-specific input which may be variously labeled "effort," "capacity," or "attention." To explain man's limited ability to carry out multiple activities at the same time, a capacity theory assumes that the total amount of attention which can be deployed at any time is limited.[21]

How does it feel to be in the flow? Csikszentmihalyi gives us some very specific aspects that he has identified by interviewing hundreds of the subjects in a number of studies. Following are the summary points he makes. These are what an individual typically feels when in a state of flow:

1. Completely involved in what we are doing—focused, concentrated.

2. A sense of ecstasy—of being outside everyday reality.

19. Csikszentmihalyi, *Finding Flow*, 117.
20. Csikszentmihalyi, *Optimal Experience*, 17.
21. Ibid., 18. Here, Csikszentmihalyi is citing Norman, *Memory and Attention*, 71.

3. Great inner clarity—knowing what needs to be done, and how well we are doing.

4. Knowing that the activity is doable—that our skills are adequate to the task.

5. A sense of serenity—no worries about oneself, and a feeling of growing beyond the boundaries of the ego.

6. Timelessness—thoroughly focused on the present, hours seem to pass by in minutes

7. Intrinsic motivation—whatever produces flow becomes its own reward.[22]

Note that he describes it with the word "ecstasy." It is, as he puts it, "stepping into an alternate state, a state of optimal performance."[23]

There you have it, a quick primer on the wonderful world of System 2 thinking and flow. Lest you slam the book shut in disgust at this point because your mind is filled with images of Zen Buddhism, chanting mantras, and a few advanced yoga moves, please take a deep breath—scratch that thought. Rather, pause for a moment and rationally consider that a philosophical system is not being advocated here. I am promoting neither an ancient Daoist tradition nor some new-age spinoff.[24] Rather, to the utter contrary, dear reader, what we have been exploring so far is simply neuroscience. Wait a second; "simply" is, perhaps, not the best word when we are delving into the cognitive arena of the brain. But, hopefully, you get the idea, and in the next chapter I will be linking all of this to a deep-rooted tradition within orthodox Christian spirituality in which elements of System 2 and flow are quite germane.

I want to bring all this talk about modes of thinking, dilating pupils, and autotelic meta-skills around to the enterprise of reading the Holy Scriptures as scripture by considering some of the elements of reading that can produce the sort of rich, spiritual dividends one desires to glean from a close and attentive reading of God's Word. Remember that such reading

22. See Csikszentmihalyi's 2004 TED Talk at http://www.ted.com/talks/mihaly_csik-szentmihalyi_on_flow.html.

23. Csikszentmihalyi, *Optimal Experience*, 32.

24. Although, a study comparing flow theory with the Daoist philosophy of Chuang-tzu has been made by W. Sun in a paper entitled, "Flow and Yu: Comparison of Csikszentmihalyi's Theory and Chuang-tzu's Philosophy," delivered at the 1987 meeting of The Anthropological Association for the Study of Play in Montreal.

was fundamental to Augustine's transformation. His reading of the Bible as scripture launched him on a trajectory inward and upward.[25] So it is that you are called to propel yourself in a like manner. As Gregory the Great said, "We should transform what we read within ourselves, so that the mind, roused by the ears, brings together and puts into practice what we have heard by means of our way of life."[26] That is what we want. We want our reading of the Holy Scriptures to become a practiced part of our inner world. Yet, this requires a slow, reflective, and calm poring over the texts. If that is the sort of experience you desire, a flow experience as you give your attention wholly to hearing the very voice of God as you read the Holy Scriptures, then it is time for you to read on and let your pupils dilate!

The Assiduity of it All

Have you ever read anything assiduously? Of course your answer will depend on what you think "assiduously" means. It is a good word. Do you have any recollection of hearing it before? As an adverb, assiduously describes an action done with close attention and care. As an adjective, an assiduous person is very diligent, very intent on whatever she or he may be doing. Does that sound familiar? Doesn't that ring of Csikszentmihalyi's description of the autotelic personality in a state of flow? Perhaps less frequently used by English speakers is the word in the form of a noun—assiduity. Did your eyes pause, ever so slightly, to look more carefully at the last word of the previous sentence because you did not immediately recognize it as being familiar to you? Have you ever even seen that word in print before your eyes quickly passed over it in the heading just above? Perhaps, or perhaps not; but again, it is a good word. Assiduity is careful, slow, persistent, focused attention to something.

Way back in the third century, Cyprian of Carthage (AD 200–258) used the Latin word from which our various English forms of the word, assiduously, derived.[27] It is a fairly famous passage in which he wrote, "May

25. Studzinski, *Reading*, 76.

26. Stock, *After Augustine*, 14–15; citing *Moralia in Iob*, 1.33.

27. The best work on Cyprian's life is Brent, *Cyprian*. For more scholarly research on Cyprian see Bakker, Van Geest, and Van Loon, *Cyprian of Carthage*. Also, one cannot go wrong by reading the man's letters and treatises. For these, see Campbell, *Complete Works*.

you be assiduous in prayer or in reading."[28] While this line has been variously translated, Cyprian is clearly admonishing that careful and focused attention be paid by us in our praying and in our reading.[29] It was actually, however, the second part of his sentence, which I did not quote, that became very widely cited and particularly well-known in the medieval period. The gist of the second part of the sentence is this—at times you speak to God, and at times he speaks to you. That is, when praying, it is you who is speaking to God, but by contrast, when you read the Holy Scriptures, it is God speaking to you.

Origen (AD 184–253) also mentions the importance of reading assiduously.[30] He was a prodigious writer. The church historian Eusebius of Caesarea (AD 263–339) mentioned a catalogue of all of Origen's works.[31] Unfortunately, that list was in one of Eusebius' works that is now lost. However, Jerome had access to that list, and he noted that Origen composed about 2,000 works.[32] More will be said about Origen later for he has many interesting things to say about the reading and interpretation of the Holy Scriptures. For now, however, it should be noted that in a letter to one of his students, Gregory of Thaumaturgus, Origen wrote, "You therefore, my true son, devote yourself first and foremost to reading the holy Scriptures; but devote yourself. For when we read holy things we need much attentiveness."[33]

---

28. Cyprian of Carthage, *Ad Donatum* 1.15 (PL 4:221). *Sit tibi vel oratio assidua vel lectio* . . . The verb, *assidua*, is an imperative from *assiduo*. I have chosen to translate that as a stative form, "be assiduous." One might also form it as an adverb in English with the sense of, "Either pray assiduously or read assiduously."

29. Robertson, *Lectio Divina*, xi. He translates the phrase as, "You should apply yourself to prayer or reading." Yet, this misses the thrust of *assidua*.

30. For nice introductions to Origen, see McGuckin, *Westminster Handbook* and Trigg, *Origen*. For more depth and details see: Lubac, *History and Spirit*; Heine, *Origen*; Martens, *Origen and Scripture*; Hanson *Allegory and Event*. For a sampling of Origen's writings, I recommend Balthasar, *Origen*.

31. Eusebius, *Historia ecclesiastica* 6.32.3.

32. Jerome (*Rufinus* 2.22) says concerning the works of Origen, "Count up the index contained in the third volume of Eusebius . . . and you will not find, I do not say six thousand, but about a third of that number of books." What is very interesting is that in Letter 33 to Paula written about AD 384, Jerome listed 786 works written by Origen. Yet some of the titles not appearing in Jerome's list, we presently have. Therefore his list could not have been a complete one.

33. Origen, "Letter of Origen to Gregory."

Thus, the importance of reading the Word of God assiduously becomes dramatically vivid to us as we fathom the awesome reality of God speaking directly to us. Engaging the Holy Scriptures as scripture does demand a certain level of assiduous reading. Remember, God is speaking to us as we read his Word.

The Intertwining of Prayer and Reading

That reciprocal notion of you speaking to God (prayer) and God speaking to you (reading) is, indeed, a forceful element. The linking of prayer and reading by Cyprian in his admonition to be careful and focused (assiduous) in both is also echoed by Jerome. The conscious intertwining of prayer and reading is a fundamental and crucial aspect to the concept of reading the Holy Scriptures as scripture, and Jerome alludes to the idea of blending the two. For example, he makes mention of this back and forth connection of prayer and holy reading in a letter written to Marcella in AD 385.[34] In a reference to Origen and his colleagues, Jerome remarked that, "Day and night they made it their habit to make reading follow upon prayer, and prayer upon reading, without a break."[35] Jerome was encouraging Marcella to emulate this sort of continual intertwining of prayer and reading.

About eighteen years later, in AD 403, Jerome wrote a letter[36] to a woman by the name of Laeta. She was the daughter-in-law of Paula, a well-known friend of Jerome.[37] Paula (the elder), also known as Saint Paula of Rome (AD 347–404) met Jerome in 382 and later moved to Bethlehem where she founded a monastery and a convent. Paula lived for about twenty years in Bethlehem, and she died there at the age of fifty-six. Laeta had a daughter who she named after the girl's grandmother. Thus, it is a little complicated,

34. Marcella (AD 325–410) was a wealthy, aristocratic widow in Rome who abandoned Roman high society to live an ascetic life of prayer and doing acts of charity. Much of her story is gleaned from Jerome's *Letter* 127. For example, Jerome noted of Marcella that, "Her ardent love for God's Scriptures surpasses all belief. . . . Meditation in the law meant for her not a mere reperusal of Scriptures, as the Jewish Pharisees think, but a carrying it out in action." (*Letter* 127.4).

35. Jerome, *Letter* 43:1 (PL 22:478) *Hoc diebus egisse vel noctibus, ut et lectio orationem susciperet et oratio lectionem.*

36. Jerome, *Letter* 107.

37. For a brief overview of Jerome's network of women readers, see for example, Studzinski, *Reading to Live*, 66–74; Stemberger, *Jews and Christians*, 101–5; LeMoine, "Jerome's Gift," 230–41; Kelly, *Jerome* 91–103.

but there are two people named Paula in the letter. It is Paula (the younger) who is the subject of Jerome's *Letter* 107. This letter by Jerome was in reply to a missive sent by Laeta who was asking the wise and learned Jerome how she might best educate her daughter. In his reply, Jerome gave some interesting advice about how to provide a proper education for the young Christian girl. It is a fascinating letter filled with all sorts of wise counsel.[38]

Jerome did not think, however, that his ambitious program for learning for the young girl could be carried out effectively in Rome. He advised Laeta to send her daughter (Paula the younger) to Bethlehem to live with the girl's grandmother (Paula the elder) and her aunt (Eustochium). Laeta took his advice and she, literally, shipped her daughter off to Palestine. The girl arrived in AD 404, and she lived there nursing the aged Jerome until 420 when he died.

In the letter of advice to Laeta concerning the education of her daughter, Jerome revisits this theme of the intertwining of prayer and reading of the Holy Scriptures, in wording quite similar to what we saw in his earlier letter to Marcella about Origen's habit of blending prayer and reading. He wrote, "Let reading follow prayer and prayer follow reading" (*Orationi lectio, lectioni succedat oratio*).[39]

Even a cursory reading of Jerome's letters makes it crystal clear that he had a considerable network of women with whom he consistently communicated as he encouraged them to be reading and studying the Holy Scriptures. This was groundbreaking in a number of respects. "Jerome thus represents a man of profoundly conservative views whose actions and convictions led to radical departures from ancient educational practices. Jerome's authority as a biblical commentator guaranteed that many devout aristocratic women could aspire to the model he provided for them: a religious life devoted to charity, good works, ascetic practices, and the study of Scripture."[40]

The man not only wrote many letters to women, he also dedicated most of his commentaries to women. This, of course, implies that they would be reading them, as he so often encouraged the women to always be studying the Scriptures. Of the twenty-three biblical commentaries by Jerome that survive, over half of them (twelve) are dedicated to women. Jerome "established a sound foundation upon which women could base

---

38. For the complete letter, see: Jerome, *Selected Letters*, 338–71.

39. Jerome, *Letter* 107:9.

40. LeMoine, "Jerome's Gift," 241.

the legitimacy of their claims for access to Scripture."[41] He understood the power of reading the Holy Scriptures, and Jerome was always admonishing and inspiring the aristocratic Roman women within his network to seriously engage the text. In this way, Jerome "pointed to new capabilities and expectations for women."[42] Take the example of Eustochium (mentioned above) who learned Hebrew so well that she was able to recite the Psalms with flawless pronunciation in their original language.[43] Thus, it should not be a surprise that Jerome dedicated two of his greatest commentaries, those on Isaiah and Ezekiel, to Eustochium.

Listening to Cyprian, Jerome, and the Old Rabbi

So, perhaps, as Cyprian and Jerome encouraged us to do, and as Origen seemingly put into practice, we ought then to try to attentively focus upon the process of holy reading and its counter link to prayer in such a way that one naturally does follow the other. The act of reading the Holy Scriptures as scripture should enthrall us. It is in this reciprocal endeavor of speaking to God (prayer) and listening to God (reading Holy Scripture), we commence to engage this tantalizing enterprise of reading the Holy Scriptures as scripture. It should create a flow experience for us.

As the old Rabbi said, "When I pray, I pray quickly, because I am talking to God; but when I read the Torah, I read slowly, because God is talking to me." This old rabbinic saying is anonymous; however, it seemingly derives from the earlier statement by Cyprian.[44] The horse sense of it clearly speaks to the notion of one combining the elements of praying and reading. Yet, the way in which they are to be combined is very instructive. While it is assumed by the rabbi that the righteous person should be praying and reading, the way in which this is done is also important. When you pray, you should keep it short because you are talking to God. However, when you read the Scriptures, oh, then you should be taking your time, poring over what you are reading. You must be ruminating, meditating, contemplating. Do not hurry; do not rush God along as he is speaking to you through his Word.

---

41. Ibid., 231.
42. Ibid., 233.
43. Kelly, *Jerome*, 97.
44. Either that, or Cyprian borrowed it from an earlier, unknown, rabbinic source.

System 2, Flow, and the Living Voice of God

Thinking with System 2 focus and entering a state of flow in which your reading experience is so focused and enjoyable that you are lost in the world of listening to the *viva vox Dei*—this is an enterprise that you, very likely, may not have fully experienced before. Experiment; be patient and persistent as you consciously move to change the way in which you have been reading the Bible. Be encouraged. Encapsulating prayer, be it ever so short (remember the rabbi's admonition), with a slow and attentive reading of the Holy Scriptures will produce a new paradigm for you that should invigorate your desire to read God's Word. In the next chapter, we will consider a very old Christian tradition of reading that may well strike a chord with you as we consider one method of reading.

6

Conceptualizing a Method

The Case of *Lectio Divina*

IT WAS MENTIONED EARLIER that there is no magic bullet, foolproof recipe, or infallible formulaic series of steps to read the Holy Scriptures as scripture. Yet, taking to heart what we have learned about the notions of how we think, what it means to experience flow, and the practice of melding prayer and holy reading, one begins to conceptualize some of the scaffolding that can lead to success in this noble enterprise of reading the Holy Scriptures as scripture.

I would like to add to this framework a very old Christian tradition from which we may well learn something. It is a method that centers itself upon how one ought to read the Holy Scriptures. The tradition is called *lectio divina*. It is a way of reading. It is sacred reading of the Holy Scriptures. It is not necessarily *the* way to read, but for some, it may offer a window of opportunity to change a few of your detrimental habits and to create some new patterns in the way you read the Holy Scriptures. It is a way of opening up yourself to the Holy Spirit as you seek to hear God's voice in the text.

While the term, *lectio divina*, may be familiar to some who identify with the Roman Catholic tradition, I think it is fair and accurate to say that, generally speaking, many Christians within a Protestant tradition may not be familiar with the term. Protestants are more likely to be better acquainted with the terminology of "having devotions." However, you will see in the end that *lectio divina* really is quite akin to what we Protestants might refer to as a particular way to have devotions. Do not let the Latin term or its traditional link to Roman Catholicism be any sort of impediment to exploring this way of reading. Wesley Kort makes a keen observation about the applicability of *lectio divina* for all believers. He writes that, "Calvin could not have accomplished what he did with his doctrine of reading Scripture if it were not for the tradition of *lectio divina*. By his doctrine of Scripture, he took this practice out of its monastic setting and inserted it into the lives of every Christian."[1] Thus, I hope that we Protestants can forthrightly acknowledge that we might be able to learn something from this practice that has incredibly old roots within Christianity.

Some have used the word "ancient" to describe the tradition. However, ancient is relative. It was in the third and fourth centuries AD that the elemental building blocks of this practice began to take root. Since I come from an academic background in which I originally focused upon ancient Near Eastern civilizations in the third millennium BC, I don't find the traditions behind *lectio divina* to be all that ancient. However, I will assent that, in terms of church history, the third century could be reckoned as ancient.

The phrase, *lectio divina*, has the meaning of "sacred reading." The way in which the phrase ultimately comes to be used is that of an activity or set of activities as a manner of reading. However, that is not the sense in the earliest uses of the term. That is to say, authors before the medieval period typically used the phrase to refer to what was being read, namely the Holy Scriptures.[2] It was only later, in the Middle Ages, that the typical use for the phrase came to describe a method of reading.

It was Guigo II, a monk of the twelfth century who is usually credited with giving *lectio divina* the systematic structure of four stages in sacred reading. He wrote a work entitled *The Ladder of Monks* in which he developed what became a rather widely held, standard formulation of the method of *lectio divina*. He did this by employing the imagery of a ladder.[3] In Guigo's design, *lectio divina* was comprised of four basic elements or stages known by four Latin words: *lectio* (reading the text), *meditatio* (meditating on the text), *oratio* (praying the text), and *contemplatio* (contemplating the text). These comprised the rungs of his ladder.

While all four of the Latin words have very recognizable English derivatives, there is more to the essence of each stage than one sees at first

1. Kort, *Take, Read*, 23.

2. For example, see Cyprian, *Of Jealousy and Envy*, 16; Ambrose, *Of the Good Death*, 1.2; Augustine, *Expositions on the Psalms*, 36.3.1.

3. Guigo, *Ladder of Monks*. Subsequent references to citations from Guigo will include the section (Roman numeral) and the page number of this edition (Arabic numeral).

glance from the mere word. In *The Ladder of Monks*, Guigo explained the sense of the four activities as follows:

- *lectio* (reading): "is the careful study of the Scriptures, concentrating all one's powers on it."

- *meditatio* (meditation): "is the busy application of the mind to seek with the help of one's own reason for knowledge of hidden truth."

- *oratio* (prayer): "is the heart's devoted turning to God to drive away evil and obtain what is good."

- *contemplatio* (contemplation): "The mind is in some sort lifted up to God and held above itself, so that it tastes the joys of everlasting sweetness."[4]

How might these elements play out practically in your quest of reading the Holy Scriptures as scripture? Imagine this scenario. You find a quiet place without distractions where you can give full attention to your reading. Pray that God would open your mind. Then you spend time reading a particular passage, perhaps aloud, two or three times. Then you take time to meditate on it, noticing words and phrases, ideas or images. Then you offer these things to God and ask for further wisdom. Finally, you contemplate it by further thought, journaling, or an artistic activity.[5]

Here is Guigo II, in his own words, as he related the story of how the idea of the ladder came to him.

> One day when I was busy working with my hands I began to think about our spiritual work, and all at once four stages in spiritual exercise came into my mind: reading, meditation, prayer and contemplation. These make a ladder for monks by which they are lifted up from earth to heaven. It has few rungs, yet its length is immense and wonderful, for its lower end rests upon the earth, but its top pierces the clouds and touches heavenly secrets.[6]

The four Latin words that are behind the four phases of activity are worth knowing well. We will explore only the first two stages, but one should internalize the terms and the essence behind the use of each one.

---

4. Ibid., II, 68.

5. I wish to express thanks here to my colleague, Katy Wehr, for offering these suggestions and insights into practicing *lectio divina*. She has been a participant in *lectio* groups and has a particular interest in this discipline.

6. Guigo, *Ladder of Monks*, II, 67–68.

I think it is a good general practice, every time you read from the Holy Scriptures, to commence with prayer in which you tell God your intent and desire to read his Word on this particular occasion as an exercise in true sacred reading (*lectio divina*). State to him your desire to be prompted by the Holy Spirit, as you carefully, attentively, and thoughtfully read the very voice of God (*viva vox Dei*). One may wish to follow the admonition of Isaac of Nineveh, a bishop in the late sixth century. He wrote, "You should not approach the words of the Holy Scriptures, which are full of mystery, without first praying something like this: 'Lord, assist me in perceiving the power here [in this text].'[7]

My aim, in this chapter however, is to focus only upon the first two rungs (*lectio* and *meditatio*) in assisting you to conceptualize a method for reading the Holy Scriptures as scripture. The final two rungs of Guigo's ladder (*oratio* and *contemplatio*) will merely be addressed in passing at the end of this chapter without any of the particulars I address concerning the first two rungs of the ladder. However, you will see that the conceptualizing of a method, as modeled in the traditional forms of *lectio divina*, entails an array of activities, any one of which does not function well without inclusion of the others.

The Act of Reading

The first term to consider is *lectio*. This Latin word is usually translated into English as the noun, "reading."[8] Yet, the fact of the matter is that the solitary English word "reading" is not, in any way, adequate to express the depth inherent in *lectio* as an activity of sacred reading. That is, a reading of the newspaper is a wholly different activity than a reading of the Holy Scriptures. Think of it; most of our readings tend to be quite superficial both in what we read and how we read it. To the contrary, there is nothing superficial about the various stages of *lectio divina*, starting with *lectio*. Do you remember the famous childlike voice heard by Augustine that triggered his conversion? The mysterious voice called out and commanded Augustine

---

7. Isaac of Nineveh, *Mystic Treatises*. See also: Brock, *Wisdom*; Wright, *Syriac Literature*.

8. The formation of the word as a noun derives from the third declension nominative form *lēctiō*.

to *tolle, lege* (Take! Read!).[9] As Augustine followed the command and read from Romans 13:13–14, "a light of certainty turned on" in his heart.[10]

But, exactly how is it that reading (*lectio*) can change us?

> How can reading the Bible cause those life changes to occur that are the essence of following Christ? The elimination of bad habits and selfish ways, the deep shift of heart in which one becomes a truly loving person, the growing docility to the Holy Spirit—how can *lectio* accomplish all these things?
>
> The succinct answer is that in *lectio* we meet the living and powerful God in an encounter that changes us. These questions remain unanswerable until we begin a regular practice of *lectio*, discovering for ourselves the unique relationship which will emerge. We can close off real encounter by not doing *lectio* or by doing it superficially. But if we simply give ourselves to the process, in humility and receptivity, *lectio* does its work in our heart.[11]

Thus, it does not simply happen. True, Augustine was converted in a moment by reading, but he subsequently gave a lifetime over to *lectio*. You have to make an investment of time into your project of *lectio*. But, really, how does one give one's self over to reading in our twenty-first century American culture? That is a serious challenge. The amazing thing is, you can do it. You can resolve and carry through on a planned and measured project of *lectio*. As we saw in chapter 4, habit formation is relatively easy. It is the breaking of old, established habits that proves more difficult, and in all likelihood you have some firmly established habits of non-*lectio*.

Guigo II considered *lectio* to be "the careful study of the Scriptures, concentrating all one's powers on it."[12] That sounds a little bit like the reader is, ideally, experiencing flow when fitfully engaged in *lectio*, and we saw the wonderful effects of flow back in chapter 4. Please do not get the idea that you need to invest hours and hours reading every day in order for the benefits of *lectio* to kick in for you. As Csikszentmihalyi noted, "The psychological effects of activities are not linear, but depend on their systemic relation to everything else we do. For instance, even though food is a source of good moods, we cannot achieve happiness by eating around the clock. Meals raise the level of happiness, but only when we spend around

9. The verbal form comes from the present active, *legō* ("I read, I gather").
10. Augustine, *Confessions*, VIII.12.
11. West, *No Moment Too Small*, 63–64.
12. Guigo II, *Ladder*, II, 68.

5 percent of our waking time eating; if we spend 100 percent of the day eating, food would quickly cease to be reward."[13] So it is with *lectio*. Do not be obsessed by your good intentions to the point that you try to overwhelm your former bad habits of non-reading by inundating yourself with *lectio*. In other words, don't feel like you must now be reading the Bible something like three hours a day in order to reap the benefits of *lectio*. That simply is not the case.

St. Benedict and Albert Einstein

Now, IT IS TRUE that there is a very old tradition that comes from the writings of St. Benedict (ca. AD 480–550) of allocating three hours a day to sacred reading.[14] Benedict composed the well-known *Rule of Saint Benedict* (RB) that laid out a number regulations for living the monastic life. If you are going to live a monastic lifestyle, then I suppose three hours a day of *lectio* could work for you. However, for most of us, the manner of life we live is not a communal, monastic lifestyle. Thus, Benedict's rules probably do not aptly apply to us in most cases. Rather, I would strongly suggest that the element of time should not be of any consequence when it comes to your personal *lectio*.

For myself, the primary concerns, rather than time, are those of attitude and concentration. The amount of time spent reading should be of little or no significance. If you enter into flow during your *lectio*, time will cease to be a matter of concern or awareness anyway. Remember that one of the key findings related to flow is that one loses a sense of time during the activity; it is enjoyable and a long time seems like a short time. A bird watcher, engrossed in the hunt for a rare sighting is not normally concerned that exactly an hour or three hours is pre-planned and incorporated into the activity. So also, the humble, seeking, concentrating reader of the Holy Scriptures need, in no way, to be counting minutes or watching the clock

13. Csikszentmihalyi, *Finding Flow*, 35–36.

14. For the life of St. Benedict see Butcher, *Man of Blessing*. The only information that is contemporaneous comes from Gregory the Great. See his *Dialogues, Book II: Saint Benedict*. A good edition to read is Kardong, *Life of Saint Benedict*. Depending on the time of year, the rule of Benedict allowed for even more than three hours a day for reading within the monastic community. There were earlier monastic guidelines that also allocated time for reading, but Benedict's three hours is a longer prescribed time. There is an interesting discussion of the three-hour guideline in Vogüé, *Rule of Saint Benedict*, 242–45.

in order to fulfill some sort of mental mandate that x number of minutes or hours of time is spent reading on any given occasion.

There is a story about Albert Einstein that produced a widely cited quotation from this physicist who gave us the theory of relativity. According to the tale, he was once asked to explain the concept of time and relativity in a simple, concise, and understandable way. He promptly replied, "When you are courting a nice girl, an hour seems like a second. When you sit on a red-hot cinder, a second seems like an hour. That's relativity."[15]

Concerning the amount of time one should dedicate to reading, a good and reasonable suggestion by Casey is to

> . . . identify a brief daily slot that we could devote to sacred reading—with a backup, if necessary. The main thing is to be realistic. Lifelong exposure to God's word is more like a marathon than a sprint. It makes more sense to get something started in an imperfect state than to procrastinate forever. It is better for morale to spend five minutes once a day and stick with it, than to plan on a longer duration and fail to find time. Momentum will develop, and with the confidence that comes from success we can modify our tactics according to our experience.[16]

The activity of *lectio* should be a joy, not a burden. Have you ever had the experience of getting into a novel that could be described as a page-turner? You wanted to keep going on, turning the next page to find out what would happen next. In the same way, reading from the pages of the Holy Scriptures can engulf the deep reader. Of course, *lectio* also brings us to reading as formation, not merely for the gleaning of information or for entertainment, but for spiritual insight and wisdom.[17] One aspect of this deep reading is that of deep listening. We want to listen to the *viva vox Dei*.

Two Modes of Reading

When was the last time you read something out loud? While it still happens from time to time, I think it is fair to say that most of our reading tends to be done silently. Yes, of course, mothers and fathers read bedtime stories to their kids out loud. People read the instructions to board games out loud to the group playing the game. In fact, there are many settings and

15. Arden, *Science, Theology, and Consciousnes*, 97.
16. Casey, *Sacred Reading*, 80.
17. Mulholland, *Shaped*. See especially chapter 5, "Information Versus Formation."

circumstances when vocal reading takes place. But if one sits down to read something like the newspaper or the latest Dan Brown novel, the reading is normally done silently. We know there are these two viable and yet different modes of reading: silent and vocal. Paul Saenger began his mesmerizing book, *Space Between Words: The Origins of Silent Reading*, by saying, "Modern reading is a silent, solitary, and rapid activity. Ancient reading was usually oral—either aloud, in groups, or individually, in a muffled voice. Reading, like any human activity, has a history."[18] While there are examples of silent reading in antiquity, the general consensus of opinion is that this was rare, and it was really not until the tenth century that reading silently became the standard mode for the activity.[19]

There is also the famous story of Augustine. He was seemingly caught off guard and impressed by the sight of Ambrose (ca. AD 340–397)[20] reading silently. It is a celebrated passage in the *Confessions*, and as we pick up the narrative, Augustine was in the presence of the great Bishop of Milan whom he clearly admired.

> There were questions I wanted to put to him, but I was unable to do so as fully as I wished, because the crowds of people who came to him on business impeded me, allowing me little opportunity either to talk or listen to him. He was habitually available to serve them in their needs, and in the very scant time that he was not with them he would be refreshing either his body with necessary food or his mind with reading. When he read his eyes would travel across the pages and his mind would explore the sense, but his voice and tongue were silent. We would sometimes be present, for he did not forbid anyone access, nor was it customary for anyone to be announced; and on these occasions we watched him reading silently. It was never otherwise, and so we too would sit for a long time in silence, for who would have the heart to interrupt a man so engrossed? . . . Another and perhaps more cogent reason for his habit of reading silently was his need to conserve his voice, which

---

18. Saenger, *Space Between Words*, 1.

19. Manguel, *History of Reading*, 43. See also: Balogh, "Voces Paginarum," 84–109, 202–40; Hendrickson, "Ancient Reading", 182–96. A contrary argument is made by Knox, "Silent Reading in Antiquity," 421–35. However, his article seems to demonstrate that while there are exceptions, it does not carry the weight of changing the consensus of opinion that reading in the ancient world strongly tended to be vocalized.

20. Good, readable biographies of Ambrose include Paredi, *Saint Ambrose* and Dudden, *Life and Times*.

was very prone to hoarseness. But whatever his reason, that man undoubtedly had a good one.[21]

Doesn't that passage portray a vivid image? There was the illustrious Ambrose, his eyes focused and intent upon the pages. He was reading, yet his lips were not uttering any sounds. His tongue was silent. Ambrose was so absorbed in this mode of reading that Augustine did not want to interrupt him. Augustine was seemingly amazed at this sight of silent reading. The way he wrote about it, this scene of Ambrose certainly caught his attention. In the episode, Augustine has been described as "an undergraduate who is brought before a teacher whom he longs to meet, only to find that he is too shy to articulate his deepest concerns."[22]

There is some debate over the exact nuance of what Augustine was really trying to say here about silent reading. Saenger is of the opinion that Ambrose was reading silently "either to seek privacy by concealing the content of his book or to rest his voice."[23] On the other hand, Mary Carruthers states, "I do not find these traits in what Augustine says, however. Instead this seems to me a sympathetic portrait of a very busy man's efforts to make time for the kind of scholarly study that refreshes him, written (we should remember) by a man who by then was himself a very busy bishop, subject to exactly the interruptions and demands he shows us in Ambrose."[24] Regardless of whichever subtle twist one favors for why Ambrose was reading silently, the fact clearly remains that we seem to have something unusual going on here that Augustine felt compelled to record. Carruthers contends that what really "surprises Augustine is that Ambrose never seemed to read in *the other way*, though others were present."[25]

It seems to me that what we have in Augustine's passage about Ambrose's silent reading is a description of a person who is in flow, engaged in the deep reading of the Holy Scriptures. Ambrose was in cavernous thought, pouring over the scriptural text in front of him. That is *lectio* as Guigo II conceptualized it, and that is exactly the sort of concentration and flow activity we want to achieve as we read the Holy Scriptures. That is the first stage—reading (*lectio*). Now we move to the second stage in Guigo's classical formulation of *lectio divina*.

21. Augustine, *Confessions*, VI.3.
22. Stock, *After Augustine*, 48–49.
23. Saenger, *Space Between Words*, 8.
24. Carruthers, *Book of Memory*, 213–14.
25. Ibid., 214.

The Acts of Meditating Upon the Holy Scriptures

In the scheme of Guigo's ladder, the second rung is meditation. The Latin term, *meditatio*, has been explained by a number of writers in a variety of ways. Thus, in the end, there is no firmly agreed upon consensus of how to tightly and concisely render the notion of *meditatio*. As a result, there are seemingly, for the deep reader, many ways and methods to engage the concept of *meditatio* without becoming hung up on a particular sequence of specific acts. If you recall, Guigo II described *meditatio* as "the busy application of the mind to seek with the help of one's own reason for knowledge of hidden truth." What kind of a process does that bring to your mind? It seems to be quite open to interpretation. Of course, Guigo's framing of *meditatio* is not the categorical word on the matter. After all, plenty of ancient writers before him wrote on the topic of *meditatio*. Guigo II simply gave us the rungs of the ladder in *lectio divina*; he did not prove to be the authoritative formulator of any rigid methodology. Therefore, let us consider a few aspects that tend to come to the forefront among the ancient and medieval writers whenever *meditatio* is the subject at hand. Again, this will not be a comprehensive examination of all of the elements of this particular stage of *lectio divina*. This little overview will introduce you to just a few representative samples of how the term has been perceived and practiced.

There would seem to be a hefty catalog of possible methods for meditating upon the Holy Scriptures, and I suspect that different techniques will work for different people. That is, there is not one way to practice *meditatio*. Yet, if we wish to generalize, we could say that the acts of a meditative reader are those by which the text is somehow internalized. The meditative reader, in some fashion, internalizes the Holy Scriptures upon which she or he is meditating.

Meditatio is something quite beyond simple memorization. However, I think memorization is an important and interesting element, and I will discuss memorizing scriptural texts a little later. But first, consider the words of Philoxenes of Mabboug, a sixth-century Syrian Christian (d. AD 523) who wrote an interesting letter to a superior in a nearby monastery. In the missive, he noted that long, focused, repetitive attention to a limited portion of the Holy Scriptures had its merits. Philoxenes wrote that "there is absolutely nothing untoward for a person to be mentally preoccupied with a single verse of the psalter for seven days and seven nights, for as it was said by our holy Fathers, 'It is better to have a single verse close at hand than to have a thousand at a distance.'"[26]

Indeed, meditative focus on a single verse for a week probably seems like a bit much for most people in our time and culture. Yet, think of it; how would such attention and focus upon a text of scripture impact you? How do you think it might transform you in some way? Have you ever, in your reading of the Bible, attempted to concentrate your focus on a particular book or chapter within a book for a period of time? Of course you probably have, although your endeavor may have lacked the quantitative degree of *meditatio* that Philoxenes was advocating. Oftentimes a weekly group Bible study, for example, will concentrate on a particular book for weeks or months. That sort of focused attention over a sustained period of time will normally afford one the opportunity to give a slow and measured reading to a specific book or set of chapters. So what Philoxenes was advocating is not unheard of in our day and age; it simply is not usually practiced at the level of intensity he was promoting. However, wouldn't it be a very interesting experiment for you to try what we might call "Philoxenes' challenge?" Try it. Pick a chapter or a set of verses and read it at least twice a day for seven days—once during the day and once at night. Of course, that is the *lectio* stage. You now should add the act of *meditatio* to that. Endeavor to internalize the text of scripture you have chosen. As Philoxenes said, read and meditate upon the chapter or verses in such a way that you have it "close at hand." Try to make it vividly applicable to you. This is an experiment—a challenge, if you will. My hunch is that you will somehow be impacted, even if in a modest way, by simply carrying through on those acts of sustained reading and meditating by internalizing the message of the text. By bringing a portion of God's Word close at hand, we allow it, in some unfathomable way, to scrutinize us. For the "principal function of the Bible is not for it to be scrutinized, but for it to examine us."[27] That is certainly one important aspect of *meditatio*.

Can You Smell the Text?

Some synesthetes can smell different colors. For other synesthetes, particular words carry a particular odor. They are, quite literally, able to smell the text. Of course, that doesn't mean when they read the word "bacon" they are

26. Graffin, "La Lettre," 465.
27. Paddison, *Scripture*, 14.

able to smell bacon. But particular words do elicit certain smells for them. As we saw back in chapter 2, the senses blend in synethetes. Likewise, when we properly engage in the reading and meditation (*lectio* and *meditatio*) of the Holy Scriptures as scripture, we are able to sense the Divine Pages in new ways.[28] We are able to taste the text. We can comprehend by smell the sense of what God is saying. We can feel the tactile message as God speaks. We can hear the voice of God whispering to us. We can see, in vivid colors, the way in which God wants us to embody his Word. The taste of the Holy Scriptures delights and fulfills us. We, in a metaphorical sense, apprehend orange proverbs and purple parables. Some psalms will be chartreuse, and other psalms will be umber.

Yes, to be sure, those are all metaphors, and the metaphors are drawn from the physical senses of the human body. Our network of the human physical senses is blended and intertwined with the spiritual and cognitive senses in an attempt to describe what is happening when we are properly reading and meditating upon the Holy Scriptures. When you read and meditate on what has been read, there is something very complicated and something very interesting that is happening. When you read and meditate, it is not like you are a photocopier. You are not just "capturing images in your mind."[29]

The synesthetic reader makes connections and garners insights from those connections where the superficial reader does not apprehend anything beyond the most basic understanding, if that, from the text being read. Your deep reading and your internalizing of the Holy Scriptures (as a spiritual synesthete) will transform your apprehension of God speaking to you.

Eating the Scrolls

I am sure you have heard the familiar saying, "You are what you eat." Eugene Peterson commences the second volume of his five-part work on spiritual theology, *Eat This Book*, with that imagery. He plainly states, "Eating a book takes it all in, assimilating it into the tissues of our lives. Readers become

28. This may be new nomenclature to you. However, it is a very ancient way of speaking of the Holy Scriptures. The phrase, *divinae paginae*, is used first by Augustine in *Enarrationes in Psalmos* (*Expositions on the Psalms*, 91 and *In euangelium Ioannis tractatus* (*Tractates on the Gospel of John*), Tr 6, n. 24. Subsequently, others (Gregory, Pschasius, Alvarus, and Rupert use the phrase. Augustine also used the phrase "The Holy Pages" (*sanctae paginae*) to refer to the Holy Scriptures.

29. Studzinski, *Reading to Live*, 6.

what they read."[30] As the writer, Joseph Epstein, nicely noted, "A biography of any literary person ought to deal at length with what he read and when, for in some sense, *we are what we read.*"[31]

Images of eating, tasting, or chewing the text are well known within Judaism and early Christianity, and these images get widely applied in later times to the practice of *meditatio.* The Latin word, *meditatio,* translates the Greek word, *meletē* (μελέτη), a noun with the meaning of "practice" or "exercise." In this way, the word was oftentimes used of an orator's or an actor's rehearsing.[32] It also can have the sense of "care" or "attention" paid by someone. Thus, there may be the double sense of carefully rehearsing, doing something over and over again. Repetition is a key element. This notion is, quite naturally, later applied to repeating a scriptural text with the aim of memorizing or internalizing it. "This process of repetitive absorption was likened to 'chewing the cud' by ruminant animals."[33] For example, as early as the Epistle of Barnabas (AD 70–135),[34] there was Christian allegorical interpretation drawn from Leviticus 11:3 and Deuteronomy 14:6 where the writer encouraged believers to do their deep hanging out with those "who know that meditation is joy, and they ruminate on the Word of the Lord."[35]

Of course, there are even earlier biblical texts that speak very vividly of the act of consuming the Word of God. The two prophets, Jeremiah and Ezekiel both eat the words. First, we have the young prophet Jeremiah

30. Peterson, *Eat This Book,* 20.

31. Wolf, *Proust and the Squid,* 5.

32. Cicero (*De oratore* 1.260) uses the verb form (*meditor*) in the sense of the relentless rehearsing by Demosthenes, the famous orator, to overcome a speech impediment. Cicero suggests that Demosthenes had trouble with saying the letter r. Perhaps he suffered a form of rhotacism and mispronounced ρ (r) as λ (l).

33. McGinn, *Mysticism,* 135.

34. Treat notes that "Since Barnabas 16:3 refers to the destruction of the temple, Barnabas must be written after 70 C.E. It must be written before its first undisputable use in Clement of Alexandria, ca. 190. Since 16:4 expects the temple to be rebuilt, it was most likely written before Hadrian built a Roman temple on the site ca. 135" ("The Epistle of Barnabas," 1:613–14).

35. *Epistle of Barnabas* 10:11. As a phrase, "deep hanging out" was coined by the Stanford University cultural anthropologist Renato Rosaldo. The term was later popularized in the discipline by Princeton anthropologist Clifford Geertz. In anthropology, deep hanging out has the sense of spending time with people in order to find out about their lives. In the *Epistle of Barnabas,* the author is admonishing Christians to spend time with those who are consuming and ruminating the Holy Scriptures. The verb used here is κολλάω (in the imperative) which can mean to "to join closely together, to be closely associated with someone or something."

declaring to the Lord that "Your words were found, and I ate them. Subsequently, your words became a joy to me and the delight of my heart. After all, I bear your name, Yahweh, God of hosts" (Jer 15:16).

When Jeremiah states that Yahweh's words were found, he is, most likely, referring to an event in the year 622 BC when a scroll of the Law (probably the book of Deuteronomy) was found in the temple during the reign of King Josiah (2 Kgs 22; 23:2). The phrase, "and I ate them" seems to refer back to Jeremiah's call (Jer 1:4–11) when Yahweh said to the prophet, "Look, I have put my words into your mouth."

Once again, also in the call narrative of the prophet, Ezekiel is commanded three times (Ezek 2:8; 3:1, 3) to eat as the divine Word of God is spoken of as a scroll.[36]

> But you, Son of Man, listen to what I say to you! You are not to be rebellious like that house of rebellion. Open up your mouth and eat what I give to you. And when I looked, whoa, there was a hand extended toward me, and there was a scroll in [it].
> He said to me, Son of Man, eat that which is offered to you. Eat this scroll, then go and speak to the house of Israel. So I opened my mouth, and he gave me the scroll to eat. Then He said to me, Son of Man, eat this scroll that I give you; fill your stomach with it. So I ate it, and in my mouth it was as sweet as honey (Ezek 2:9; 3:1–4).

The earliest biblical text that alludes to eating or consuming the Word of God is in Deuteronomy when Moses declared to the Israelite community that,

> He humbled you by allowing you to hunger and then by providing you with manna to eat. Neither you nor your ancestors were acquainted with the stuff in order that you might understand that one does not live by bread alone, but rather by every word that comes from the mouth of Yahweh (Deut 8:3).

Finally, one finds in the New Testament, in the Revelation, John is instructed to consume a scroll.

> Then the voice that I had heard from heaven spoke to me again, saying, "Go, take the scroll that is open in the hand of the angel who is standing on the sea and on the land." So I went to the angel and told him to give me the little scroll; and he said to me, "Take it, and eat; it will be bitter to your stomach, but sweet as honey in

36. See Davis, *Swallowing the Scroll* and Hecker, *Mystical Bodies*.

your mouth." So I took the little scroll from the hand of the angel and ate it; it was sweet as honey in my mouth, but when I had eaten it, my stomach was made bitter (Rev 10:8–10 NRSV).

Eating the Book; eating the Word of God—here is another example of the synesthesia metaphor working well for the activity of reading the Holy Scriptures as scripture. Leclerq saw the activities of *lectio* (reading) and *meditatio* (meditation) as being virtually inseparable. It is the combination of the two acts that "inscribes, so to speak, the sacred text in the body and in the soul."[37] The fusing of the two activities, in tandem with the text, is likened to "a kind of mastication which releases its full savor."[38] That is, there is a certain piquancy or sharp taste to text, and its full flavor is not released under normal circumstances. For example, glibly speed reading the biblical text in order to stay on a schedule to complete a goal of reading the Bible in a calendar year will never yield the sweet savory taste found in the measured, attentive, and focused reading and meditation garnered through a process like that of *lectio divina*.

A Taste of Honey

There is another sense of taste image that became widely used. John was told that the scroll would taste as sweet as honey. When Ezekiel ate the scroll, he mentioned how it had a taste as sweet as honey. Guigo II's remarks on the fourfold process he popularized also drew upon the sense of taste, and he, too, alluded to the savor of sweetness. He stated that "Reading, as it were, puts food whole into the mouth, meditation chews it and breaks it up, prayer extracts its flavor, contemplation is the sweetness itself which gladdens and refreshes."[39]

However, as one might expect, it was Origen at the lead of all those Christian commentators, and there are many of them, who picked up on the image and language of honey.[40] More will be said about Origen later as he is, more often than not, at the root of colorful language and spiritual insights

---

37. Leclercq, *Love of Learning*, 73.
38. Ibid.
39. Guigo, *The Ladder*, III, 69.
40. For many examples, see Lubac, *Medieval Exegesis*, 2:163–67.

to which many later Christian writers allude. Origen points out that for the faithful, "the sweetness of honey is found" within the Word of God.[41]

Augustine also gets into the act of describing the sensory experience of tasting the Holy Scriptures. He tells us to read the Word of God because it is "sweeter than honey, more satisfying than any type of bread, and you will also discover that it gives more robust flavor than any vintage of fine wine."[42] Indeed, the Holy Scriptures are sometimes compared to the sweetness of honey, and sometimes they are compared to bread. Ambrose, Augustine's mentor, noticed this and remarked that both metaphors are apt in that the Word of God is as bread because of its strength, but it is also honey because of its extreme sweetness.[43] In a great quote, Adam Scotus (ca. AD 1140–1212) cites a bishop by the name of Bruno of Segni (AD 1047–1123) saying, "The dominant taste of Scripture is that of flour mixed with honey; for what is sweeter than honey? And what stronger than bread made of wheat? Scripture is therefore soundly composed of what is sweet to taste and strong at nourishing."[44]

Thus, the image of the Holy Scriptures as yielding a taste for the one consuming God's Word is widely used within Judaism and Christianity. Again, we see that the synesthetic reader, the deep reader who is meditating upon the Holy Scriptures, will draw a variety of succulent and satisfying tastes and flavors from God's Word. In this way, the words of the psalmist make perfectly good sense.

> Oh my, how I love your Torah!
>
> All day it is my meditation.
>
> How incredibly smooth is your word on the roof of my mouth,
>
> It is even sweeter than honey in my mouth (Ps 119: 97, 103).

Becoming a Meditative Reader of Scripture

It seems that *lectio* and *meditatio* meld together in such a way that one cannot easily separate the second activity from the first activity. How, then,

41. Origen, *Homiliae in Exodum* 216 (PL CXLIV, 540B). While Origen originally wrote in Greek, some of his writings survive only in Latin translations. Thus, the phrase quoted here is the Latin, *fidelibus dulcedo mellis invenitur.*

42. Augustine, *Sermons* 38 (PL 40, 1304).

43. Lubac, *Medieval Exegesis*, 2:166.

44. Ibid. He cites the Latin, *dulcis ad gustandum et fortis ad alendum.*

does one become an effective meditative reader? Since *meditatio* is difficult to tightly define, that is a challenging question. However, Hugh of St. Victor (AD 1096–1141) gives a very laudable go at it when he writes, "Meditation is sustained thought along planned lines. . . . Meditation takes its start from reading, but is bound by none of the rules or precepts of reading. Meditation delights to range along open ground where it fixes its free gaze upon the contemplation of truth, drawing together now these, now those causes of things, or now penetrating into profundities, leaving nothing doubtful, nothing obscure."[45]

Illich notes that Hugh "distinguishes between the pilgrimage and the stroll, the strenuous *lectio* and the leisurely *meditatio*. He distinguishes the two styles of movement but stresses their similarity."[46] Therefore, the two elements are different, but they are part of the same *lectio divina*. In fact, Hugh reminds us of a very important element that should be present within the activity of *meditation*, namely memorization.

Memories

If you have ever memorized a text such as a poem, lines in a play, or some Bible verses, you know that something quite extraordinary has transpired. You captured that text and internalized it in such a way that you have it immediately at hand. Of course, "at hand" is metaphorical language. More literally, in some rather inexplicable way, you now have the text in your mind, and you are capable of communicating it to someone else. You have internalized the text. It is, in some strange way, yours. It is in you.

Unfortunately, our culture today is not big on memorizing texts. People used to memorize phone numbers. That does not happen anymore; and why should it? You have all your phone numbers in the contact list of your iPhone. People used to memorize Scripture verses. That does not seem to happen very much anymore either. After all, one can, almost immediately, call up any verse on one's phone if you have a Bible app loaded on it. There is no need to memorize it; at least that is the common school of thought. In today's world, we have gained the ability to easily retrieve a text. However, at the same time, we have largely lost the aspect of internalizing a text that is gained through memorization. In my opinion, it is not a good tradeoff.

---

45. Hugh, *Didascalicon*, 92–93 cited in Illich, *Vineyard*, 52.
46. Illich, *Vineyard*, 63.

Many people think that, for one reason or another, they are not good at memorizing, and so they avoid it—rather like the plague.[47] But that is exactly like the preconception that many people would have if they were told to participate in some new activity such as running a mile for time or painting a picture in oils on a canvas. Yet, we know that with practice, one will consistently improve performance in virtually any endeavor. It is the same with memorization; practice makes better.

Memorization of scriptural texts was, however, an integral element of *meditatio* from the earliest times. Memorization of readings with constant review was done until entire books of the Bible were memorized.[48] Jerome was a staunch advocate of memorization. He advised Laeta that her daughter, Paula, should memorize entire books, starting with the Psalter.[49] While that may seem outrageously difficult to us, the fact of the matter is that most members of any monastic community had the book of Psalms memorized. For example, according to the monastic Rule of Ferreolus which dates from the sixth century, "every psalm should be held in memory."[50] Jerome was not asking the young girl to do anything unusual or extreme.

In the medieval period, as in the classical world of Greece and Rome, memorization was a highly regarded craft. It was thought that certain methodologies and tools could enhance and refine one's recollection, and many writers gave attention to memory.[51] Mary Carruthers' magnificent work, *The Book of Memory*, gives us a very detailed look at the art of memory in medieval culture. She highlights a number of the leading proponents of how-to manuals and their various methods for enhancing one's memory. For example, she notes the case of Hugh of St. Victor, who we met earlier in this chapter. Hugh is significant in any discussion on memory because he is the first of the medieval writers to retrieve and employ ideas from many of the classical methodologies for memory training.[52] Carruthers describes

---

47. I am generalizing based on my experience with students over the past thirty-four years. I usually have some sort of memorization project as a part of many of my courses. I have found that, for the most part, students do not like to memorize, and they have the preconception that they will not be very good at it.

48. Robertson, *Lectio Divina*, 84.

49. Jerome, *Letter* 107:12.

50. Ferreolus, *Regula* 11 (PL 66:963). *Quin etiam psalmos totos memoriter teneat.*

51. This is, of course, also the case today. Just do an internet search for "improve memory" or search the keyword "memory" on Amazon.com, and you will be quite overwhelmed with the number of guides available to improve one's memory.

52. Illich, *Vineyard*, 45. See also, Zinn, "Hugh of Saint Victor," 211–34.

how Hugh presented us with a wonderful model for merging together the "process of Scriptural reading, moral development, and memory training in the single image of Noah's ark."[53] In a rather massive work entitled *De arca Noe*, he presented memorizing as a prelude to wisdom. Hugh would have us mentally construct an ark, board by board, as a means of cultivating the mind and the heart of the Christian. He writes, "The Ark of Wisdom has three storeys that represent three stages of moral judgment. . . . I am in the first storey of the ark when I begin to love to mediate on (that is memorize) Scripture."[54]

The merits of memorizing texts from the Holy Scriptures are manifold, and Hugh speaks of the process and value of being able to internalize what is gained through *lectio* and *meditatio*. He argues that the very being of the reader is transformed in the process. So that, "When the virtue I display in works is mine internally as well, when my goodness is completely habitual and necessary to me, then I ascend to the third storey, where knowledge and virtue become essential parts of me."[55] For Hugh of St. Victor, *meditatio*, which is "the process of memory-training, storage, and retrieval" produces the complete internalizing of the Holy Scriptures.[56]

It has been argued that in religious reading, ideally, the best rereading is done by memory.[57] When a scripture is memorized, it stays with you in a way that it provides a context for how you live. In a sense, there is a wonderful, transformational element that is now within you when you have memorized a text from the Holy Scriptures. Therefore, I would like to challenge you to begin a new project—start memorizing. Again, as in the practice of *lectio*, it is not the quantitative measure that is important here. If you have never memorized much of anything, the process may be difficult and challenging at the start. However, even if you were to memorize only one verse in the next three months, that would prove to be transformational for you. You will have internalized a portion of God's Word that you will carry with you for all time. You will have woven that thought from God into your very being, and you will be, in some inscrutable way, different. If you are a complete novice to the practice, try memorizing short segments at first. Hugh of St. Victor recommended this, although he certainly was

53. Caruthers, *Book of Memory*, 53.

54. Hugh, *De archa Noe*, II,v as cited in Carruthers, *Book of Memory*, 203.

55. Carruthers, *Book of Memory*, 203.

56. Ibid.

57. Griffiths, *Religious Reading*, 46.

not the first to do so.[58] Remember, "Any long text can be treated as though it were composed of a number of short ones."[59]

Meditatio: It's Like Banging My Head Against a Wall

I must confess; I have a pattern of behavior that is more than a little embarrassing. Not that it happens every time, but with some measure of regularity, I will fall asleep in bed while reading. That is not the embarrassing part. Now, of course, I know that this is a very common phenomenon among people. Indeed, I am quite confident that a good share of the readers of this sentence have experienced falling asleep while reading. In that way, we are kindred spirits. I like to read in bed, and I usually fall asleep while reading. My problem is, and again, I am sure it is not unique to me, so I know there are others of you out there who will sincerely relate to my plight—my problem is that I will oftentimes jerk backward at the moment of sleep, and I will rather violently bang my head on the wall behind me. We do not have a headboard, but I think I understand how that name was derived.

Yes, I like to read sitting up in the bed, but this produces an amplified collision as the movement into sleep usually is immediately preceded by a slight forward lean that, when quickly followed by the backward thrust of the cranium upon losing consciousness, produces a rather impressive velocity. Thud! O, that I were alone at that moment; were that the case, it would not be an embarrassment, except to me alone. I have actually learned to live with personal embarrassing episodes, those that nobody else witnesses. The latest such incident happened even this afternoon. I was attempting to move the garden hose while it was on, and it started to writhe when I awkwardly lost my grip on the nozzle. I got sprayed, nay, drenched, before I was able to contain the twisting, spitting serpent. I took a gusher right in the face and down the front of my pants. I looked around, and no one was present to take in the moment at my expense. The neighbors were not watching. It was embarrassing, but only to me. I have those sorts of episodes all the time, and I have learned to live with that. It is the banging of the head against the wall that is truly embarrassing. Why? Because every time, I mean every time, I have done that my wife, Patty, has heard the thud.

58. For example, the Roman rhetorician Quintilian (ca. AD 35–100) who wrote a magisterial manual, known as the *Institutio Oratoria*, also addressed the merits of brevity in memorization.

59. Caruthers, *Book of Memory*, 104.

Sometimes, after the collision, I hear a muted giggle from the living room if she is staying up a little later. There is usually a delay of a few seconds between the thud and the giggle as I am sure she is trying to discern if a tree has just fallen against the house or if I were merely reading. Sometimes there is just silence from the other room, but I know that in her heart she is laughing out loud. Other times she is right there, right next to me at the moment of impact where there is volume and a slight shock wave from the concussion. I tell you, it is embarrassing.

So, what does banging my head against the wall have to do with reading the Holy Scriptures as scripture? Are you wondering how I am going to make a link to *meditatio*? What I have learned is that usually, between Augustine and Jerome, one can find a relevant text to most of life's little situations. So it is in my case of head banging. Let me allude to Jerome who was encouraging Eustochium, in a very long letter, on ways of holy living. In his writing, he let her know that reading the Holy Scriptures was paramount for the Christian to know God. He encouraged her to always be reading, and he admonished her to, "let sleep steal upon you with a book in your hand, and let the sacred page catch your drooping head."[60] Now, he did not say anything about banging one's head on the wall, but he was making a point that there is much to be gained by arranging for the last thoughts of day to be drawn from the Holy Scriptures. There is something powerful about the final thoughts in your mind that are present at the moment of transition into sleep. Perhaps, as meditative readers, I would like to suggest that we could be well served by allowing the mind to move from conscious, deliberative internalizing of the Holy Scriptures directly into that soft web of sleep.

Two More Rungs

There are four rungs to Guigo's ladder and his systematized approach to *lectio divina*. We have, so far, surveyed a few elements of the first two rungs: *lectio* and *meditatio*. Now we will take a much briefer look at the final two rungs: *oratio* and *contemplatio*. These last two activities, while no less important than reading and meditation, are not the focal points of *lectio divina* as I want to present it in this work. Indeed, entire books and chapters have addressed just these two concluding stages. However, my intent here

60. Jerome, *Letter* 22:17.

has been to address the first two movements and simply mention the final two activities in passing.

Oratio is prayer, and I have already mentioned how I feel strongly that prayer, even the briefest of petitions, should always precede *lectio* and *meditatio*. Back in chapter 5 we saw how Jerome compelled us, in a famous line, to "Let reading follow prayer and prayer follow reading" (*Orationi lectio, lectioni succedat oratio*).[61] What better, more intuitive advice might one heed regarding the interlacing of *oratio* and *lectio*?

As we read and pray, the Holy Scriptures provide our core and normative entrance into the mode through which God will reveal himself to us.[62] This is why the combining of Guigo's four rungs is so valuable. He noted that in order for meditation to be fruitful, it must be followed by devoted prayer.[63] Prayer was generally seen as a natural and heartfelt response to the inspiration one found in the process of *lectio* and *meditatio*.[64]

Finally, there is *contemplatio*. Of all of the rungs on Guigo's ladder, this one has, perhaps, received the widest array of commentary. There is a measure of danger in the word; some may envision something quite mystical happening at this stage. Some may perceive this element as quite rare or unique and actualized by only a few of the more spiritual elite or perhaps a few of the more flakey Christians. Such is definitely not the case. "Contemplation is certainly the peak of this entire activity. It is not something superimposed from without but is like a delicious fruit that ripens on the tree of Bible reading. And it is a normal fruit—provided we do not understand the term to mean extraordinary mystical graces. There is in fact, a form of contemplation available to all. It is a normal complement of the Christian life taken seriously."[65]

As Guigo conceptualized it, our contemplation should, in some way, elevate the mind toward God.[66] Others have seen this stage as the *praxis* or "doing" element within *lectio divina*. In that sense, it means actually living out what we have gained from our *lectio*, *meditatio*, and *oratio*. For example, Peterson writes, "Contemplation in the schema of *lectio divina* means living

---

61. Jerome, *Letter* 107:9.

62. Peterson, *Eat This Book*, 104.

63. Guigo, *Ladder*, XIII, 81–82.

64. Studzinski, *Reading to Live*, 169.

65. Magrassi, *Praying the Bible*, 116.

66. Guigo, *Ladder*, II, 68.

the read/meditated/prayed text in the everyday, ordinary world."[67] Thus, there is "an organic union between the word 'read' and the word 'lived.'"[68] I like this view of *contemplatio* as it brings a very pragmatic element into one's Christian life. It unites the hearing of the Word and the doing of the Word in much the same way we are steered by James when he writes, "But be doers of the word, and not hearers only, deceiving yourselves" (James 1:22).

Many Methods

A point to be repeated, and thus emphasized, is that *lectio divina* should not be perceived as a rigid step-by-step methodology that needs to be closely and routinely followed in order to be an effective reader of the Holy Scriptures as scripture. There are many avenues of reading that can produce the kind of fruit we want to reap from our reading of God's Word. To be sure, "It would be pointless to ask the ancients for concrete and detailed methods of reading . . . The ancients apparently distrusted methods that were too rigid, that bound the human mind to a series of well-defined attitudes. Perhaps they were afraid of extinguishing the spontaneous freedom of the children of God in dialogue with the Father."[69]

Yet, regardless of how closely one follows the elements of *lectio divina* introduced above, the bottom line is that reading the Holy Scriptures as scripture does take a commitment to invest time in the enterprise. Many people would like to learn a foreign language, but they are unwilling or unable to engage in the regular, sustained exercise of using the language that the endeavor demands. In the same way,

> *Lectio divina* demands a solid commitment of time. The process is void if it is confined to spasmodic periods of no more than a few minutes. To generate its specific results it requires a certain density of experience–especially at the beginning of the journey. It is like the idea of the critical mass in nuclear physics: without a certain quantity of fissionable material no chain reaction follows. The formation of mind and heart that is due to *lectio divina* is realized only after a solid investment of time.[70]

67. Peterson, *Eat This Book*, 109.

68. Ibid.

69. Magrassi, *Praying the Bible*, 103.

70. Casey, *Sacred Reading*, 21.

Lectio divina is, to be sure, about the formation of the mind and the heart. That is the goal. One should not be overwhelmed by excitement and enthusiasm for *lectio divina* as a kind of ultimate spiritual diet plan. *Lectio divina* in antiquity and in its modern practice is simply a tool, a suggestion, one avenue. It is not a biblically mandated operation of carefully orchestrated steps designed as the ultimate pathway to spiritual enlightenment. I want to be clear. I am not advocating that only a dedicated effort in meticulously following the monastic footprints of *lectio divina* will lead to a true reading of the Holy Scriptures as scripture. However, for some, this brief introduction to the conceptual elements comprising this very old tradition of reading may ignite a cognitive and spiritual response of invigorating one's resolve to explore new ways of reading that you simply have not previously tried.

This chapter has been nothing more than a sketchy, simplistic introduction to one aspect of sacred reading that you may not have had much association with or knowledge of before. There are, absolutely, a number of very good books focusing on *lectio divina* that give a much fuller and richer account of the tradition than what you have found in this section. The design here has been to whet your appetite a bit. Throughout this chapter I have drawn a few quips and quotes from some sources that I would highly recommend to those who desire to explore more fully the depths and caverns of *lectio divina*. In no way is the basic survey contained in this book to be reckoned as a comprehensive account of the matter. Rather, this work is for the explorer who will launch out into some new terrain having been intrigued or perhaps tickled by something here or there within its pages. Remember, the goal of this book is to be a catalyst in nudging you toward a deeper relationship with God by making some changes in the way you read the Bible. Casey gives us a good warning with regard to our program of *lectio divina*. He states that it "is an element in a lifelong process of turning toward God: its effects are discernible only in the long term. Equally, the effect of the absence of *lectio* may not be apparent to us until it is too late."[71]

Reading the Bible can be difficult, and it truly is a formidable enterprise to read the Holy Scriptures as scripture. There is much that goes into this endeavor as it is multifaceted. In the next two chapters you will read about several unusual characteristics of the Holy Text that make a proper reading of it a challenging undertaking. The Bible is, after all, a fractal work (chapter 7) of sfumato (chapter 8). Doesn't that make you want to read the next two chapters?

71. Ibid., 9.

7

The Fractal Nature of
the Holy Scriptures

Fractal Theology?

I WAS READING AN interesting book the other day.[1] The work focused upon the relationship of culture and technology in the modern world. Not too far into the book, I came upon a section in which the author was discussing our rapidly changing culture, especially change due to technology, and in the course of his discussion he cited some examples using analogies of fractal geometry. I am certainly not a mathematician, but I do enjoy dabbling in academic disciplines peripheral to mine. I had heard the term "fractal" used a number of times before, and I knew that it was associated with geometry. However, beyond that, I really had no understanding of even the rudiments of the concept. Fractals were foreign to me. My world of geometry was, at the time, pretty Euclidian. In fact, my entire worldview, my theology, my life was oftentimes way too Euclidian—too simplistic, too limited, too neat. As I am constantly discovering, the world is an incredibly complex place. If I have learned anything from reading about the physical universe, I have learned that we do not live in a simple, understandable, neat place. Yet, this does not confound me or discourage me. In fact, it has the opposite effect. As I was soon to discover, fractals would enhance my worldview, my theology, my life.

One of the things for which I am very thankful is the fact that I enjoy new discoveries, and I really am a rather curious fellow, or should I say, a fellow who is curious. I should clarify; I am curious about many things, but

1. Hardison, *Disappearing*.

I am not curious about everything. Yet, being the inquisitive sort, I set off to find the primary source alluded to in the book that I was reading. After all, I always advise students to take this step. After a quick trip to the library I secured a copy of the bibliographic source, and I set out to learn about fractals from the horse's mouth—so to speak. It seems the person to read is a mathematician by the name of Benoit B. Mandelbrot.[2]

How Long is the Coastline of Britain?

Now, this is seemingly a straightforward question. Look it up in an atlas, look it up in an almanac, or search on the Internet, like I did, and you find out the coastline of Britain is about 3,000 kilometers long. But, in this life, things are not always as they seem. In fact, Mandelbrot has argued that the coastline of Britain is not approximately 3,000 kilometers long. Amazingly, he says that the coastline of Britain is infinitely long!

In his work *The Fractal Geometry of Nature*, I came across a chapter with the enticing title, "How Long Is the Coast of Britain?" What at first seemed to me like a fairly straightforward question, in fact, developed into a labyrinth-like maze of immensely complex considerations.

To express simply and concisely the essence of fractal geometry is no easy task, and I suspect that you would rather that I did not exhaust myself trying. So I won't—exhaust myself that is. But, do be patient as I attempt to illustrate the concept; it will be worth it for the concept, indeed, merits some pondering. I found it to open a window into nature, and even more enticing, I found it to provide some interesting and original metaphors for thinking about the Holy Scriptures.

Perhaps Mandelbrot's example of the measuring of the coastline of Britain would be a good starting point. If someone gave you the task of measuring the coastline around Britain, how would you do it? You could, I suppose, take a couple of yardsticks and start by placing them end to end. By doing this around the entire coast you would ultimately arrive at a total distance around the place. But now suppose you did the same thing—this time with a twelve-inch ruler. Would you get the same distance? No, you would not. As you walked around the second time, measuring with the one-foot ruler, you would be able to fit that measuring device into some nooks and crannies into which the yardstick would not have fit. As you came to some jagged rocks you could be more precise with the one-foot ruler than you

2. Mandelbrot, *Fractal Geometry*.

had been with the yardstick. Now suppose you did the measuring again—this time with a six-inch ruler. And again, what if you did it again using a one-inch ruler? You see, every time you measure, even avoiding all human error, your measurements will differ. What if you used a microscope and measured the coastline in microns? Mandelbrot makes the argument that, in fact, the coastline of Britain is infinitely long. This is where Euclid goes out the window because his nice, neat shapes like circles and squares do not very often represent nature. Indeed, if the coastline of Britain were a Euclidean shape you could ultimately get your results converging fine enough so that the Euclidean straight-line measurements would, for all practical purposes, give you the length of the coastline of Britain. But Euclidean thinking does not really deal well with the reality of nature. Most things in nature approximate coastlines, not circles and squares.

Here is where it gets tricky. Whereas you and I have always known that there are three dimensions, Mandelbrot would argue that there are, seemingly, fractions of dimensions. Hence, the coastline of Britain might have a dimension of 1.26 for instance. How he arrives at the number of the fraction is too weighty for me; if you are intrigued, read Mandelbrot. But the point to be made is this—in measuring fractal forms the number that results is observer dependent. This should ring of Einstein to you. Fractal geometry seems to be a wonderful illustration of the nature of the universe given the mind-boggling absurdities of relativity and sub-atomic particle physics. One quick example will probably be enough to keep you up later than usual tonight. If there is anything to the general theory of relativity, time and distance depend on the observer. That is to say, how long a yardstick is depends on the observer. So it is, according to Mandelbrot, with measuring the coastline of Britain, Euclid's universe just does not suffice.

Mandelbrot's point is that nature rarely reflects the Euclidian geometry of straight lines. One could cite the example of the border between Portugal and Spain. The Portuguese atlas shows the border as being 20 percent longer than the Spanish atlas. You see, the Spanish surveyors based their measurements on a larger unit of distance than the Portuguese and therefore measured fewer squiggles in the line defining the border.[3] What appears as a straightforward, simple question (how long is the coastline of Britain?) actually produces an answer that is totally unexpected. The coastline of Britain is infinitely long. Early in his book, Mandelbrot exudes a measure of childlike glee (even without tone and facial expression) that

3. Hardison, *Disappearing*, 62.

he has "confirmed Blaise Pascal's observation that imagination tires before nature."[4] Think about it, and you will agree; the fractal nature of things is enough to boggle the mind. I can understand why it would make a mathematician like Mandelbrot a bit giddy. After all, it certainly made the great mathematician/Christian philosopher, Blaise Pascal, sit up and take note.[5]

Augustine on the Fractal Nature of the Holy Scriptures

Euclid's universe, as it turns out, was too neat and too simple. Mandelbrot's fractals reflect something much more gruesome in complexity. Of course, it is not just fractals that cause the problem. One could just as easily speak of cosmology, quantum physics, string theory, even D-branes—those sorts of things.[6] The befuddling structure of God's creation is seemingly just that—befuddling. It is, in several senses, never ending. This is the point, the analogical thought linking all of this to the nature of the Holy Scriptures. Just as you can always measure the coastline of Britain in a higher magnification because of the fractal nature of it, so also the Holy Scriptures hold for us an unlimited source that all of the spiritual and scholarly scouring of a lifetime will not exhaust. In that sense, the Holy Scriptures are fractal in nature. While the language of fractals is not used, Augustine, way back in the fifth century, spoke of the Holy Scriptures in a sense that can only be described as fractal-like.

Presently, there is no unified theory in quantum physics. Scientists have pursued that elusive prize, and they have found it, so far, to be wanting. Nor is there a unified theory of Scripture. Yes, while there can be some measure of unity on certain of the basics, just as there is in elementary physics, there remains the reality that the Holy Scriptures are limitless in the exercise of interpretation. Augustine understood this, and it is exactly the point of the following story of his correspondence with a pagan Roman bureaucrat. Augustine understood the fractal nature of the Holy Scriptures.

4. Mandelbrot, *Fractal Geometry*, 4.

5. If you are not familiar with Pascal, you may well want to investigate him. You should read his work entitled, *Pensées* (Thoughts). There are a number of good English translations available. Perhaps the best biography of Pascal is O'Connell, *Blaise Pascal*; see also, Adamson, *Thinker about God* and Davidson, *Blaise Pascal*.

6. See, for example: Greene, *Fabric of the Cosmos*; Davies and Brown, *Superstrings*; Johnson, *D-branes*; and my favorite—Musser, *Idiot's Guide to String Theory*.

The Case of the Pagan Roman Bureaucrat

In AD 411, or perhaps 412, Augustine wrote an important letter to a fellow by the name of Volusianus. He was a young, witty, and influential Roman aristocrat who had recently been appointed to the position of proconsul in North Africa, the turf of Bishop Augustine. It seems that Volusianus came to this post shortly before 412. "It is thought to be his first accomplishment to merit address as *illustris,* and Augustine addressed him as such" in his first letter to the new Roman official.[7] The good Bishop took note of the talents of Volusianus, and he initiated cordial and respectful communication with him. Now, Augustine knew this guy was a pagan, but he also knew that Volusianus' mother was a Christian. Augustine also knew this fledgling upstart had a very bright future in front of him. I also suspect that Augustine saw a little bit of himself in the young, talented fellow.[8] Listen to the tone and the gentle encouragement to study the Holy Scriptures that Augustine pens in the opening of the letter.

> To his illustrious lord and rightly most excellent son, Volusianus, Bishop Augustine sends greetings,
>
> With regard to your well-being, which I desire both in this world and in Christ, I perhaps even myself am not surpassed by the prayers of your mother. Hence, in rendering to your merits the duty of sending my greetings, I exhort you, as much as I can, not to hesitate to devote your care to the truly and certainly holy writings. For they are something sincere and solid and do not allure the mind by obscure language, nor do they make any tottering inanity resound with the false beauty of rhetoric. They deeply move someone who is eager not for words but for the truth.[9]

Then the wise Bishop Augustine opened the window of opportunity for Volusianus to write to him if he had any questions while reading the Holy Scriptures. Augustine wrote, "But if some question arises for you either when you are reading them or when you are pondering them, for the

7. Weber, "Albinus," 478.

8. Augustine's work, *Confessions,* yields many intriguing similarities between the pre-conversion intellectual life of Augustine and that of Volusianus. This may be one reason he takes such an interest him; he saw some characteristics in the young Volusianus that brought him back to his younger days (see books II and III). One might surmise that Augustine perceived the great potential the new proconsul had as a future Christian scholar, and as his own conversion experience was triggered by the reading of the Holy Scriptures, so Augustine encouraged Volusianus to read the Word of God.

9. Augustine, *Letters,* 132.

resolution of which I may seem useful, write to me in order that I may write back."[10]

Volusianus was an interesting character who was caught in the seams between two worlds—the ancient Roman pagan tradition and the relatively new Christian world. As an aristocratic Roman, he was hanging out with a group of friends, many of whom could be described as intellectual Roman pagans who were skeptical, if not cynical, of the Christian way. The cynicism of Volusianus against Christianity was clear; yet he respected the great learning of Augustine.

Peter Brown, is one of the truly great scholars on the age of Augustine.[11] He described Volusianus and his situation as follows:

> The paganism of Volusianus seems to have been taken for granted. He appears with his father in the ostensibly self-confident circle of pagans to which Rutilius Namatianus expressed his belief in the permanence of Rome—after the Gothic sack of 410. And yet, he belongs to a completely new generation: he was, perhaps, born in the early 380's—that is, after the official suppression of paganism. He is treated by Augustine, in 412, with great tact and esteem; on the surface, he belongs to a Christian family consisting of his mother, sister and niece; the exchange of letters contains only what the intermediary could regard as "threadbare arguments"—arguments such as could be made from within Christianity itself; the correspondence is later referred to by Augustine as "my letters on the virginity of Mary to the illustrious Volusianus, whom I mention with esteem and affection." And yet, despite his caution, Volusianus seems to have remained loyal to a tradition which may have begun with his father. He had stickled at the Incarnation, and the closely related problem of the Virgin Birth; but so, also, had his father before him. Thus we see two generations of Roman pagans provoking from the greatest Christian thinkers of their time— Ambrose and Augustine, respectively—impeccable statements of the central doctrine of the new religion.[12]

Volusianus was certainly no slouch. Indeed, he "was surely one of the best known individuals in fifth-century Roman society."[13] How would he

10. Ibid.

11. See, for example, a few of Brown's notable works: *Through the Eye of a Needle*; *Poverty and Leadership*; *Rise of Western Christendom*; *Power and Persuasion*; *Late Antiquity*; *Religion and Society*; *Augustine of Hippo*.

12. Brown, "Aspects," 7–8.

13. Weber, "Albinus," 478.

react to Augustine's reaching out to him and encouraging him to read the Holy Scriptures?

When the End is the Beginning

Volusianus did write back to the bishop. As he described the situation to Augustine in his letter of reply, he felt there was a need for the wise and learned man to address some of the questions from the group of young Roman aristocrats that seemed to be challenging the very core of Christianity.

> While our conversation delayed over these ideas, one of the many asked, "And who is perfectly imbued with the wisdom of Christianity who can resolve certain ambiguous points on which I am stuck and can strengthen my hesitant assent with true or probable grounds for belief?" We were stunned and silent. Then he suddenly burst forth with this: "I wonder whether the Lord and ruler of the world filled the body of an inviolate woman, whether she endured those long annoyances over ten month, and whether, though a virgin, she nonetheless had the child in the ordinary manner of giving birth and after this her virginity remained intact."[14]

The consensus of opinion is that Volusianus was writing a bit tongue in cheek, or perhaps, even baiting Augustine somewhat in this reply. It clearly was not the case of only one unnamed individual in his clique who was sporting rhetorical fun at some of the doctrines he mentioned. Volusianus, too, was skeptical, and even somewhat resentful, of the Christian faith.

> In many ways Volusianus lived in what was already a post-pagan world. . . . But he continued to harbor grave doubts as to the truth of Christianity. He also doubted the political advisability of a Christian empire. His criticisms were first aired in a salon of cultivated gentlemen in Carthage. Volusianus voiced the resentment of pagans, in both Rome and Africa, who believed the fall of Rome had happened because of neglect of the worship of the gods.[15]

Yet, while he was a tad brash, he was truly a formable mind of the age. "The breadth of Volusianus' *auctoritas* was remarkable as well. Letters debating with Bishop Augustine of Hippo on the dogma of the Incarnation mark Volusianus among the pagan intelligentsia capable enough to

---

14. Augustine, *Letters*, 135.2.
15. Brown, *Through the Eye*, 359.

match wits with one of the greatest minds of the century and strong willed enough to defy the arguments of Augustine and persistent family pressures to convert to Christianity."[16]

Augustine's reply was magisterial, yet humble (always a good combination). He laid out for Volusianus, and for the rest of us, the majesty of the Holy Scriptures. He touts the never-ending depth of God's Word:

> For such is the depth of the Christian Scriptures, that even if I were attempting to study them and nothing else from early boyhood to decrepit old age, with the utmost leisure, the most unwearied zeal, and talents greater than I have, I would be still daily making progress in discovering their treasures; not that there is so great difficulty in coming through them to know the things necessary to salvation, but when any one has accepted these truths with the faith that is indispensable as the foundation of a life of piety and uprightness, so many things which are veiled under manifold shadows of mystery remain to be inquired into by those who are advancing in the study, and so great is the depth of wisdom not only in the words in which these have been expressed, but also in the things themselves, that the experience of the oldest, the ablest, and the most zealous students of Scripture illustrates what Scripture itself has said: "When a man has done, then he begins" (Sirach 18:6).[17]

This is an amazing snippet of a letter written by a truly monumental Christian thinker. Augustine stated, in effect, that there is no end to the treasures within the Bible. It is the fractal nature of the Holy Scriptures that he really described here. One cannot exhaust them; even the most intelligent, the ablest, or the oldest one among us is unable to reach the end of their meaning. Notice, he concluded this segment of the letter with a quotation from the Septuagint, from the book of Sirach, that drives home the point that when it comes to studying, interpreting, and understanding the Holy Scriptures, the end is really nothing but the beginning.

16. Weber, "Albinus," 479. Weber uses *auctoritas* here in the sense of "authority."

17. Augustine, *Letters*, 137.1.3.

Augustine's Full Circle

One should appreciate how Augustine had come full circle in his life in order to write that sentiment.[18] As a youngster he had rejected the Holy Scriptures because they did not measure up to the literary style and artistry of Cicero. Listen to how Augustine described his initial attitude toward the Bible and compare that with his viewpoint looking back with the perspective of a transformed man:

> I decided to apply myself to the study of the Holy Scriptures to see what it was like. What I discovered was not something to be grasped by the proud or the immature, but something veiled in mysteries, humbling as one enters and sublime as one advances. I was not one of those able to enter by bending my neck to negotiate the steps. For when I directed my attention to the Scripture I did not feel as I do now; it did not appear to me worthy of being compared to the dignity of Marcus Tullius Cicero. My sophisticated pride shrank from its literary style, and my trained wit was unable to penetrate its inner meaning. The Scripture is designed to help spiritual little ones to grow, but I couldn't stand the thought of being a "little one." Puffed up in arrogance as I was, I looked upon myself as one of the greats.[19]

Indeed, Augustine did not want Volusianus to have that same debilitating attitude toward the Holy Scriptures that he had originally experienced. Volusianus was young, brash, and intellectually very talented—just like Augustine had been in his youth so many years ago. For that reason, the letter quoted above in which he implored Volusianus to read the Scriptures is laced with allusions to Cicero.[20] Nothing got lost in the mind of Augustine, and here, he fed Volusianus exactly what the young Roman needed. As Cameron notes, this "passage plays on Cicero's portrait of the ideal rhetor in *De oratore* 1.21.95."[21] The wise, old Bishop was lobbing Cicero right before the face of one who might have needed it most at that moment.

18. Cameron, *Christ Meets Me*, 5.

19. Augustine, *Confessions*, III.5.9.

20. Cameron, *Christ Meets Me*, 4.

21. Ibid., 294.

As the World Turns

This back and forth correspondence with Volusianus was, fundamentally, a watershed sequence of events, actually, more for Augustine than for Volusianus. While there was not a large number of letters involved in the interchange, the exchanges with the young Roman pagan did dramatically impact Augustine.[22] It triggered his writing of one of the classic works of Western civilization, *The City of God*.[23] The brief correspondence with the talented bureaucrat "sowed the seed" as "Volusianus' questions had prompted Augustine to form plans for a large-scale work to detail Christianity's place in the world and its relationship to Rome."[24] The year following his exchanges with Volusianus, Augustine "wrote the first of the work's thousand pages and spent the next decade writing the rest."[25]

Volusianus came from a world in which the stability of Rome, the stability of the world as far as he was concerned, had recently been shaken to the core. While the entrance by the Visigoths through the gates of Rome in AD 410 commenced a true shifting in the world, the "sack of Rome," as the event is widely known, is a bit of a misnomer. Rome was not really sacked; it was, more technically, looted. No churches were ravaged, and people were treated humanely as the barbarians entered the city. This raises

22. Five letters comprise the interactions of Augustine's dealings with Volusianus. The first letter (132) was written by Augustine, addressed to Volusianus, encouraging him to read the Scriptures. The second letter (135) was written by Volusianus with some questions on doctrine. The third letter (136) was from an imperial commissioner by the name of Marcellinus to Augustine in which he relays some further questions by Volusianus. The fourth letter (137) is Augustine's long reply to Volusianus' questions. The fifth letter (138) was written by Augustine to Marcellinus in reply to letter 136.

23. *The City of God* (*De Civitate Dei*) has the full title *The City of God Against the Pagans* (*De Civitate Dei contra Paganos*). In this remarkable work, Augustine explained Christianity's role in the face of other, worldly based religions and philosophies. He especially focused on the relationship of the church with the Roman government. Alaric and the Visigoths had entered Rome on August 24, 410. That event was a game changer, and it set many Romans into a state of shock and introspection. Many people from within the old circles of Roman society interpreted what happened as a divine punishment for abandoning traditional Roman religion for the new wave of change, namely Christianity. But Augustine forcefully made the point that it was not Christianity that led to the fall of the city. In *The City of God*, he consoled Christians, explaining that, even if a cataclysmic event such as the fall of Rome, or any earthly empire for that matter, was imperiled, it was God's city, the heavenly Jerusalem, that would triumph in the end. For a good translation see *City of God against the Pagans* translated by Dyson.

24. Cameron, *Christ Meets Me*, 4.

25. Ibid., 5.

a little-known aspect to the Gothic invasion of Rome; the soldiers under Alaric were largely Christian. Yes, you read that correctly. Is that how you had envisioned it? What image was in your mind when you heard of the great barbarian sack of Rome in 410? I suspect you were not thinking of them as Christians. Yet, there is plenty of evidence for a great and pervasive spreading and acceptance of the Gospel throughout the Gothic culture quite early. One finds Athanasius (ca. AD 296–373)[26] labeling the Goths among the people groups reached by the proclamation of the Gospel.[27]

The invading barbarians were only in the city for about three days. Understanding the colorful character of Alaric is a key to understanding the events of Rome's fall, the so-called sack. Yes, Alaric was a Goth, but he was also a legitimate Roman general. He sported the highest level of command in the Roman army, that of *magister militum* (Master of the Soldiers). Some of his soldiers who were led by Alaric as they invaded the city in 410 were, earlier, the very same ones he had led in the service of Rome.[28] Basically, Alaric simply allowed his troops to enter the city and clean out things of worth. "Far from being a bloodbath, the Visigothic sack of Rome was a chillingly well-conducted act of spoliation. The gilded statues of the Forum vanished. Huge loads of cash along with gold and silver plate left the city when the Visigoths marched out three days later."[29]

Yet, to be sure, the world had changed because of that event. Volusianus knew it; Augustine knew it—even Jerome in far off Palestine knew it. In a letter to Principia, Jerome remarked that, "The city that had taken the entire world had now, itself, been taken."[30] In another place, he lamented that, "the whole world seems to have perished in one city."[31] This was the *Sitz im Leben* of the Augustine–Volusianus relationship.[32] One was, perhaps, the

---

26. Some good works on Athanasius include: Gwynn, *Athanasius of Alexandria*; Leithart, *Athanasius*; Weinandy, *Athanasius*; Anatolios, *Athanasius*.

27. Athanasius, *De incarntione*, 51.1. For a masterful summary of origin of Christianity among the Goths, see Andreas Schwarcz, "Cult and Religion." For more on the Goths see Heather, *The Goths*; Heather, *Goths and Romans*; Thompson, *Visigoths*.

28. Kulikowski, *Rome's Gothic Wars*. See this work for a clear, concise, and highly entertaining description of the lead up to and the culmination of the invasion by Alaric.

29. Brown, *Through the Eye*, 294.

30. Jerome, *Letter* 127.12. *Capitur urbs, quae totum cepit orbem.*

31. Jerome, *Commentary on Ezekiel*, I. Pref. (PL 25:16).

32. A German phrase widely used in biblical studies that has the meaning of "the setting in life" or "the life situation." The term was coined by a famous biblical scholar by the name of Herman Gunkel in the early twentieth century.

brightest of a new generation of Roman officials in a post-Roman world; the other was a man transformed by his reading of the Holy Scriptures as scripture.

In *Letter* 137, Augustine laid out for Volusianus the very key to his hermeneutical method—his way of reading the Holy Scriptures. After all, Augustine had learned that the key was, in fact, learning how to read the Holy Scriptures! As Cameron put it, "Hindsight had taught him that what he had actually needed was instruction in *how to read*; the odd collection of writings required first submitting to its humble, earthy style. But Scripture not only counsels humility, it also imparts it."[33] Thus, Augustine attempted to pass on this invaluable lesson as he wrote Volusianus,

> But as to its way of communicating, Holy Scripture is composed
> in style that is accessible to everyone, even if only a few plumb
> its depths . . . it doesn't mount up with the kind of exalted speech
> that sluggish and untrained minds dare not pretend to think. . . .
> Instead, it invites everyone with its humble discourse, and feeds
> them all, not only with passages whose meanings stand out plain-
> ly, but also with ones enveloped in secrecy. It does this so that all
> readers can be exercised in the truth—the same truth shared out
> equally in obvious texts and hidden ones.[34]

The end of the story of Volusianus is uncertain. There is a written tradition that he became a Christian just before he died. Peter Brown, in a somewhat skeptical sounding voice, stated, "Yet if we are to believe the *Vita Melaniae Iunioris,* Volusianus was eventually converted on his deathbed by his niece, Melania the Younger, when on an official mission to Constantinople in 437."[35]

Fractals, Augustine, and the Nature of the Holy Scriptures

We, perhaps, do not really know the true end of Volusianus. However, we do have the meager remnants of his interactions with the mind of Augustine. The great Bishop clearly pointed the young aristocrat in the right direction—the same direction that had led to Augustine's own conversion and personal transformation—reading the Holy Scriptures as scripture.

33. Cameron, *Christ Meets Me,* 5.
34. Augustine, *Letters,* 137.1.18.
35. Brown, "Aspects," 8.

Mandelbot has introduced us to the world of fractals in nature. Augustine pointed to the complexity of Holy Scriptures and a need of reading them in such a way that the *viva vox Dei* will penetrate our mind and our heart. This has led to the figural image of the Bible as a fractal structure, limitless (like the coastline of Britain) in its complexity and depth.

If one embraces this metaphor of the Holy Scriptures as a fractal structure, then one can move forward, appreciating the expanse of God's Word to us. And to be sure, it seems this expanse is immeasurable, fractal-like, in its scope and reach. Augustine knew this. He knew of the paradoxical "clear" and "unclear" aspects of the Holy Scriptures.[36] This leads us to the next chapter in which the *sfumato* of the Holy Scriptures is considered.

36. Augustine, *Letters*, 137.1.3. Augustine uses the terms *aperta* and *operta* in the sense of clear (open) and unclear (closed) passages of Scripture.

8

The *Sfumato* of the
Holy Scriptures

What's da Vinci Got That I Don't Have?

I GOT AN INTERESTING book from my sister for Christmas a number of years ago. It had a catchy title—*How to Think like Leonardo da Vinci*. The day after Christmas, I started paging through the thing. The author, Michael J. Gelb, presented what he called the "seven da Vincian principles."[1] He named these principles using da Vinci's native language, Italian. The one that caught my attention immediately was called *sfumato*. Being a native English speaker, I could pretty well figure out the essence of the other six terms he used: *curiosità, dimostrazione, sensazione, art/scienza, corporalita, connessione*. Yet, *sfumato* threw me a bit. I surmised that it was the *sf* sequence of letters at the beginning of the word that caused my cognitive dissonance. You don't see too many English words with *sf* at the beginning. In fact, I could not think of any, so I lifted the handy *Webster's Ninth* off the shelf and began paging toward the s section. I got detained for a minute at "selcouth." They say if you want to make a new word a part of your vocabulary you should use it two or three times a day for the first week. While that may sound like a bit of a selcouth idea to you, I found that it really works.

I began turning the pages again, and finally, after "sexy," I found a handful of words that began with *sf*. Now I suppose that some music majors and instrumentalists know "sforzando," but it was a new one to me.[2]

---

1. Gelb, *How to Think*.

2. There are a number of musical terms which are loanwords borrowed from Italian. For example, Fromkin and Rodman cite the following: *opera, piano, virtuoso, balcony,*

Wouldn't that be a killer Scrabble word to play? I could see using it if some-one had played "for" or "do." As I ran my finger down the column, past sforzando, I actually found sfumato. While Italian in origin, it is also an English word; that is, sfumato is what is known as a loanword. A loanword comes from a broader linguistic concept called borrowing. Linguistic bor-rowing is a universally observed process in which one language "takes and incorporates some linguistic element from another."[3]

Sfumato—it means "the definition of form without abrupt outline by the blending of one tone into another." Granted, it might be tough to work that word into a conversation. Yet, its relationship to da Vinci's style of paint-ing makes it, I think, a pretty good label for one of the principles for think-ing like Leonardo. You see, sfumato is used by art historians to describe the mysterious, hazy feel and look common to many of da Vinci's paintings. Sfumato means literally, "going up in smoke," and to achieve this smoky, uncertain, vague effect, he vigilantly applied numerous paper-thin layers of paint. It gave his paintings an enigmatic feel.[4] Gelb selected this word to talk about da Vinci's propensity to embrace ambiguity, paradox, and uncertainty. Do you want to think like Leonardo? Then, according to Gelb, you need to be able to confront paradox, ambiguity, and uncertainty. Guess what? There is quite a bit of that in the Holy Scriptures, especially when one speaks of interpreting the Bible. That is the direction of this chapter.

The da Vincian principle of sfumato, as Gelb employs it, aims at over-coming the challenge of living with simplicity *and* complexity at the same time. Gelb urges the reader to use that paradox to one's own advantage rather than having it elicit angst in your life. Indeed, life is often composed of paradox, opposites, ambiguity, and uncertainty. "Leonardo's ceaseless questioning and insistence on using his senses to explore experience led him to many great insights and discoveries, but they also led him to con-front the vastness of the unknown and ultimately the unknowable. Yet his phenomenal ability to hold the tension of opposites, to embrace uncertain-ty, ambiguity, and the paradox, was a critical characteristic of his genius."[5]

---

and *mezzanine.*

3. Arlotto, *Introduction*, 185. See Arlotto's chapter 5 on "Borrowing" for a fuller lin-guistic accounting of the phenomenon. See also, Fromkin and Rodman, *Introduction*, 309–12.

4. To see a good example of sfumato as a technique, search Google images for "St. John the Baptist by Leonardo da Vinci."

5. Gelb, *How to Think*, 143.

As Gelb points out, there is joy and sorrow, intimacy and independence, strength and weakness, good and evil. These polar experiences comprise life. Unfortunately, many people do not deal well with polarity, ambiguity, or paradox. I have noticed that many students do not handle ambiguity very well these days. It gnaws at them, and it stymies their creative abilities. Rather, as Gelb argues, the da Vinci-like thinker will embrace the ambiguity, the problem of paradox, the element of uncertainty.

The Sfumato of the Holy Scriptures

It oftentimes happens that when people read the Holy Scriptures, they sense the tension of sfumato within the text. It can be disturbing, frustrating, even bewildering. However, that troubling reality need not exasperate or hinder the reader who penetrates the biblical text in order to hear the living voice of God speaking quite directly. The Augustinian-like reader of the Bible is aware and understands that this dynamic exists within the pages of the Bible and embraces that aspect of the Holy Scriptures. To be sure, a pensive, measured, prayerful, and prolonged reading of the Holy Scriptures with a heightened awareness and an appreciation of the sfumato within will facilitate a blending of different senses. That combining of various senses is exactly the sort of synesthetic experience one sometimes needs in order to apprehend something that is unclear as though it were clear.

Remember, $5 + 2 =$ yellow was not immediately clear to you when you were first presented with it. However, once you read (back in chapter 2) about synesthesia, the equation made sense; you then apprehended the unclear aspect of the formula. Consider now, for example, the message from Prov 26:4–5 where one finds contradiction and the uncertainty of sfumato. Yet, with an appreciation of sfumato, the synesthetic reader engages the apparent incongruity, and, perhaps in that sense, what one finds in these verses is simply a set of orange proverbs.

> Do not answer a fool according to his folly,
>   otherwise, you may become just like him.
>
> Answer a fool according to his folly,
>   otherwise, he will be wise in his own eyes.

Many people who have read these verses see nothing but utter contradiction. Especially because these two particular proverbs occur one directly after the other, the reader is rather slapped in the face by the ambiguity; the juxtaposition magnifies the incongruity.[6] If these verses had been separated within the Book of Proverbs by a distance of five or six chapters, then the abruptness of the glaring contradiction would not have been quite so vivid. The reader would, perhaps, have had plenty of time to forget the command of verse 4 not to answer the fool before coming across the command to answer the fool.

As it is, the two contradictory sayings are right next to each other, and as a result, a lot of ink has been spilled over these two verses exactly because they are virtual opposites. This alone is enough to turn off some people from reading the Holy Scriptures. "It's full of contradictions," they wail, sometimes citing this particular case. To that Augustine would have replied, "Yes, indeed. There are contradictions, ambiguities, and paradoxes." Actually, that is a paraphrase of a hypothetical response by Augustine; he did not actually say that. He did, however, say, "casual readers are misled by problems and ambiguities of many kinds, mistaking one thing for another."[7] These contradictory proverbs present exactly the sort of unclear or mixed message found in the Bible that may frustrate the usual reader. But for you, your goal is not to be simply a casual reader. You want to read the Holy Scriptures as scripture, and the sfumato of the biblical texts will enhance, rather than frustrate, that enterprise. The reality of ambiguities and contradictions needs to be coupled to the spirit of the reader who has a seeking and patient heart and simply yearns to hear God speak through his Word. When those elements are coupled, it can produce a richer and deeper reading of the Holy Scriptures. "Augustine argues that God allowed obscurities and ambiguities to be present in Scripture so that those who are intellectually proud might be humbled by the labor of interpretation, and so that the message of Scripture might not be disdained because it seemed too simple."[8]

Part of the majesty of the Holy Scriptures is their fractal nature, and we know that fractal structures are not simple. The Holy Scriptures, themselves, contain the paradox of complexity and simplicity. Remember Augustine's categories of clear and unclear? "These were Augustine's most basic hermeneutical categories."[9] He was very keenly aware of the pres-

6. For a discussion on the nature of contradictory proverbs across cultures, see Katz, "Analycity and Contradiction," and Yankah, "Do Proverbs Contradict?," 127–41.

7. Augustine, *On Christian Teaching*, 32.

8. Levering, *Theology of Augustine*, 14.

9. Cameron, *Christ Meets Me*, 7.

ence of sfumato within the Holy Scriptures; he knew certain passages of the Bible can be staggeringly ambiguous. Yet, remember always, while there is the complexity of the text, there is also the simplicity of the Gospel.

Don't Do X, Do X!

Now, let us circle back to our example of Prov 26:4–5. In this case, we find two proverbs that present the reader with a seemingly blatant contradiction. Read them again.

> Do not answer a fool according to his folly,
> otherwise, you may become just like him.

> Answer a fool according to his folly,
> otherwise, he will be wise in his own eyes.

The sfumato here should entice the wise reader to take a second and third look in order to ponder what sort of relationship there is between the two verses. Of course, on the surface, a contradiction looms, but the deliberative reader knows to go deeper. The superficial, quick and casual reader sees only incongruity. In fact, in the Talmud there is a serious discussion about banning or removing from circulation the book of Proverbs just because of the glaring contradiction.

> They also wanted to ban the Book of Proverbs because there are statements in it that are self-contradictory. Yet, they ultimately did not ban it—why? They said, "Wasn't there the same sort of thing in Ecclesiastes? Yet, we were able reconcile (the contradictions) there. Let's also dig deeper in this case. How is it that we have a contradiction (in Proverbs)?" It is written, "Do not answer a fool according to his folly." Yet, it is also written, "Answer a fool according to his folly."[10]

However, in the end, they clearly decided not to ban the book because of contradictions within it. In this case, the rabbis ultimately decided the two proverbs presented two very separate scenarios. As they interpreted them, the proverbs taken together meant that in matters related to the Torah, one *should not* answer back to the fool (verse 4). However, in regards to any of the ordinary issues of daily life, one *should* answer the fool (verse 5). Thus, they did, seemingly, catch on to the notion of how most proverbs

10. *Shabbat* 30b.

work across cultures—they are not meant necessarily to be universal truths, but rather, they are geared for specific situations. The rabbis' bifurcation into the two categories of Torah and everything else is a bit restrictive, but at least it leans away "from the simplistic dualistic dogmatism to a situationally nuanced wisdom."[11] To be properly understood, there needs to be a deeper understanding that there is, universally, a time-sensitive aspect to proverbs. "Proverbs are right only if they are stated to the right person at the right time."[12]

To their credit, the rabbis did come to a solution, and they did not ban the book of Proverbs. But this is a good example of some interpreters who had difficulty dealing with the idea of sfumato within the Word of God. The reaction of wanting to reject the book solely because of a contradiction is right in line with readers who cannot even fathom that such a thing would come from God. Rather, being aware of and appreciating the sfumato within the text energizes the careful reader to consider deeper issues rather than simply succumbing to the face value of something like contradictory statements.

Thus, there are really two levels of sfumato one finds in Prov 26:4–5. First, there is the blatant, stark contradiction of the two imperatives 1) Don't answer, and 2) Answer! Secondly, there is the ambiguity of fine distinctions that may underlie the two statements. What, exactly, is it that calls for these contradictory actions? Is it only the Torah versus everyday issues distinction that can account for the statements? No; there are many variables, and to be sure, many readers have made suggestions to resolve the relationship between the two verses. For example, there is a later explanation within Jewish tradition that interprets the proverbs in a totally different context. The *Midrash on Proverbs*[13] says that you do not answer the fool in a situation when there are other people around who know both you and the fool. In that case, those people may well consider you and the fool to be alike. You should, however, answer the fool when both of you are in the company of people you do not know.[14] Of course, we are not told the rationale for the juxtaposition of the contradictory instructions. We do not know the

11. Hildebrandt, "Genre of Proverbs," 535.

12. Longman, "Book of Proverbs," 543.

13. The dating of the *Midrash on Proverbs* (*Midrash Mishle*–מדרש משלי) is difficult. It may have originated in the ninth century AD, but the earliest mention of it comes from the first half of the eleventh century. See Strack and Stemberger, *Talmud and Midrash*, 352–53.

14. Visotzky, *Midrash on Proverbs*, 102.

particular scenario the editor(s) of the book of Proverbs may have held in mind. As Michael Fox notes, "One might propose that a great many distinctions are possible, and the editor is leaving it to the reader to draw them, for wisdom is relative to the situation."[15]

Beginning the Framework

This is the point where you should begin to appreciate the sfumato that is so much a part of the Bible. Perhaps in the past, you found the uncertainty or the ambiguity of certain texts within the Holy Scriptures to be frustrating. But now, things have changed just a bit. You are slowly but surely becoming a new reader. You are amending some existing patterns of how you have read the Bible in the past (chapter 4). A framework of orientation (chapter 3), flow (chapter 5), and *lectio divina* (chapter 6) is beginning to give some basic shape to this new enterprise of reading the Holy Scriptures as scripture. Hopefully, you are commencing a movement toward a Scripture-filled life. Yet, an awareness of the complexity of the enterprise is now growing as you consider the fractal aspects (chapter 7) and the sfumato (chapter 8) of God's Word. The realization of the fact that "God has structured Scripture in order to be endlessly profound and spiritually challenging as well"[16] is beginning to sink into your mind and heart. Good! You are walking down the right trail, but as you are aware, it is a never-ending trail. Remember, this book is a mere introduction, designed to plant in your mind and in your heart a few new ideas about what it means to be reading the Holy Scriptures as scripture. A variety of disparate elements of the enterprise have been introduced, but these have been explained and explored only on a very superficial level.

Just Being Aware of It is Not Enough

Just being aware of sfumato is not enough. The enterprise of reading the Holy Scriptures as scripture involves a complex scaffolding of various elements. You must engage the process as an "intensive reader,"[17] and as

15. Fox, *Proverbs*, 793. Fox speaks of an editor because the various collections of proverbs were edited together into its present form. It is an editor who made the final decision to place the two verses next to each other.

16. Treier, *Theological Interpretation*, 45.

17. O'Keefe and Reno, *Sanctified Vision*, 19.

such, the Holy Scriptures will absorb your attention. Think of the peculiar melding of simplicity and complexity within the pages of the Bible. These two concepts form a spectrum of human experience and thought. From my frame of reference, simplicity is nice while complexity can be trying. Yet, even in life's simplest moments there can be complexity. I know many people who make conscious decisions that complicate their lives; it often seems that they actually prefer complexity. Yet, life can be simple too. While I know my life is not all that simple, I like to think that, given a choice, I tend to make decisions that lead toward simplicity. I have read a few things that speak well to the one who prefers simplicity.[18] For instance, I was impressed with Robert Fulghum's pithy list in his work, *All I Really Need to Know I Learned in Kindergarten*. He said that he learned most of what is necessary to live a meaningful life in kindergarten. This is what he learned:

Share everything.

Play fair.

Put things back where you found them.

Clean up your own mess.

Don't take things that aren't yours.

Say you're sorry when you hurt somebody.

Wash your hands before you eat.

Flush.

Warm cookies and cold milk are good for you.

Live a balanced life—learn some and think some and draw and paint and sing and dance and play and work every day some.

Take a nap every afternoon.

When you go out into the world, watch out for traffic, hold hands, and stick together.

Be aware of wonder. Remember the little seed in the Styrofoam cup: The roots go down and the plant goes up and nobody really knows how or why, but we are all like that.

Goldfish and hamsters and white mice and even the little seed in the Styrofoam cup—they all die. So do we.

18. Perhaps the best work I have found on the concept is Foster, *Freedom of Simplicity*.

And then remember the Dick-and-Jane books and the first word you learned—the biggest word of all—LOOK.[19]

You cannot get too much simpler than that. Then there is the complexity factor. Oftentimes while I am teaching, I get into the complexity of the biblical text—things like variant readings, ancient manuscripts, scribal errors, etc. Make no bones about it, the text is complicated; it is fractal. Add to that the notion from Augustine that there are clear and unclear texts. On top of all of that, there is sfumato lurking among the pages of the Bible. But then I tell the students always to remember that there is the complexity of the text, and there is the simplicity of the Gospel. There you have it; in my opinion, it is the mother of all sfumato—the biblical text is complicated, the Gospel is not. In a way, Jesus' Sermon on the Mount is a bit like the kindergarten list. Jesus keeps it simple. Yet, even doing the simple things is a challenge. I don't know about you, but I have a tough enough time with the simple stuff; I do not always want to be worried about the complicated things. Students get frustrated with me when they ask perplexing, complicated questions because, generally, I do not have a clue. When I tell them that I do not have a clue they get a funny, almost pained expression on their face. I mean, they want me to explain something in the book of Revelation, and I'm sitting there trying to figure how I can get through the day without getting angry at somebody. They want to know if the resurrections in Rev 20:4–5 are both bodily resurrections, and I'm struggling with something as simple as seeing that speck of sawdust in my brother's eye.[20]

Sfumato—it is a funny word. I really think that I do have a bit of Leonardo's love of sfumato in me. Some of the really big uncertainties of life don't bother me in the slightest. Ambiguity does not really annoy me too much. I enjoy, or maybe better, I appreciate a good paradox. I also think a certain sfumato comes with age. Freshmen students do not have much patience for sfumato; college students generally have a pretty low threshold for ambiguity. I suspect that Leonardo was, at least, in his late forties before he got his sfumato act together.

In the next chapter, we will explore the vast world of hermeneutics and issues of how one should interpret the Holy Scriptures given our working presupposition that there is an element of sfumato within the pages of the Holy Scriptures.

19. Fulghum, *All I Really Need*, 2–3.
20. See Matt 5:22; 7:3.

9

The Lamb, the Elephant, and Biblical Interpretation

A New Labyrinth to Explore—Biblical Interpretation

THERE IS ANOTHER VERY important aspect to the enterprise of reading the Holy Scriptures as scripture. The reader must interpret that which is being read. When it comes to actually interpreting the Bible, one enters a fascinating yet complex labyrinth. This domain is usually labeled *hermeneutics,* or it is sometimes simply called *biblical interpretation.*[1] Hermeneutics is a very broad field of study in which one can investigate any text, not just the Bible. For that reason, the phrase *biblical hermeneutics* is sometimes used to specify that it is the Bible, in particular, that is being interpreted. While we agree that the nature of the Holy Scriptures is unique, the fact is that "biblical language is ordinary language and, as such, inherently ambiguous."[2] Therefore, reading involves interpretation. As it cleverly has been put, "To be human is to interpret."[3]

---

1. The term comes from the Greek verb meaning "I translate" or "I interpret" (hermēneuō–ἑρμηνεύω). The literature on hermeneutics is very substantial and of quite a variety. For the true beginner, I recommend you start with Camery-Hoggatt, *Reading the Good Book Well.* This is an entertaining and understandable introduction to some of the issues and topics within the field of hermeneutics. Other books, good for a beginner, include: Jasper, *Introduction to Hermeneutics;* Virkler, *Hermeneutics;* Goldsworthy, *Gospel-Centered Hermeneutics;* and Brown, *Scripture as Communication.* For the more advanced and ambitious readers, I recommend: Porter and Robinson, *Hermeneutics;* Thiselton, *New Horizons;* Thiselton, *Hermeneutics;* Vanhoozer, *Is There a Meaning;* Vanhoozer, *First Theology;* and Osborne, *Hermeneutical Spiral.*

2. Leithart, *Deep Exegesis,* 9.

3. Smith, *Fall of Interpretation,* 159.

This chapter aims at providing a small sampling of issues that I find particularly interesting. What you will read here is, by no means, any attempt to provide an overview of the entire field of biblical interpretation. One should consult some of the books suggested in footnote 1 for a more complete perspective on hermeneutics. For, indeed, it does take an entire book to provide an adequate presentation of the field. I am not seeking to provide such a broad look within this chapter. My hunch is that most readers will be relative novices to the world of hermeneutics, and a complete survey might well prove to be a bit overwhelming because of the depth and complexity of the topic of biblical interpretation. Rather, I aim to raise awareness that you are interpreting when you read the Holy Scriptures as scripture. I aim, also, to whet your appetite somewhat for further study on the topic.

Where should one begin? Introducing hermeneutics is difficult because the field of study is totally nonlinear; there is no good place to jump into the discussion. I might start, for example, by suggesting that there is wide variety of opinion about the matter of subjectivity. What else might one expect? Yet, subjectivity is important in hermeneutics.[4] When humans read or see something, there is a subjective, interpretive process that occurs. Do you remember the story about Kepler and Brahe in chapter 2? They saw the same sunrise but interpreted that event very differently. When it comes to interpreting the Holy Scriptures, one is in for a roller coaster of a ride for as I. Howard Marshall noted, "There is great uncertainty about this entire general area of hermeneutics and interpretation, not only in the narrower sector of biblical studies, but also in the broader field of literary studies and philosophy."[5]

I will introduce only a few thoughts about the process of reading and interpreting. Do not expect a list of how-to rules for biblical interpretation in this chapter. This book is a simple, beginning look at a complex enterprise, namely reading the Holy Scriptures as scripture. The design of this book is to launch you on a quest; it is not a reference work that compiles all the answers one may seek while on the journey. Interpreting the texts within the Bible is a part of that lofty enterprise. As a reader, you are also an

---

4. I thank my colleague, Dr. Glen Menzies, who provided a number of useful insights on this matter of subjectivity. He asked, "Isn't there a difference between the subjectivity of appropriation and the subjectivity that erases the lines between what is true and what is not?" He also noted that there are several types of subjectivity: 1) seeks to conform what is inside of me to something on the outside; 2) seeks to conform what is outside to my own internal requirements.

5. Marshall, *Beyond the Bible*, 12.

interpreter. How should you best go about that business? What are some of the issues at hand?

Richard Briggs borrowed the phrase, "the hermeneutic of self-involvement," from Anthony Thiselton[6] in order to label the procedure in which "we invest ourselves in the text, and in the process we are changed."[7] That phrase does capture an important nuance of what it means to be reading the Holy Scriptures as scripture. It means that you, as an Augustinian type of reader, will invest yourself in the Bible, and as a result you will be changed. That is exactly what happened to Augustine. He read, and he was transformed. This hermeneutic of self-involvement assumes that you will engage the interpretive stage as a deep reader who is properly oriented (chapter 3) and reading with a measure of patience (chapter 4) while employing a method (chapter 5) that works for you and yields enduring results through a transformation in the heart and in the mind, à la Augustine.

But there are also dangers lurking within the world of hermeneutics. One should be warned that it is not a sacrosanct science of principles of interpretation so culled and refined that the mere running through a checklist of dos and don'ts will yield the proper interpretation of a scriptural text. No, that is not the case. Consider the following notion. "Modern hermeneutics has often aspired to a kind of scientific objectivity in interpretation, one that goes along with the obsession with method. If interpretation is a scientific or quasi-scientific enterprise, it does not depend on any character development or religious commitment in the interpreter."[8]

The point here is that there *is* something very important to who the interpreter is. Not all interpreters are the same. Anyone can read the Bible; not everyone comes to the Holy Scriptures with the same regard for the Word, or for God, as far as that goes.

Is He Joking?

The Christian reader who engages the Holy Scriptures in humility as the *viva vox Dei* will interpret the text differently from the non-Christian reader. As Leithart put it, "Interpretive skills can be taught and improved, but

6. Thiselton, *New Horizons*, 272–312. Thiselton was Briggs' supervisor for his dissertation, so I suspect it was borrowing by suggestion.

7. Briggs, *Reading the Bible Wisely*, 121.

8. Leithart, *Deep Exegesis*, 139.

only the glad of heart make good readers."[9] In his vivid example, he notes that pedophiles can read the Bible and employ hermeneutic principles, but they will not "get the text" in the same way that a committed follower of the Lord who is a deep reader will get the text. In the world of biblical hermeneutics, not all interpreters are equal. Such is the case with a non-Christian reader because "analysis and teaching might improve things marginally, but that person's main problem is not a technical but a spiritual one . . . and the only real solution is conversion."[10] So it is the case that *anyone* can do hermeneutics, but there are qualitatively different levels of spiritual engagement in the process among readers. Leithart uses the analogy that reading the Holy Scriptures is somewhat like hearing a joke. "If interpretation is more like getting a joke than it is like dissecting a frog, then only certain kinds of people will be good interpreters."[11] As a reader of the Holy Scriptures as scripture, you will be a good interpreter in large measure because you have, as in Leithart's example, "the hermeneutical equivalent to a good sense of humor."[12]

But what about differences of interpretation among those who are committed followers of Jesus and are deep readers of the Holy Scriptures as scripture? Why can there be differences among such a set of interpreters? You and I may read the same passage and come to different conclusions about the interpretation of the text. How can that be?

The Lamb and the Elephant

The church fathers and other biblical interpreters through the ages have variously understood the nature of the interpreter's act, but they generally all recognized that there exists a reader's subjectivity in the interpretive process. Bernard of Clairvaux (AD 1090–1153) was one such interpreter of the Holy Scriptures.[13] Aware that the sense of the words read from within the Bible can vary according to the various experiences, circumstances and needs of the reader, Bernard noted that "In the sea of sacred reading, the

9. Ibid.

10. Ibid.

11. Ibid.

12. Ibid.

13. For the life of Bernard, see: Evans, *Bernard of Clairvaux*; Lane, *Theologian of the Cross*; Sommerfeldt, *Life of the Mind*; For a sampling of Bernard's writings see: Evans, *Selected Works*; Pennington, *Bernard of Clairvaux*; Thornton and Varenne, *Honey and Salt*.

lamb can walk, and the elephant can swim."[14] The gist of this very witty observation will be our next point of focus, namely the phenomenon of multiple meanings. Bernard's phrase is a very intriguing one; why a lamb and an elephant? What is the illustration meant to convey?

Bernard was no interpretive slouch, and he was quite cognizant of the multiplicity of hermeneutical concerns and methods before the reader. He also understood that each reader brought a unique set of qualities and experiences to the interpretive process. I believe that what he was getting at here is the idea that the depth of the Holy Scriptures is immense, like that of the ocean, and there is ample room for two very different interpreters to make their way through the text. In other words, the example points to the fact that interpreters are different, and that can easily lead to divergent readings of a text. "St. Bernard was well aware that the sense of the words read would vary according to the different needs of different readers, yet the Scriptures by their very nature can profit all of them in different ways."[15] In this way, I am the lamb and you are the elephant. Or, if you prefer, you are the lamb and I am the elephant. I do not much care because that is not the point. Whichever role you want to take on, I will be the other critter, okay? The point is that whoever the lamb or the elephant may be, it seems they may differ in the *meaning* that they derive from the biblical text.

What Is The Meaning of "Meaning"?

What is the meaning of the word, "meaning"? This is actually not as stupid a question as it might first sound, and this may be the place where you begin to appreciate the important roles philosophy and linguistics have historically played in the hermeneutical enterprise. The question (What is the meaning of the word, "meaning"?) may bring to mind the famous response by President Clinton during the Monica Lewinsky debacle. From the *Congressional Record* we read:

> President Clinton was questioned by his own counsel during this deposition:

---

14. St. Bernard of Clairvaux, *Sermo de diversis* 94.2 (PL 183); *In hoc sacrae lectionis pelage agnus ambulat, et elephans natat.* The verb, *ambulat*, is curious here. Usually taken as "walked," the imagery here suggests the action is in the water. It can also mean to sail so, perhaps, something like "paddled" might be a good turn of the phrase in this context.

15. Sandor, "Lectio Divina," 110.

BENNETT: In [Lewinsky's] affidavit, she says this; "I have never had a sexual relationship with the President . . ." Is that a true and accurate statement as far as you can see it?

CLINTON: That is absolutely true.

Seven months later in testimony before the grand jury, Clinton said the truth of such denials depends on what the meaning of "is" is.[16]

The President uttered the now almost legendary statement, "It depends on what the meaning of 'is' is." In the face of that seemingly ridiculous response, many accused him of simply wielding sophistry in an evasive reply.[17] Was it mere sophistry? Aristotle, in *Metaphysics*, defined sophistry as "wisdom in appearance only." But a popular understanding of the word might be something more like what the actor Jeremy Sisto, playing Julius Caesar, said in the 2002 TV miniseries *Caesar*. At one point he quipped, "Sophistry? Doesn't that mean you know how to tell fancy lies?" Whatever one thinks of Clinton, he was alluding to a rather well-known and complicated problem within philosophical linguistics and hermeneutics. Either wittingly or unwittingly, he made reference to the issue of "meaning" by simply asking the famous question.

In speaking of biblical hermeneutics or biblical interpretation, one might consider that the interpretation of a text gives one the meaning of the text. This way of viewing things has been labelled as *naïve realism*. That phrase has been variously defined, but the horse sense of the expression is that it represents the philosophical point of view of the average person.[18] Naïve realism has also been labelled as "common sense realism." There is much that is appealing about this way of thinking, and one may be tempted to throw out the muddling aspects of the enterprise in which we are engaged by even asking such a ludicrous question as "What is the meaning of meaning"? However, perhaps, it should be branded as a deep question rather than a ludicrous question.

Whereas the safe realm of naïve realism might suggest that words carry their meaning with them, the world of quantum physics has certainly demonstrated that everything is not simply as our senses apprehend things.

16. *Congressional Record*, V. 144, Pt. 19, October 19, 1998 to December 19, 1998, 28013.

17. Soccio, *Archetypes*, 84.

18. Mach, *Analysis*, 37. His definition actually uses the phrase, "the average man."

The same seems to be true in the world of linguistics. Thiselton has noted that "As Saussure has shown decisively in one way, and Wittgenstein convincingly in another way, the meaning of a word depends not on what it is in itself but on its relation to other words and to other sentences which form its context."[19]

The Significance of Meaning

The theory of meaning is one of the thorniest and most disputed in the realm of philosophical linguistics. Naturally, the school of thought one follows in thinking about meaning drastically impacts one's hermeneutical frame of reference. The problems of meaning are manifold. First of all, there is widespread disagreement about something as basic as the sense of meaning. Meaning has been variously described with regard to its significance, reference, intention, ideas, and uses.[20] I will spare you in that none of these aspects of meaning will be discussed here. That is quite beyond the scope of this book. However, there is another significant problem with having a meeting of the minds about meaning. There is the issue of what it is that actually determines the meaning of a text. No matter what one believes about the nature of meaning, there is still the question of what it is that determines the meaning. This is a quagmire to be sure. Coming from various points of view, "at least eight factors, singly or in combination, have been identified as determining it: authors, audiences, contexts, communities, languages, texts, truth conditions, and cultural functions."[21]

Thus, there certainly seems to be significance to meaning. The previous sentence is much wittier than you may have first surmised. There is a play on the words "meaning" and "significance" that is drawn from a fairly well-known issue in philosophical linguistics and hermeneutics. The name most often associated with the meaning/significance issue is that of E. D. Hirsch (b. 1928). He wrote a couple significant and meaningful books that are often cited and usually alluded to in other hermeneutical works.[22] Hirsch wrote, "Meaning is that which is represented by a text; it is what the author meant by his use of a particular sign sequence; it is what the signs represent. Significance, on the other hand, names a relationship be-

19. Thiselton, "Semantics," 78–79.
20. Gracia, "Meaning," 492–99.
21. Ibid., 495.
22. Hirsch, *Validity*; and Hirsch, *Aim*.

tween that meaning and a person, or a conception, or a situation, or indeed anything imaginable."[23]

Evangelicals have, in general, sided with E. D. Hirsch on most of his views. In fact, "Hirsch's *Validity in Interpretation* has dominated conservative Protestant hermeneutics for several decades."[24] Yet, the maze of hermeneutics is so fantastically dense that, at this stage, you may wish not to put all of your eggs into Hirsch's hermeneutical basket. As is true with many aspects of life, things are often more complicated than one thinks, or would wish, and that is certainly true about biblical hermeneutics. An apt observation about the nature of the beast is that,

> If words like "literal," or "meaning," or even "text" itself are beginning to become a little more difficult and problematic for you, then we are actually getting somewhere, for it is the business of hermeneutics to get us to think rather more carefully than we are wont to do about just such words, and so perhaps to be a little less absolute in our claims to understand them. Hermeneutics warns us also about taking too simply and straightforwardly the idea that a text is just exactly what it was intended to be in the mind and intention of its author, as if understanding the letters of Paul were equivalent to entering into the mind and purposes of the apostle himself.[25]

Of course, there are many others who have contributed in a rich variety of ways to the hermeneutic bouillabaisse. In a rather famous and oft-cited article, Krister Stendahl (1921–2008) raised the issue of what the text meant compared to what the text means.[26] This meant/means dichotomy presents the reader with what might be described as a two-stage perspective of interpretation in which the past and the present are somewhat at odds with each other. This issue raised by Stendahl seems to have gotten the hermeneutical ball rolling, and there was much thinking and writing done during the second half of the twentieth century on some very key elements in hermeneutics. Several other very influential individuals of the last century who also spiced up the discussion on meaning and the nature of hermeneutics in general were Hans-Georg Gadamer (1900–2002) and Paul

23. Hirsch, *Validity*, 8. My colleague, Dr. Glen Menzies, suggested that it might well be mentioned that Hirsch "insisted that 'meaning' must be located within some consciousness or another. Basically, this means that meaning must be located either within the author or the reader. It is even problematic to speak of meaning within a 'text.'"

24. Treier, *Theological Interpretation*, 134.

25. Jasper, *Hermeneutics*, 13.

26. Stendahl, "Biblical Theology."

Ricoeur (1913–2005). Virtually any book on hermeneutics will include some sort of discussion about the contributions of these two fellows.

Any worthwhile presentation that would comprehensively summarize the thought of Gadamer and Ricoeur would probably require a book in itself. Even the barest recapping of their main contributions is widely beyond the scope of this chapter; after all, this section is a mere sampling of only a few of the myriad of issues within the discipline of biblical interpretation. Gadamer and Ricoeur are formidable figures, and if you have really caught the fever of wanting to explore more, you could investigate a couple of their best-known works.[27] Gadamer's hermeneutical method "moves from the author and the text to the union of text and reader, with roots in the present rather than in the past."[28] In Gadamer's words (albeit translated words), "All reading involves application, so that a person reading a text is himself part of the meaning he apprehends. He belongs to the text that he is reading."[29] That plays some rather nasty tricks with Hirsch's take on the meaning of a text. Yet, even Hirsch, somewhat of an archrival to Gadamer, admits to the man's importance by stating that Gadamer "has published the most substantial treatise on hermeneutic theory that has come from Germany in this century."[30] Indeed, Gadamer's influence has reached even into the realm of Pentecostal hermeneutics.[31] Ricoeur's influence has also penetrated into the evangelical and Pentecostal hermeneutical realms, although probably not to the extent of Gadamer.[32]

Suffice it to say, the aim of these past few paragraphs that mention the likes of Hirsch, Stendahl, Gadamer, and Ricoeur is simply to introduce

27. In the case of Gadamer, his most-often alluded to work is entitled *Truth and Method*. Let me warn you; it is dense and difficult. Ricoeur's most influential works are more scattered, but you could sample some of his writing in Valdes, *Ricoeur Reader*. Some secondary works on Ricoeur that could be useful are: Kearney, *Paul Recoeur*; Vanhoozer, *Biblical Narrative*; Stiver, *Theology after Ricoeur*.

28. Osborne, *Hermeneutical Spiral*, 471.

29. Gadamer, *Truth and Method*, 340.

30. Hirsch, *Validity*, 245.

31. See for example: Sheppard, "Biblical Interpretation," 121–41; Archer, *Pentecostal Hermeneutic*. See also Oliverio, *Theological Hermeneutics*, 196 who remarks concerning Pentecostal scholar Timothy Cargal that in his "hermeneutic there is a subtle yet important shift in the location of 'meaning' in the biblical texts away from the intention of the biblical author toward its locale in the interaction between text and reader, and the legacy of the hermeneutic tradition following Gadamer can be seen here."

32. This is in the sense of influence, not the number of citations. For example, Ricoeur is alluded to more often than Gadamer in a work such as Yong, *Spirit-Word-Community*.

you to a few of the key players from the twentieth century in the world of biblical hermeneutics. However, it is clearly the case that theoretical hermeneutics did not resolve itself at the end of the last century in spite of the efforts of those mentioned.

New groundbreakers are emerging and aggressively tackling the daunting maze of hermeneutics. There is an exciting, relatively new movement in the field that is oriented toward what has been described as theological interpretation.[33] This program was kick-started in the 1990s with the appearance of several key works. Two books in particular that I would recommend (Fowl's *Engaging Scripture: A Model for Theological Interpretation* and Kevin J. Vanhoozer's *Is There a Meaning in This Text?*) have both produced impressive interest.[34] As we plow ahead in the twenty-first century, one might well suspect (and, in fact, eagerly anticipate) that the march forward in biblical hermeneutics might evolve into something of an about-face, looking back into the past with much more careful consideration given to biblical interpretation as practiced by the patristic and medieval interpreters of the Holy Scriptures. Wow! Why would I say that?

Many Doors and A Lot of Keyholes

Seemingly, "a text does not have a single door nor a single key."[35] In that respect, I tend to agree with Treier who suggests that neither Gadamer, nor any other thinker for that matter, is entirely correct when it comes to untangling the Gordian knot of hermeneutics.[36] There is great diversity in hermeneutical thought, and "The history of hermeneutical variety manifests different ways of emphasizing or coordinating the author, the texts, and/or the reader."[37] "However, as James K. A. Smith notes, Christians too often shy away from all forms of interpretative plurality, assuming them to be products of humanity's fall into sin. One gets the idea that we would have no need for interpretation in an ideal world. But in some respects

---

33. See for example: Treier, *Theological Interpretation*; Green, *Practicing Theological Interpretation*; Adam et al., *Reading Scripture*; Fowl, *Theological Interpretation*.

34. Fowl, *Engaging Scripture*; Vanhoozer, *Is There a Meaning*.

35. Bovon, *Exegesis*, 1.

36. Treier, *Theological Interpretation*, 148.

37. Ibid., 135.

diversity is a creational and Pentecostal reality: redemption does not remove interpretation . . ."[38]

This raises an interesting and legitimate question. Is the *meaning* of any particular biblical text (the word, *meaning*, here with a singular sense about it) found solely "in the inspired human author's intention at the point of the text's composition"?[39] That is, can there be multiple meanings in a text from the Holy Scriptures?

Ancient Traditions of Multiple Meanings

This actually does bring us back to the patristic and medieval practices of interpretation. The concept that there are multiple possible meanings in the texts of the Holy Scriptures is a very ancient one that oozes out of Judaism and into Christianity.[40] Many ancient Christian interpreters "defended the proposition, so alien to modern biblical studies, that the meaning of scripture in the mind of the prophet who first uttered it is only one of its possible meanings and may not, in certain circumstances, even be its primary or, most important meaning."[41]

Early Jewish exegesis seems to have set a standard to explore the text by attempting to draw out from it the maximum number of potential interpretations. In the Talmud one finds statements that attest to meaning beyond the literal sense. For example, one reads in the Babylonian Talmud, "As the hammer causes many sparks to fly, so the word of Scripture has a manifold sense."[42]

So it was, in somewhat of a like manner, within early Christianity. The reading of the Bible was certainly influenced by Jewish exegetical methods, and early Christian interpreters sought a diversity of readings from within a given text. This goes all the way back to Paul. For "in regard to Paul's reading of the Old Testament, whether one uses the term 'allegory' or not, some type of 'counter-conventional interpretation' was both practiced and recognized by the first Christians."[43] Of course, the fact of the matter is that

38. Ibid., 148. Treier cites Smith, *Fall of Interpretation*.

39. Oliverio, *Theological Hermeneutics*, 194.

40. Multiple meanings certainly also ooze out of the classical world. For example, Homer's *Iliad* was widely read in classical antiquity as containing multiple meanings.

41. Steinmetz, "Superiority of Pre-Critical Exegesis," 27.

42. *Sanhedrin* 34b.

43. Fowl, *Engaging Scripture*, 26.

Paul does, indeed, use the word allegory, and that provides an impetus for others to follow him on that path.[44]

Thus, very early on in Christian interpretive traditions, there existed an openness to apprehending multiple senses within the Holy Scriptures. Essentially, there were two recognized domains: the letter and the spirit. The letter represented the *literal sense* of the scripture under consideration. This was universally recognized to be the first and primary sense to be considered when reading and interpreting the text. "The letter teaches events" is the way Nicholas of Lyra (ca. AD 1270–1349) put it.[45] Nichols is an extremely significant, if not widely unknown, individual. Highly regarded, it has been said that he was the "greatest biblical exegete of the fourteenth century and perhaps the greatest in the West since Jerome."[46]

Thus, "The letter teaches us what was done."[47] The *literal sense* is virtually synonymous with what has been called the *historical sense* as the "two words [*littera* and *historia*] are practically interchangeable, and we pass easily from the one to the other."[48] The phrase, the *plain sense*, even though it does have a broader meaning than only the historic aspect of the text, is widely used to speak of what we call the *literal sense*.[49] In this way, the *literal sense* refers to the meaning of the words themselves as expressed by the human authors. This also becomes known as the *historical/grammatical* sense.

While the primary and initial way of reading was to seek out the *literal sense* of the text, there clearly was also what became known in English as the *spiritual sense* within the text of the Holy Scriptures. This one word (spiritual) in English is used to capture the essence of three distinct senses of scripture that were labeled with three separate terms. The *literal sense* along with the three spiritual senses produced a fourfold hermeneutical structure to reading the Bible. This fourfold construction of the possible senses of the Holy Scriptures goes back, at least, as far as John Cassian (ca.

---

44. In Galatians 4:24 Paul uses the word *allēgoroumena* (ἀλληγορούμενα) which is a passive participle of the verb "to speak allegorically" (ἀλληγορεῖν). He uses the term to describe the two women, Hagar and Sarah, as two covenants.

45. Lubac, *Medieval Exegesis*, 2:257.

46. Krey and Smith, *Nicholas of Lyra*, 1.

47. Lubac, *Medieval Exegesis*, 2:41.

48. Ibid.

49. Greene-McCreight, "Literal Sense," 455–56. For more detail on the plain sense, see especially chapter 1 ("Plain Sense" in Christian Interpretation of Scripture) in Greene-McCreight, *Ad Litteram*.

AD 360–435), a contemporary of Augustine.[50] The three elements of the spiritual sense that became widely accepted over time and were ensconced in biblical interpretation by the medieval period were: 1) the allegorical sense, 2) the tropological or moral sense, and 3) the anagogic or future sense. Thus, taken together with the literal sense, there were the four senses of scripture.

Cassian employed all four of these terms as he wrote in a famous example, "The one Jerusalem can be understood in four different ways, in the historical sense as the city of the Jews, in allegory as the Church of Christ, in anagoge as the heavenly city of God 'which is the mother of us all' (Gal 4:26), in the tropological sense as the human soul."[51] After Cassian, these three terms (allegorical, anagogical, tropological) became generally used to denote various aspects of the broader spiritual sense of a text. In fact, a little ditty in Latin that captured the essence behind the three terms became an extremely popular and widely cited medieval poem. As de Lubac remarks, "Its form was meant to act as an aid to memory and was at once popular and quasi-scholastic. The saying went like this:

Littera gesta docet	The letter shows events
Quid credas allegoria	allegory what you should believe,
Moralia quid agas	Morality teaches what you should do
Quo tendas anagogia	anagogy what mark you should be aiming for.[52]

Notice that *moralia* is used instead of *tropologia*. That is due only to the meter scheme of the poem. However, not all is made crystal clear by using the various terms. The exact sense and nuance of the various terms was elusive and slippery. It seems that these so-called technical terms were not so technically used. "The actual use of the senses is complex and poorly understood. We would greatly benefit from knowing how the senses were used in practice, by various authors, and what purpose they served. . . . Why was the theory of the senses preserved, in a fairly straightforward form, when their actual use was so clearly varied?"[53]

An example of the lines being somewhat fuzzy in discerning the exact borders of the four senses in the text is noted by Treier who comments that

50. For a very good and readable biographical work on Cassian, see Stewart, *Cassian the Monk*. Another good, standard work on Cassian is Chadwick, *John Cassian*.

51. Cassian, *Conferences*, 160.

52. Lubac, *Medieval Exegesis*, 1:1.

53. Krey and Smith, *Nicholas of Lyra*, 17.

ORANGE PROVERBS & PURPLE PARABLES

"many premodern challenges that were handled with interpretations once seen as 'allegorical' can today fit under the categories such as 'metaphor' or 'figurative' language."[54] Chapter 10 will explore the amazing aspects of metaphor that simply fill the pages of the Holy Scriptures. But for now, let us simplify things. There is widespread agreement that there are two basic senses to scripture—the literal sense and the spiritual sense. This is case however one might define, delimit or expand the various elements within the spiritual sense.

No, I Mean Literally!

The literal sense, so it is generally thought, can be uncovered and rightly understood by correctly using the appropriate interpretive tools at one's disposal. Here is where knowledge of the original languages, archaeological evidence, literary and historical analysis, etc., will lead the attuned and disciplined reader/interpreter to the plain sense of the text. This is a hugely important part of the enterprise, and one must not shirk from the hard and disciplined work required to arrive at a proper understanding of the literal sense of the text.

The importance of this aspect of biblical interpretation cannot be diminished. Remember that in the patristic and medieval periods, virtually everyone agreed that the literal sense was the first and primary of the biblical senses to be sought in the text. In the words of Hugh of St. Victor, this "is the first of the biblical senses: the 'first signification.'"[55] Hugh stressed the necessity to build upon one's careful reading of the literal sense. He stated that, "Nor do I think that you will be able to become perfectly sensitive to the allegory unless you have first been grounded in history."[56] This is exactly the sentiment made clear even by Origen and echoed through the ages by the likes of Augustine, Jerome, and Gregory.[57] The classic example of articulating the need to start and then subsequently draw upon the literal sense comes from St. Thomas Aquinas. He wrote that "all the senses are founded upon the one, the literal sense. From that alone should any argument be

54. Treier, *Theological Interpretation*, 54.

55. Lubac, *Medieval Exegesis*, 2:41. Here Lubac is citing Hugh's *Didascallion* Bk. VI c. iii (PL, CLXXXVI, 801A - *primam significationem*).

56. Hugh of St. Victor, *Didascallion*, 136.

57. For a host of citations supporting the primacy of the literal sense see Lubac, *Medieval Exegesis*, 2:44.

drawn, and not from those intended in allegory."[58] Thomas did, however, recognize that there could be a legitimate spiritual sense about the text. He noted that when the words on the pages (i.e., the literal sense) had "further signification," then the spiritual sense was meant.

So it is that the "precritical interpreters did not approach the Bible without various limits. For the most part, they insisted that spiritual readings must be consistent with the literal sense."[59] For example, "Augustine held that the articles of faith, along with that which Christians are to love and to hope, are practically all given in the plain passages of Scripture. The Bible's normative theological content is therefore part of its 'clear' sense."[60] The letter (literal sense) came first; the spirit (spiritual sense) was to be drawn from that. So it was that through the patristic and medieval periods some interpreters, such as Hugh of St. Victor, leaned more on the literal interpretation while others, such as Bernard of Clairvaux, leaned more on the spiritual interpretation. But it is important to understand that the two broad senses were seen as working side by side and were both viable options for the interpreter to come to an understanding of the Holy Scriptures.

The Spiritual Sense—A Light Goes On In Augustine's Mind

We have already seen that, as a young man, Augustine rejected the Bible. We know he rejected it, in part, because it lacked the artistic use of the Latin language he had been taught to appreciate. For Augustine, the Bible was not like reading Cicero (106–43 BC) or Virgil (70–19 BC) because, frankly, it just was not up to the literary standards that he had come to see in works like *Hortensius* or *The Aeneid*.[61] He simply saw the Bible as an inferior literary work compared to the highly refined Latin of the classics in which he had been trained. As he put it, "When I studied the Bible

---

58. Aquinas, *Summa Theologiae*, I.1.10, ad. 1.

59. Treier, *Theological Interpretation*, 52.

60. Preus, *Shadow to Promise*, 13.

61. *Hortensius* is a now lost work of Cicero's that Augustine first read while he was studying rhetoric at Carthage (*Confessions*, III.4.7). Virgil's epic poem, the *Aeneid* is generally considered to be one of the most important works in all of Latin literature. The piece had a significant impact on Augustine who made a number of references to it in his writings.

and compared it with Cicero's dignified prose, it seemed to me unworthy."[62] Cicero's *Hortensius* had a huge impact on Augustine, for as he wrote, "At the age of eighteen, in the school of rhetoric, I took up the study of Cicero's work called the *Hortensius*, and after reading it I was inflamed thenceforth with such a love of philosophy that I thought of giving myself without delay to philosophical studies."[63]

There was another reason, beyond the literary issues, that dissuaded the pre-conversion Augustine from embracing the Holy Scriptures. To put it bluntly, he found the Old Testament to be rather obscure. As he said it, "My trained wit was unable to penetrate its inner meaning."[64] It is very interesting to note that perhaps the most influential non-biblical Christian writer of all time found the Holy Scriptures to be impenetrable at that particular (pre-conversion) stage of his life.

What was the turning point? What was it that changed Augustine, arguably the most prolific and significant Christian interpreter ever, from somebody who did not understand the text into one of the most insightful biblical exegetes ever? Without a doubt, his conversion experience profoundly transformed him. However, I think the argument can be made that, other than his conversion, it was the impact that Ambrose's preaching had upon him. In AD 384, thirty-year-old Augustine moved to Milan where he came under the influence of Bishop Ambrose. A gifted orator, the bishop was also a person of prayer who led a simple, very austere and exemplary life, and as a result, Ambrose was incredibly popular with the people.[65] Augustine heard preaching by the famous bishop that was quite unlike anything he had ever heard. What was it in Ambrose's preaching that so struck Augustine? It was that Ambrose utilized the spiritual sense of the Holy Scriptures in his sermons. That is largely what opened the window of Augustine's mind to be able to make sense of the Old Testament. Listen to how Augustine, himself, described it.

> This realization was particularly keen when once, and again, and indeed frequently, I heard some difficult passage of the Old Testament explained figuratively; such passages had been death to me because I was taking them literally. As I listened to many such

62. Augustine, *Confessions*, III.5.9.

63. Taylor, "*Hortensius* of Cicero," 491. This cites Augustine, *De Beata Vita* (1.4) which predates his *Confessions*.

64. Augustine, *Confessions*, III.5.9.

65. Dudden, *St. Ambrose*, 107–15.

> scriptural texts being interpreted in a spiritual sense I confronted
> my own attitude, or at least that despair which had led me to be-
> lieve that no resistance whatever could be offered to people who
> loathed and derided the law and the prophets.[66]

And again,

> I delighted to hear Ambrose often asserting in his sermons to the
> people, as a principle on which he must insist emphatically, the
> letter is death-dealing, but the spirit gives life. This he would tell
> them as he drew aside the veil of mystery and opened to them
> the spiritual meaning of the passages which taken literally, would
> seem to mislead.[67]

For Augustine, the spiritual sense of the Holy Scriptures ignited a light that
enabled him to understand and embrace the majesty of God's Word in a
profoundly new way.

The Multiple Senses of the Holy Scriptures

Remember, the synesthete is able to blend various senses. The metaphor
employed throughout this book is that of you being a synesthete when you
are reading the Holy Scriptures as scripture. This synesthetic reading happens, in part, when you blend the two particular domains—the literal and
the spiritual senses. Historically the church has recognized both the literal
and the spiritual senses within the Holy Scriptures. Yet not everyone has
embraced the structure of the fourfold senses of the Holy Scriptures that
were outlined above. A variety of models could be cited. For example, Origen articulated a three-part model for the senses of scripture. His threefold
theory of the senses of scripture, included 1) the literal, 2) the moral, and 3)
the spiritual. This corresponded, by analogy, to the body, the soul, and the
spirit of a person.[68] Of course, any consideration of the person and work of
Origen usually ignites some fireworks. Suffice it to say, Origen oftentimes
got bad reviews for what many, over the centuries, have seen as his over-
extravagant use of allegory, a part of his third category (spiritual). In one
of the better books I have seen defending Origen and his propensity to al-
legorize, the great scholar, Henri de Lubac, carefully examined the evidence

66. Augustine, *Confessions*, V.14.24.
67. Ibid., VI.4.6.
68. Vaccaro, "Digging for Buried Treasure," 763.

and came to the conclusion that Origen was not so bad after all.[69] However, for dramatic effect and to paint a picture of the widespread rejection of the man, de Lubac began his book by quoting a series of anathemas flung by others against Origen. The book commences, "'Extravagances', 'puerile play', 'strange ramblings', 'wild imagination': Many discover nothing else in the interminable pages of Origen's commentaries and homilies. The allegorization those pages never cease to make from the given biblical information is to their eyes nothing but an immense and tedious misinterpretation. It proceeds entirely, they think, from a 'chimerical method'; it is the fruit of 'fallacious hermeneutics.'"[70]

But, perhaps, cooler heads could prevail. I have changed my opinion about a number of things throughout my life, and lately, I have changed my opinion about Origen. De Lubac's very measured and reasoned appeal to what Origen was doing has altered some of my long-held faulty assumptions about him as a biblical interpreter. While we typically do not think of him that way, Origen first read the text literally. He said that, "the really historical episodes are, in Scripture, much more numerous than those that contain a purely spiritual sense."[71] There is no doubt that "Origen, a complex and important figure, sought to maintain the importance of the literal, historical sense throughout the Bible. However, influenced by aspects of Greek dualism and literary theory as well as religious priorities, he freely pursued a 'Spiritual' sense in the text by means of allegorical interpretation."[72]

To be sure, Origen, has come under a steady attack for, how should one say, his dramatic excesses in use of allegory. Yet, we need to remember that "Whatever be made of Origen's exaggerations and flaws, there is no doubt that the church owes to him a fundamental attitude toward the OT that, despite the eclipse of recent centuries, is still the most faithful to the viewpoint of the NT. This is true because the church reads with faith the mystery of Christ already present in an anticipated manner in the history of Israel."[73]

---

69. Lubac, *History and Spirit*. It should be noted that Lubac's conclusion is from page 427 through page 507—a hint that it is a long, complicated, detailed, but magisterial work on Origen.

70. Ibid., 1.

71. Ibid., 116. De Lubac is citing Origen's *Peri Archon* (*First Principles*) 4.3.4.

72. Treier, *Theological Interpretation*, 46.

73. Martin, "Spiritual Sense," 770.

As a helpful rule of thumb for discerning where the lines of the literal sense and the various aspects of the spiritual sense, such as allegory, begin and end as you are reading the Holy Scriptures, remember this. "For both Paul and Augustine, allegory lies not only in words, but more importantly in events themselves. History and allegory are not antithetical, but complementary."[74] That is, the two great domains of the letter and the spirit work together in the mind and the heart of the deep reader of God's Word.

The point here was not to engage in a debate about Origen. The point has been to suggest that in order to read fully the Holy Scriptures as scripture there needs to be an active engagement with both the literal and the spiritual senses of the text. However one chooses to talk about what the makeup of the spiritual sense is and what terminology should be used to describe it, there is definitely a reality of the letter and spirit residing within the Holy Scriptures. There do seem to be multiple meanings to the text.

How Augustine May Have Hit the Nail on the Head

I like to think that Augustine may have, indeed, hit the nail on the head. All this talk of multiple meanings, and the notion that there are potentially different meanings for different readers could, perhaps, unnerve the person who has always come to the Holy Scriptures with a strictly literalist or only a historical-critical approach. The presumption of multiple meanings does raise some very legitimate questions. What are the parameters? Does anything go? To be sure, not everything goes! There are reasonable boundaries, and I really like Augustine's approach. For him, who so amazingly delved into the heart of the Holy Scriptures, it was, above all else, the double command articulated by Jesus in Matt 22:35–40 that comprised the guidelines.[75] If you recall the episode, it centered on the infamous question by the lawyer. "Which is the greatest commandment in the Law?" Jesus' reply of melding two commands into one answer sets the tone for everything we are to do. "Love God with all your being," and "love your neighbor as yourself" may be a key to biblical interpretation for followers of Jesus. How is it that this double command for love can be a key to negotiating the quagmire of biblical interpretation?

74. Van Fleteren, "Principles," 7.

75. This story is common to all three of synoptic gospels. It occurs also in Luke 10:2–28 and in Mark 12:28–31.

For Augustine, loving God and loving your neighbor was to be the basic rule of thumb for interpretation.[76] As far as Augustine was concerned, whoever the exegete or interpreter might be, whether you, or me, or the guy down the street, if the basic rule of loving God and neighbor is faithfully employed in the reading and interpreting of the Holy Scriptures, then, in all likelihood, the outcome is going to be quite acceptable.[77] Now, you should understand, it was not Augustine's intent to say this hermeneutic of love "prevents the interpreter from making mistakes, but rather, that it keeps the interpreter on or close to the right road."[78]

Thus, if we recognize, as Augustine so acutely did, that love, God's love, is the source of the Holy Scriptures, then our reading and interpreting of those sacred words will be well guided. As Stock fittingly noted concerning Augustine's hermeneutic of love, "It is not the purpose of love to generate interpretation, but vice versa. Yet the models of reading and loving operate in a similar way."[79] Unfortunately, explorations of what that should really look like are wanting. "What would interpretation governed by the law of love look like? Strangely, Augustine does not say."[80] As Jacobs remarks, "An account of the hermeneutics of love is one of the great unwritten chapters in the history of Christian theology."[81] Perhaps as we engage in the enterprise of reading the Holy Scriptures as scripture, we can endeavor to explore further Augustine's tantalizing notion of the hermeneutic of love.

Multiple Meanings Through the Holy Spirit?

What kind of hermeneutical approach does all this talk of multiple meanings lead us into if we are to be reading the Holy Scriptures as scripture? Generally speaking, most biblical interpreters agree that one does not simply jettison the original, literal, historical-grammatical meaning of the text in favor of other meanings. For example, Bill Oliverio has noted, in

---

76. I made the verb in this sentence singular even though there appear to be two subjects (loving God and loving neighbor). In fact, I take those two elements to be collective, that is, they go together as one whole. At least, that seems to be one of the points Jesus is making here.

77. Glidden, "Augustine's Hermeneutics," 135–57.

78. Jacobs, *Theology of Reading*, 154.

79. Stock, *Augustine the Reader*, 185.

80. Jacobs, *Theology of Reading*, 11.

81. Ibid.

speaking of Amos Yong's hermeneutical project, "While holding to the original intent and reception of a text as a center of gravity for its meaning, he also claims that a pluralizing hermeneutic is needed to handle the biblical texts because of the plurality of their sources, as well as his openness to the multiple readings inherent in many texts."[82]

The literal meaning is definitely to be the center of gravity in our enterprise of reading the Holy Scriptures as scripture. Yet, as Oliverio observed, "Yong holds that texts vary on a continuum between closed readings (those closely connected with the author's intention) and more open reading (those directed toward the reader's response).[83] The idea of an open reading as utilized by Yong is a derivation of Umberto Eco's notion of an open text, and the two phrases (open reading and open text) could be used synonymously.[84]

With this view in mind, the case of St. Francis of Assisi is interesting. If you remember the story, he read the text "Go and sell your goods," and then he went and did just that.[85] Leithart sees this as a misreading by Francis. In an endnote, Leithart remarked, "Of course, misreadings may have happy results. Few would take 'Go and sell your goods' the way St. Francis did, but most are glad that he understood it the way he did."[86] However, the question must be asked, was it truly a misreading by Francis? I would argue that, no, it was not a misreading by Francis. Rather, the Holy Spirit did, in fact, act in the interpretive process in a way particular to Francis' reading of the text. That is, the Holy Spirit worked in Francis to elicit his interpretation that was formulated, in part, by his application. There was a certain praxis in Francis' interpretive package that was driven by the Spirit. However, it seems that the Holy Spirit does not instruct everyone just so. This raises a very interesting issue, the premise of which is that the Holy Spirit can and does work in individuals via peculiar and specific twists of interpretation. That is, the Holy Spirit is a part of the interpretive process for the one who reads the Holy Scriptures as scripture. "Augustine everywhere assumes that texts embody an author's communicative intentions and that it is the task of interpretation to clarify these. Yet, this in no way inhibits the semantic

82. Oliverio, *Theological Hermeneutics*, 242–43.

83. Ibid., 243.

84. Eco, *Role of the Reader*.

85. A couple of the best, most recent, works on Francis' life and writings include: Thompson, *Francis of Assisi*; Rusconi, *Sources and Writings*; Vauchez, *Medieval Saint*.

86. Leithart, *Deep Exegesis*, 221.

abundance intended and disclosed by the Holy Spirit, beyond what was consciously intended by the human author."[87]

There is a very real and unfortunate propensity for casual readers of the Holy Scriptures to completely forgo any work of the Holy Spirit that might potentially be a part of the interpretive enterprise. With certain ways of reading the Holy Scriptures we are in danger of "slighting the Spirit's present action upon Scripture, rendering Scripture merely a 'mechanical creation' running on fuel deposited there and then rather than having its location in a present reality continually at work through the Spirit."[88]

On the contrary, deep readers of the Holy Scriptures as scripture weave into the interpretive process an openness to the work of the Spirit. As Yong has noted, "Central to the Christian tradition is the conviction that theological understanding is a gift of God the Spirit (I Cor 2:9–16) whereby the interpreter relies on the gracious (charismatic) activity of the Spirit to reveal and illumine divine truths. This requires the interpreter to be open to the unpredictable movements of the Spirit who "breaks in to" (or "breaks through") the interpreter's situation and enables interpretive activity to commence in and through the same Spirit."[89] It seems that the Christian reader of the Holy Scriptures as scripture,

> receives from the Church the sacred books of Scripture, which contain both the Law and the Prophets and the apostolic witness to Jesus Christ and the Church. The books that compose the New Testament assert that Jesus is the Messiah who fulfills the Law and the Prophets. The New Testament books thus not only require interpretation themselves, they also advance hermeneutical claims regarding the Scriptures of Israel. The words and deeds that Scripture reports must be interpreted if we are to understand their historical and theological significance.[90]

There most definitely needs to be an interpretive element in the process of your reading the Holy Scriptures as scripture. As you become a deep reader, you will want to actively engage the interpretive element of this complex enterprise we have been considering. Weave into your reading Augustine's hermeneutic of love and be open to the reality of the Holy Spirit working in your personal interpretive process. Before reading, pray for the

87. Watson, "Authors, Readers Hermeneutics," 123.
88. Paddison, *Scripture*, 11.
89. Yong, *Spirit-Word-Community*, 222.
90. Levering, *Theology of Augustine*, 1.

Holy Spirit to give you insight, and do not be afraid to act upon your reading as did Francis of Assisi. Do not despair over the seeming difficulty of this endeavor. After all, Augustine gave us somewhat of a punch line for the entire enterprise of reading the Holy Scriptures as scripture. He encouraged us that if one has truly been "taught of God" (Isa 54:13; John 6:45), then it has been given to that one "to know what he ought to do and to do what he knows; he not only has the power to come but does come; he not only believes what ought to be loved, but loves what he believes."[91]

---

91. Fortin, "Hermeneutics of Love," 6. Fortin is citing Augustine, *De gratia Christi* (On the Grace of Christ) 13.14; 14.15; and 12.13.

10

Mapping the Metaphorical World

The Power of Metaphor

EUGENE PETERSON, CREATOR OF *The Message: The Bible in Contemporary Language* writes that, "If we don't understand how metaphor works we will misunderstand most of what we read in the Bible."[1] If you were to take that statement halfway seriously, you would get a sense of the importance of metaphor in the Holy Scriptures. It is not just Peterson who says this; biblical scholars from all historical eras have recognized the powerful role of metaphors.

The Holy Scriptures are inundated with metaphorical language, and Peterson is, perhaps, correct—there will be a lot of misunderstanding if you do not grasp metaphor as you read your Bible. Consider the fact that, "What appears to be history may be metaphor or figure instead, and the interpreter who confuses metaphor with literal fact is an interpreter who is simply incompetent."[2]

Of course, metaphor is the whole basis behind the title and theme I use in this book. There are not really proverbs that are orange, and there are not, literally, such things as purple parables. When I say you should be reading the Holy Scriptures as a synesthete, that is a metaphor. It means I am encouraging you to become a deep reader who is making new network connections as you cultivate your enterprise of reading the Holy Scriptures as scripture. In that way, your senses will be combining thoughts and ideas in new ways so that connections you did not make in your old way of

1. Peterson, *Eat This Book*, 93.
2. Steinmetz, "Pre-Critical Exegesis," 28.

reading are now popping into your mind and heart as you are cognitively and spiritually processing as a synesthete. Orange proverbs and purple parables are metaphors for apprehending in a new way the *viva vox Dei*.

Multi-Colored Psalms

Have you ever read a mauve psalm? Yes, we agree, there are not psalms that are literally mauve in color—again with the metaphor. However, I wish to use one of the psalms as an example for discussing metaphors and their importance within the Holy Scriptures. For me, the particular psalm I wish to discuss is crimson; it will be some other color for you because synesthetes do not share the same perceptions of color. That is, one synesthete may see the emotion produced by the reading of a particular psalm as blue, while another synesthete with the same type of synesthesia (i.e., emotion is perceived as color) may well see streaks of mauve and burnt orange during the reading of the same psalm.

Augustine: The Synesthetic Psalm Reader

When it comes to the psalms it is Augustine who, perhaps more than any other individual, elicits in me a sense of befuddling awe and bewildering respect. For in his work, *Expositions of the Psalms*[3] we have a commentary of truly biblical proportions. Augustine's work on the psalms is larger than all the other patristic commentaries on the psalms combined! Augustine was so prolific, in fact, that it was said, in a little ditty written in his honor, that nobody could possibly read everything he had written. The gist of one of the lines in Isidore of Seville's poem extolling Augustine sounds something like this according to my paraphrase—"Any guy who says that he has read all of Augustine is lying."[4] I suspect that great line still holds quite true

---

3 Augustine, *Expositions*. The Latin title is *Enarrationes in Psalmos*.

4. *Mentitur qui se totum legisse fatetur* is the first line of a little poem attributed to Isidore of Seville (ca. AD 560–636). In its entirety, it reads: "He lies, who avers that he has read all of you. In fact, what reader can even have all your works? For you shine, Augustine, in the glory of a thousand volumes: your books themselves bear witness to what I say. However much one may like to have volumes of books of many authors, if you have Augustine [O reader], he is enough for you." This translation is from Newton, *Scriptorium*, 80.

to this very day. If you want to read everything Augustine has written, you certainly cannot be watching much television.

Just think of this commentary on the psalms produced by Augustine. The guy slogged through the writing of this massive undertaking for almost thirty years. Along the way, other writings projects of his took a backseat. He delayed them in favor of working on the psalms project because he envisioned his work on the psalms to be of the utmost priority for the public. In Letter 169 Augustine wrote, "Indeed, so unwilling am I to turn away from my work on the psalms, that I will not give attention at the moment even to the books on the Trinity, which I have long had in mind and have not yet completed, because they require a great amount of labor, and I believe that they are of a nature to be understood only by few. Such work claims my attention less urgently than my writings on the psalms which may, I hope, be useful to very many people."[5]

Augustine ate, drank, slept, and prayed the psalms. The guy flooded all of his writings with thoughts from the psalms to the point that he peppered his entire literary bouillabaisse with the seasoning of more than 10,000 savory citations from the psalms.[6] Clearly, it may be argued, Augustine internalized the entire Psalter. He also "got" metaphor. If anybody can be said to connect with the picturesque language of the psalms with all their figural phrases, it is Augustine. He certainly seems to have filled out the images in the psalms to a fuller extent than, perhaps, anyone else before or since.

Beyond all of that, what I particularly admire about Augustine is how he cut to the chase when it came to what he considered the paramount goal of biblical interpretation. As he understood it, and as he articulated it in his work *On Christian Teaching* (*De doctrina Christiana*), everything centered on the love of God and love of neighbor.[7] As William Brown put it in his work, *Seeing the Psalms*, Augustine's mode of interpretation was a "hermeneutic of love."[8] This is what propelled Augustine's interpretive lens.

5. Teske, *Letters*, 169.

6. Bouvy. "Enarrationes," 419. Bouvy's quotation is cited in Augustine, *Exposition*, 13.

7. Augustine, *Christian Teaching*, 1.36.40.

8. Brown, *Seeing the Psalms*, 12.

Psalm 1 in Stunning Crimson

Augustine starts his look at Psalm 1 with a christological bang. The well-known opening of the psalm begins, "Blessed is the one who has not walked in the counsel of the wicked." Augustine comments, "This statement should be understood as referring to our Lord Jesus Christ."[9] Thus, the starting point for Augustine and "this one who is blessed" in Psalm 1 is then, by extension, every person. Anyone is blessed who embraces the way of Christ.

And so it is that Augustine sends us on our way into the Psalter, and it is, to be sure, a delightful romp through the figurally drenched texts. Along the way, Augustine picks from the lush sentences a myriad of metaphors that are simply oozing with interpretive juices. As noted by Boulding, "The first procedure to be considered is one much practiced by Augustine in his theological exposition of the words of a psalm: the development of its picturesque speech, the heightening of its colorful similes and metaphors."[10] Thus, whereas the Old Testament may sketch with pencil a thought using simile or metaphor, Augustine often colorized it in somewhat like an artist working in Photoshop. Perhaps that is why I see crimson when I recite Psalm 1.

Conceptual Metaphors: They Border on Magic

There is a challenge for modern interpreters. We must attempt to penetrate the mind of the ancients, layering through the various linguistic strata in order to recover the archaeological artifact of the metaphor in order to be able to understand its cognitive function. In that sense, the metaphor is an ancient pot shard, and we must properly read the recovered shards in order to correctly identify the vessel's function and better understand the strata in which the pot of a given text existed.

It certainly is no secret that the Bible is awash with metaphor. Of course, that is no great surprise either, for as Lakoff and Johnson noted in their earth-rattling 1980 book, *Metaphors We Live By*, "Our ordinary conceptual system, in terms of which we both think and act, is fundamentally metaphorical in nature."[11] Suffice it to say, I am a relative novice in the world of cognitive linguistics and the specific subfield of conceptual metaphor theory (CMT). However, even a novice or beginning learner like

9. Augustine, *Expositions*, 67.

10. Ibid., 38.

11. Lakoff and Johnson, *Metaphors*, 3.

me can have one's interest piqued by an innovative book. And, to be sure, my world of metaphor theory was invigorated and energized by Lakoff and Johnson's work in a profound way as they convincingly made the case that we humans are innately metaphorical thinkers.

Thus, it is quite natural to find a good share of metaphor within the pages of the Holy Scriptures. To play the poker card, the Bible is royally flush with metaphor. David Yellin, in his *Selected Writings*,[12] suggested that there are about a thousand images in the Bible. Van Hecke noted there are interrelated bundles of metaphor that may facilitate a greater clarity of how the ancient writers conceptualized reality.[13] For example, Psalm 1 speaks of a tree, fruit, leaves, and chaff, and as Yellin, who seems to have counted everything, observed there are about 250 images from the world of plants in the Bible. To be sure, this would seem to be a cluster of juicy Chardonnay grapes, ripe for the picking. I love the quote by José Ortega y Gasset.[14] He said, "Metaphor is the greatest power available to man; it borders on magic; it is like a creative tool left by God in the minds of His creatures."[15]

Indeed, metaphor is in the mind. As Feldman put it in his jaw-dropping book, *From Molecule to Metaphor: A Neural Theory of Language*, "There is now very strong evidence that essentially all of our cultural, abstract, and theoretical concepts derive their meanings by mapping through metaphor."[16] As Feldman further notes, as of today, no one really "knows the details of how words or sentences are processed in the brain, and there is no known methodology for finding out."[17] Yet, the argument is being made these days by those working in cognitive linguistics that metaphorical thinking seems to be an innate and all-encompassing cognitive activity in humans.

Still, while human cognition seemingly employs an innate metaphorical structuring, the actual metaphors we use are learned. They are based on experiences, culture, and the like. Now, this is the point to be made as we, seemingly, have drifted a bit into the forest of CMT. It is a somewhat

12. Available only in Hebrew as *Ketuvim Nivcharim*–כתובים נבחרים.

13. Hecke, *Metaphor*, 38.

14. He was an important Spanish philosopher in the twentieth century (1883–1955). Besides influencing the likes of Martin Heidegger, he also had considerable sway upon a group of significant Spanish poets known as the Generation of '27.

15. Weiss, *Bible From Within*, 132.

16. Feldman, *Molecule to Metaphor*, 46.

17. Ibid., xii.

foreboding terrain. It is filled with the drooping vines of Chomskian-like nomenclature and the thick, sticky muck of the human mind. If you are like me, as we suddenly find ourselves, seemingly, wandering off the main road of deep, Augustinian reading of the Bible into the broad and menacing woods of cognitive linguistics, I feel that a very brief overview of CMT would be a worthwhile and calming element for all of us. For as you will see, the enterprise of reading the Holy Scriptures as scripture does, in fact, demand an informed appreciation of language and the mind.

A Thirty Second Primer on Conceptual Metaphor Theory

Within this secluded yet alluring jungle of CMT, the current state of understanding is that, generally speaking, two species of domains dominate the landscape of jargon employed in the field. First there is what is called the *source domain*—this is the conceptual domain from which we draw our metaphorical expressions. For example, we might consider the computer as the source for making a connection to the second or *target domain*, for instance, the human mind. When the source and the target are mapped together, a conceptual metaphor is created. In this case, "the mind is a computer" equals the metaphor.

In Psalm 1, the blessed man, that being the target, is set up as a tree yielding fruit, that being the source. Also in our psalm, the wicked, set up as the target, are mapped with a source that is chaff. Thus, the target is the conceptual domain that we attempt to better understand or describe through the linking of it to a source domain (as in love is a journey, or the wicked are chaff). In addition to the important concepts of the source and target domains, another key notion of current conceptual metaphor theory is the idea of mapping. Mapping is the systematic set of correspondences that exist between the source and the target domain.

That is about a thirty second primer on conceptual metaphor theory—there is a source, a target, and mapping. However, let me assure you that CMT is much more complicated, and nobody I have read is suggesting that there is anything like a unified theory of metaphor upon which all interested parties agree. It is true, though, that a primary tenet of current CMT is that metaphors are matters of thought and not merely of language. Hence, the proper phrase is *conceptual* metaphor. So it is that in *Metaphors We Live By*, and in their later book, *Philosophy in the Flesh*, Lakoff and

Johnson hypothesize that certain very basic conceptual metaphors arise from correlations in our everyday experiences.[18]

Indeed, primary "metaphors seem to arise spontaneously and automatically without our even being aware of them."[19] In fact, Lakoff and Johnson argue that metaphor is a neural phenomenon. They write, "You don't have a choice as to whether to think metaphorically."[20] As they say it, "Because metaphorical maps are part of our brains, we *will* think and speak metaphorically whether we want to or not. Further, since our brains are embodied, our metaphors will reflect our commonplace experiences in the world."[21]

A fundamental notion of conceptual metaphor theory seems to be this element of mapping or systematic metaphorical correspondences between ideas. Another of the luminaries in cognitive linguistics who has written extensively on this concept of mapping is Gilles Fauconnier. In his book, *Mappings in Thought and Language*, he argues the idea that "mappings between domains are at the very heart of the unique human cognitive faculty of producing, transferring, and processing meaning."[22] In processing the meaning of Psalm 1, we are engaging mental mappings through the imagery of trees, fruit, leaves, and chaff.

Rotten Chaff in Psalm 1

In this section, I direct your attention to a single metaphor—that of the wicked being chaff. We will take a look at a few examples of this metaphor within the Holy Scriptures, and in the process, I would also like to introduce to you what appears to me to be the earliest attestations of metaphorical mapping involving chaff in a few texts from the ancient Mesopotamian cultural sphere. These examples will occur in some texts that predate the earliest biblical texts by a considerable margin. That is, the biblical writers borrowed an already existing metaphor within their writings when employing the metaphorical image of chaff.

Many biblical interpreters have seen Psalm 1 as establishing a link with the entire Psalter, and much has been said about the first psalm functioning

18. Lakoff and Johnson, *Philosophy in the Flesh.*

19. Lakoff and Johnson, *Metaphors*, 257.

20. Ibid., 256.

21. Ibid., 257.

22. Fauconnier, *Mappings*, 1.

as an introduction to the book of Psalms. The point has been presented that Psalm 1 manifests an "orienting power" largely through the use of "metaphor and image."[23] Indeed, Basil the Great (AD 329–379) used a series of metaphors to demonstrate the relationship of Psalm 1 to the rest of the Psalter. For Basil, Psalm 1 was the foundation of the house, it was the keel of the boat, and it was the heart within a body.[24]

Psalm 1 is brief, but it delivers a pungent punch. This powerful piece rings with majesty as it draws one's heart to God's Torah. Read and absorb its frank and colorful declaration of a great divide—the stark contrast between the righteous ones and evil doers.

> Blessed is the one who has not walked in the way of the wicked,
>   the one who has not stood in the path of sinners—nor has sat
>   in the seat of scorners.
>
> Rather, that person's delight is in the Torah of the Lord,
>   and in his Torah this one meditates day and night.
>
> This individual will be like a tree, planted near streams of water,
>   yielding its fruit in its season.
>
> Its leaf will not wither,
>   and all that this person does will prosper.
>
> Not so the wicked.
>
> Rather, they are like chaff that the wind drives away.
>
> Therefore, the wicked will not rise in the judgment,
>   nor sinners in the congregation of the righteous.
>
> For Yahweh knows the way of the righteous,
>   but the way of the wicked will perish.

The botanical imagery is flying fast and furious. There are trees, fruit, leaves, and chaff. In his book, *Seeing the Psalms*, William P. Brown has an entire chapter on the tree of Psalm 1 in which he explores the metaphorical use of the image.[25] He also briefly notes that the chaff serves as an antitype of the tree. It is, to be sure, a metaphorical antonym, and here I wish to play just a bit with the use of chaff as a source domain.

---

23. Brown, *Seeing the Psalms*, 55.

24. Blaising and Hardin, *Psalms 1–50*, 2.

25. Brown, *Seeing the Psalms*, 55–79.

Over the centuries, there have been a number of suggestions concerning the images employed by the writer in this particular psalm. For example, the fruit of the tree has been variously suggested to be:

- faith and works (John of Damascus)
- wisdom (Methodius of Olympus)
- churches (Augustine)
- immortality (Hilary of Poitiers)
- the resurrection (Caesarius)
- the mystical and spiritual sense of the Scriptures (Didymus the Blind)
- the meaning of Scriptures (Jerome)

While, yes, technically speaking, "like a tree" (v. 3)[26] and "like chaff" (v. 4)[27] are similes, I have always had the intuitive sense that even if a metaphor and simile are textually different, they are functionally the same. Janet Soskice has advocated this in her work, *Metaphor and Religious Language*,[28] and it has also been argued elsewhere that simile is simply a "form of metaphor."[29]

The chaff in our psalm is clearly mapped to the wicked. And indeed, chaff usually signifies the wicked or the destruction of evil doers. Here is a sampling of Old Testament texts that employ this metaphor:[30]

> . . . your enemies, those who hate you . . . O my God, make them like whirling dust, like chaff before the wind (Ps 83:2, 13).

> Let them be like chaff before the wind, with the angel of the Lord driving them out (Ps 35:5).

> The nations roar like the roaring of many waters, but he will rebuke them, and they will flee far away, chased like chaff on the mountains before the wind and whirling dust before the storm (Isa 17:13).

> But the multitude of your foes shall be like small dust, and the multitude of tyrants like flying chaff (Isa 29:5).

---

26. Hebrew *keèts*–כעץ.

27. Hebrew *kemots*–כמץ.

28. Soskice, *Metaphor*, 59.

29. Brown, *Seeing the Psalms*, 7, citing Kysar, *Stumbling*, 30.

30. The following are all citations from the NRSV.

Therefore they shall be like the morning mist or like the dew that goes away early, like chaff that swirls from the threshing floor or like smoke from a window (Hos 13:3).

I will scatter you like chaff driven by the wind from the desert (Jer 13:24).

Gather together, gather, O shameless nation, before you are driven away like the drifting chaff, before there comes upon you the fierce anger of the Lord (Zeph 2:1–2).

The plans of the wicked are repugnant to me . . . How often are they like straw before the wind, and like chaff that the storm carries away? (Job 21:16b, 18).

Thus, it is that within the pages of the Holy Scriptures the wicked are, literally, gone with the wind. They are chaff, and the image is well used and clearly mapped. This metaphorical image also feeds into an additional biblical metaphor. Conceptual metaphor theory recognizes that there are patterns of association established through metaphor, and a widely used conceptual metaphor one finds woven throughout the biblical text is that of harvest as judgment. For example,

For thus says the Lord of hosts, the God of Israel: Daughter Babylon is like a threshing floor at the time when it is trodden; yet a little while and the time of her harvest will come (Jer 51:33).

The New Testament writers also pick up on this imagery. Thus, we read,

His winnowing fork is in his hand, and he will clear his threshing floor and will gather his wheat into the granary; but the chaff he will burn with unquenchable fire (Matt 3:12)

The wicked as chaff and judgment as a harvest form part of a larger cluster of metaphorical images that are experientially related. This is exactly the sort of thing Fauconnier says is typical in what he calls "metaphoric integrations."[31]

---

31. Fauconnier and Turner, *Way We Think*, 154.

The Sumerians Are Coming; The Sumerians Are Coming!

The biblical writers were certainly not the inventors of the metaphorical imagery that uses chaff as a source domain. The use of chaff in this manner is extremely ancient, much older than our biblical texts. In fact, I would say that our first written lessons in metaphor come from those wily Sumerians, those inventors of writing (ca. 3300 BC), who left us baked metaphors impressed in clay. We see the Sumerian clay tablets gushing with figural language. It is not entirely surprising that the Sumerians, who seem to have invented almost everything,[32] draw for us the earliest attested cognitive map connecting chaff to worthless things, to anything that is inconsequential and will pass away, just as the evil doers are portrayed in the biblical text.

Sumerian economic texts are packed plumb-full of agricultural information. By the end of the third millennium BC a highly structured economic bureaucracy had developed within the Sumerian city-states. There was a royal sector of the economy in which grain production and distribution was carefully tracked and painstakingly recorded. In the Ur III period, a number of economic texts make many references to chaff, the Sumerian word for which was *in-bul-bul*.[33]

In the agricultural world of the Sumerians, they would use threshing carts to separate the cereal grains from the stalks and then use heavy threshing sleds drawn by oxen to further dislodge the grain. In the economic texts, chaff was exclusively used in the literal, non-metaphorical sense. However, in literary texts, Sumerian *in-bul-bul* is used by the black-headed people to signify worthlessness.[34] It was something that is of no value, and it is clearly used as a metaphorical source domain.

For example, in a hymn to Nergal, the great god destroys the brick and mortar of cities that are his enemies, and they drift away like chaff.[35] In a Sumerian proverb, we see the case of a woman who apparently performed

---

32. This is, of course, tongue in cheek. They did not invent everything; but do see Kramer, *History Begins at Sumer* for an impressive list of Sumerian firsts.

33. Also known as the neo-Sumerian period, the Ur III phase of Sumerian history lasts roughly from about 2100 to 2000 BC.

34. This term, the black-headed people, was the nomenclature that the Sumerians used to refer to themselves.

35. Nergal was one of hundreds of deities recognized by the Sumerians. He was later worshipped throughout all of Mesopotamia by other people groups such as the Assyrians and Babylonians. Nergal is mentioned 2 Kgs 17:30.

some sort of ritual for the king.[36] It is not entirely clear what exactly she did, but it is certain that *whatever* she did, it was not good. The text of the proverb ends, "How did Enlil, the great lord, act toward her? He despised her very foundations, just like the foundations of chaff."[37] The use of chaff as a metaphor for something of insignificant value is seen in a proverb from Ur.

> A house-hold slave was treated with contempt. He wept.
>
> All he had was chaff in his hands, so he grimaced his teeth in anger.[38]

In another, rather enigmatic proverb, Enlil, the Sumerian god of breath and wind, creates something that is metaphorically chaff. The proverb reads:

> What did Enlil make? Chaff!
>
> The lance has struck. It went into the flesh.[39]

What is it that Enlil, created? One might be tempted to suggest that it seems to be mankind. Yet, nowhere else in Sumerian literature, as far as I am presently aware, is Enlil presented as a creator of humans. A final example of the Sumerians mapping chaff to vanity, nothingness, worthlessness in one of their proverbs is this one:

> Second-hand clothes are what the child of a slave-girl gets; they will (ultimately wear out) and fall off her; becoming nothing but chaff.[40]

Without a doubt, the original metaphorical mapping of chaff began in remote antiquity, probably way before the invention of writing. I can imagine some poor guy in the Neolithic period, out in his field near Jarmo about the end of the eighth millennium.[41] He was working like a dog to

36. Lambert, *Babylonian Wisdom*. See tablet SP 3.45 = BM 38596.

37. Ibid.

38. Gadd, and Kramer, *Ur Excavation Texts*, tablet 279.

39. Alster, *Proverbs*, collection 3 (c.6.1.03), A.3.25.51. This is tablet 4677 in the Yale Babylonian Collection.

40. Ibid., collection 4 (c.6.1.04), 4.43.

41. Jarmo is the archaeological site that yielded some of our first information about the domestication of plants that occurred in the Near East sometime in the eighth millennium BC. The ancient village flourished during the archaeological period known as the Neolithic. The site of Jarmo is located in the foothills of the Zagros mountain range in northern Iraq, not too far from the modern city of Kirkuk. See Braidwood, "Jarmo," 189–95. A bit outdated, but still a useful survey of the Neolithic Period in the Near East is Mellaart, *Neolithic*.

get that rotten chaff separated from the barley spikes, and he cursed the worthless stuff as some of it floated away in a light breeze. At the same time, his no-good thieving son-in-law who was a worthless scoundrel wandered by. Suddenly, a new neural network connection was made in his mind, and presto, a conceptual metaphor had been created. He mapped chaff to the evil, useless son-in-law.

Sumerians, Augustine, Donne and the Power of Metaphor

At this point, I suspect a reader or two may be wondering why in the world I included this rather exotic excursus on Sumerians using the metaphor of chaff. One who might simply have wanted to learn a little something about the reading of the Holy Scriptures as scripture may feel that she or he has been pulled rather far afield by this digression. One of the things I have learned in over thirty years of teaching is that peripheral excursions can be very fruitful for the curious student; so I do not hesitate to use them. Such an excursion, which is seemingly off the main path, may entice an individual to think about something in a new way. Yet, this chapter was not a mere serendipitous stumbling into the Oz-like world of the cognitive sciences and the earliest documented use of a particular metaphor by the Sumerians. Augustine never even heard of the Sumerians, but I suspect he too would have drawn some examples and insights from their texts had they been discovered during his lifetime.[42] In fact, some of the things talked about in this chapter are exactly the sorts of ideas that Augustine wrote about. My hunch is that very few of us understand or enjoy metaphor more than Augustine did. In fact, modern-day conceptual metaphor theory harkens back, in many ways, to some of the things Augustine had to say about the nature of language and the figural aspects of it.[43] Augustine conveys to us an understanding that earthly "teaching is best understood through a

---

42. Augustine defended the legitimate use of secular learning by citing the biblical example of the seizure of Egyptian gold by the Israelites leaving Egypt. From that, Augustine argues that Christians should use secular learning. Thus, he champions the notion that Christians have the right to employ the learning of the pagans, which is to say, non-Christian texts "may be accepted and kept for conversion to Christian purposes" (*accipere atque habere licuerit in usum convertenda christianum*) (*On Christian Teaching*, II.40.60).

43. Augustine, *On Christian Teaching*, especially books I–III.

metaphor of pointing," where the teacher facilitates a discussion or provides information that points the way to understanding.[44]

Perhaps then, there may not be too many better ways to ease into the conclusion of this chapter than to point you to a quote from John Donne (1572–1631)[45] who, by the way, drew upon Augustine at almost every turn. He leaned so heavily on Augustine that it has been estimated that, in his sermons alone, he alluded to the great Bishop of Hippo more than seven hundred times.[46] Hear the words of Donne as he speaks of God's metaphorical use of language to us in his Holy Scriptures.

> My God, my God, thou art a direct God, may I not say a literal God, a God that wouldst be understood literally and according to the plain sense of all that thou sayest? But thou art also (Lord, I intend it to thy glory, and let no profane misinterpreter abuse it to thy diminution), thou art a figurative, a metaphorical God too; a God in whose words there is such a height of figures, such voyages, such peregrinations to fetch remote and precious metaphors, such extensions, such spreadings, such curtains of allegories, such third heavens of hyperboles, so harmonious elocutions, so retired and so reserved expressions, so commanding persuasions, so persuading commandments, such sinews even in thy milk, and such things in thy words, as all profane authors seem of the seed of the serpent that creeps, thou art the Dove that flies. O, what words but thine can express the inexpressible texture and composition of thy word.
>
> *Devotions Upon Emergent Occasions,*
> *Expostulation 19*

Without a doubt, "St. Augustine is above all others the Father to whom Donne turned most constantly,"[47] and in the above quotation, Donne borrowed closely from Augustine's language of awe and respect for the power of metaphor.

Therefore, as we endeavor to become more proficient in reading the Holy Scriptures as scripture, this chapter has pointed you to the necessity for childlike awe at the wonder of language, the brain, and how the two of

44. Drucker, "Teaching," 132.

45. John Donne, the English poet is, perhaps, best known for the famous lines contained in *Devotions Upon Emergent Occasions* XVII, "No man is an island, entire of itself;" and "never send to know for whom the bell tolls; it tolls for thee."

46. Jungman, "Mining for Augustinian Gold," 16.

47. Simpson and Potter, *Sermons*, 10:346.

them work together to produce metaphors that fill our Bible. As Feldman writes, "Each of us is the world's greatest expert on one human mind—our own. But Nature (or God if you'd prefer) did not endow us with the ability to comprehend how our minds work. When it comes to the mental processes involved in understanding the meaning of the text, scientists cannot explain even the basics, such as how the meaning of a word is represented in the brain."[48]

Indeed, it seems Ortega y Gasset simply and superbly expressed it when he said, "Metaphor is the greatest power available to man; it borders on magic; it is like a creative tool left by God in the minds of His creatures."[49] As you read the Holy Scriptures as scripture, continue to discern and enjoy the creative tool of metaphor that God has given to us.

48. Feldman, *From Molecule to Metaphor*, 3.
49. Weiss, *Bible From Within*, 132.

11

Toward the Virtuous
Act of Reading

Generating Virtue

THE SHAPING OF THE individual into a virtuous reader is one of the natural outcomes achieved as one engages the enterprise of reading the Holy Scriptures as scripture over a sustained period of time. The act of generating virtue by means of reading the biblical text, God's Word, is certainly not an unreasonable expectation. In fact, it should be our eager expectation. Yet, there is a bit of a chicken and egg scenario when one considers the role of virtue in the enterprise. It would seem that the reader needs to bring certain interpretive virtues such as honesty, openness, attention, obedience, and humility into the act of reading.[1] Beyond that, it would also seem that the act of reading the Holy Scriptures as scripture elicits virtue within the individual. There is, then, a reciprocal relationship.

People of faith are implored to add virtue to their faith. "For this very reason, make every effort to supplement your faith with virtue . . ." (2 Pet 1:5). The main verb, "supplement," is an imperative form (*epichopēgēsate*– ἐπιχορηγήσατε), and it has the sense of "to provide at one's own expense." What is it that we are to provide? What is it that we are to add to our faith? It is virtue (*aretē* – ἀρετή), and *aretē* is that "uncommon character worthy of praise, excellence of character."[2]

---

1. Briggs, *Virtuous Reader*, 19 and Vanhoozer, *Is There a Meaning*, 376–77.
2. Arndt and Gingrich, *Lexicon*, 105.

Millennial Vice and Virtue in Reading

This chapter will juxtapose vice and virtue within the enterprise of reading the Holy Scriptures as scripture. The premise is that there are vices that impede and virtues that enhance the activity of reading, and it is important for the deep reader of the Bible to be aware of both vices and virtues inherent within the enterprise. I suppose that there is, legitimately, a long catalog of vices one could list for the reader to avoid. However, in this chapter, attention will be drawn to only one particular vice. It is, however, a foible that easily seeps into the mind and the heart of even the most virtuous of deep, Augustinian-type readers who altruistically want to read the Holy Scriptures as scripture.

Without sugarcoating it, let me propose that the vice is egotism—the human propensity toward self-centeredness. This particular vice is like a deep trench that is actually difficult to see. Unfortunately, the American culture, itself, seems to pave a wide road that leads directly to the rim of this ditch. For example, in a recent study, Twenge and Campbell noted that there is a "relentless rise of narcissism in our culture. . . . The United States is currently suffering an epidemic of narcissism."[3] Of all the vices I could have selected, why would I bring this particular one into focus in this concluding chapter? There is a reason.

Egotism is closely related to narcissism, a term that is much in vogue by those who attempt to characterize particular generational groups. For example, the newest generational cohort that has been studied is that of the Millennials. They are identified as that group born between 1984 and 2003.[4] Interestingly, a distinguishing feature of Millennials, as a group, is that they tend to be a very narcissistic, self-centered group.[5] For example, in Twenge's study, "She had analyzed some 15,000 students' responses to a questionnaire called the Narcissistic Personality Inventory between 1987 and 2006. The inventory contained statements like, 'I think I am a special person,' 'I can live my life any way I want to,' and 'If I ruled the world, it would be a better place.' Over time, the percentage who scored high had risen substantially."[6]

3. Twenge and Campbell, *Narcissism Epidemic*, 1–2.

4. See Strauss and Howe, *Millennials Rising*. The dates may fluctuate depending on who one reads, but the benchmark is generally considered to be Strauss and Howe.

5. Twenge, *Generation Me*, 68–74. The academic study of generational traits seems to have been jump started by Strauss and Howe, *Generations*.

6. Hoover, "Millennial Muddle."

Please do not be alarmed; I am not going to be harping against Millennials. To the contrary, in fact, I anticipate and hope that the largest generational group reading from this book will be Millennials. To be sure, I have been teaching Millennials for over a decade now, and I find them generally quite endearing. Yet, there is some convincing data on the rise of narcissistic behavior within that particular age cohort. Of course, we know that generational qualifying is generalizing, and we speak of patterns within a group, not of individuals. Yet, there are definitely group patterns. One must also take into account some factors other than age. One particular study, quite perceptively, points out that the common traits by which Millennials, as a cohort, have been labeled are really traits for white, suburban, affluent individuals born 1983–2004.[7] That is, there are other cultural forces beyond age that pull upon individuals.

To be clear, I think it is a fair statement that, regardless of our age cohort, all of us are prone to wander in the direction of egotism. Every one of us, as a deep reader of the Holy Scriptures needs to be cognizant of the tug that egotism has upon us. The bottom line is that we all tend to exhibit behavioral traits that stem from what I like to call the Ptolemy Factor.

The Ptolemy Factor

The Ptolemy Factor is, I believe, hugely influential in the lives of human beings generally, and it is extremely detrimental to one's reading of the Holy Scriptures as scripture. The good news is that the Ptolemy Factor can be mitigated by a variety of components basic to the cultivation of the Christian life. But what is this Ptolemy Factor; how does one best describe it? Actually, I coined the phrase as a result of an idea I had for cartoon. Here is the backstory.

An interesting fellow with the catchy name of Claudius Ptolemaeus was born about AD 90. Better-known simply as Ptolemy, he is actually famous because he believed the wrong thing. He believed the Sun circled the Earth. Sometime during our elementary school years, the curriculum of the day usually introduces something the students already know, namely that the Earth goes around the Sun. Most kids have seen enough old *Star Trek* movies to know a bit about the universe, but sixth-grade textbooks oftentimes introduce students to another guy named Copernicus (AD 1473–1543). The young students are taught how he finally set things

7. Ibid.

straight by proving that the Sun, rather than the Earth, is the center of our solar system. The old notion, the now laughable idea that the Earth was the center of the solar system, is virtually mocked. In the science and history books, Ptolemy is given credit for advocating a system for the cosmos that the modern mind sees as ludicrous. Poor Ptolemy; how could anyone have ever believed that yarn?

Actually, Ptolemy's system made a lot of sense; it seemed to support everyday experience. In what is widely considered to be one of the hundred most influential books written since World War II, Thomas Kuhn in his work, *The Structure of Scientific Revolutions*, wrote that "No other ancient system had performed so well; for the stars, Ptolematic astronomy is still widely used today as an engineering approximation; for the planets, Ptolemy's predictions were as good as Copernicus'. But to be admirably successful is never, for a scientific theory, to be completely successful."[8]

Ptolemy: Champion of the Geocentric View

Some time ago I had a brilliant idea for a one-frame cartoon. Now, my daughter will tell you that she is the one who first thought up this particular cartoon, but she simply is not remembering it correctly. I think *my idea* has a rather "Larsonesque" sense to it. Clearly, I have been affected by Gary Larson's cartoons. After all, what late twentieth-century American has not been influenced, on some level, by *The Far Side*? My wife, Patty, is a great fan of *The Far Side*. Whereas some collect great art, she has collected the works of Gary Larson. I am particularly fond of his renditions of prehistoric man. On my office door at the university I used to post the various Larson cartoons that portrayed those prehistoric characters with the wonderful names of Zonk, Gork, and the rest. However, while I had this great idea for a cartoon, I had never gotten around to drawing it. The problem is, I do not draw very well. I'm still in my stick-figure phase. However, if you use your imagination, I'll try to paint for you an image of the cartoon using words; after all, it is the thought of the cartoon that makes it funny, not the artwork.

Picture, in your mind, Ptolemy sitting in his cluttered library with all kinds of books on physics, geometry, and astronomy on his shelf. He is intently playing with a model of the solar system. He clearly has just had some sort of scientific breakthrough! You can see the various planets and sun that rotate around each other. You know that type of model they used

8. Kuhn, *Structure of Scientific Revolutions*, 68.

in the third grade, right? The teacher turned a little crank and the planets moved in their orbits. Of course, in the cartoon, the model is constructed all wrong. It is built after the Ptolemaic image of the universe. The Earth is in the center, and on his model, and the Sun in its orbit goes around the Earth. In fact, everything rotates around the Earth. Now picture Ptolemy's hen-pecking wife learning over him, and she scowls at him, "Why must everything always revolve around you?"

Get it? Ptolemy's solar system is designed so that everything revolves around him; he is the center of all things. That's narcissism; that is the Ptolemy Factor. That is a funny cartoon, whether you chuckled or not.

This solar system in which the Sun rotates around the Earth is known as the geocentric model, and Ptolemy was its champion architect. Yet, in all fairness to Ptolemy, it should be pointed out that he did not invent the geocentric model; he merely made it work better than anyone else had before. Credit for the geocentric model must be given more broadly to the Greeks and more particularly to the widely known and accepted Aristotelian physics. Little is it known that not all early thinkers were duped into advocating a geocentric model. For instance, Aritarchus of Samos (310–230 BC) advocated a heliocentric theory that turned out to be not so different from that of Copernicus.

The funny thing about the Ptolemaic (geocentric) model is that it was a *really good* model, i.e., it worked quite well. As one of my favorite authors, Daniel Boorstin, wrote in his significant book, *The Discoverers*, "Why did Nicholaus Copernicus (1473–1543) go to so much trouble to displace a system that was amply supported by everyday experience, by tradition, and by authority?"[9] As he noted, "those who would remain unpersuaded by Copernicus were simply being sensible."[10] Indeed, such was the case, and it should be sobering and enlightening to us that our senses can be so deceived.

The first aspect of the Ptolemy Factor I would like to address can be explained this way. Like Ptolemy, you think you are right. In fact, all of the perceptual evidence indicates you are right. However, you are wrong. In Ptolemy's case, he thought the Earth was the center of the solar system. When one looks up into the heavens from the Earth, it certainly does appear that is, indeed, the case. After all, it does seem that the Sun is moving around the Earth. Yet, that is not the case. Your senses, your brain, your

9. Boorstin, *Discoverers*, 296.
10. Ibid.

instincts have all been fooled; you have been bamboozled. What you believed to be true, is not true. That is, reality is a bit counterintuitive when it comes to how one perceives the relationship between the Earth and the Sun. Now, it seems quite evident that nobody holds something to be true that they "know" is false. Think about it. Do you knowingly hold as true something that you are positive is false? I seriously doubt it.

Another, very important aspect of the Ptolemy factor is this notion of narcissism, or self-centeredness. Just as it was pointed out by his wife in my cartoon, in Ptolemy's model of the universe, everything revolved around him (in that he was on the Earth). This is a common human malady. The American culture tends to accentuate the problem, and the reader of the Holy Scriptures as scripture needs to be acutely conscious of the danger. Why? Why this particular vice?

Being a Virtuous Reader

It is a virtuous reader who reads the Holy Scriptures as scripture, and it requires a measure of acumen to be a virtuous reader. It takes reading with a particular slant and attitude. You cannot read selfishly; you must read charitably. As Jacobs nicely put it, "But what makes the difference between a reading that is manipulative and selfish and one that is charitable? . . . Fundamentally, it is the reader's will that determines the moral form the reading takes. . . . That one can read charitably only if one's will is guided by charity is a pretty obvious point, yet it is neglected in hermeneutical theory even more than the charitable imperative itself."[11]

As one who is seeking to become a faithful, deep reader in this enterprise, it is good that you should be keenly aware of several related vices of the reader which arise out of the Ptolemy factor. For example, pride and sloth have been labeled as two grave sins often committed by the reader. "Pride is a corrupting influence on the interpreter for a number of reasons. First, it encourages us to think that we have got the correct meaning before we have made the appropriate effort to recover it. Pride typically does not wait to listen; it knows."[12] I use the Ptolemy factor and the vice of egotism or self-centeredness as my example because the virtue I wish to highlight seems to be at the very opposite end of the spectrum. Vanhoozer has noted

11. Jacobs, *Theology of Reading*, 31.
12. Vanhoozer, *Is There a Meaning*, 462.

that "Humility is a specifically Christian contribution to hermeneutics."[13] In fact, humility is, perhaps, one of the key virtues to be developed by the deep reader of the Holy Scriptures as scripture.

Contrary to the effects of the Ptolemy Factor, the reading and interpreting of the Holy Scriptures as scripture should be grounded in the Augustinian principle of charity. "Indeed, interpretation ultimately depends upon the theological virtues of faith, hope, and love."[14] Back in chapter 9, it was suggested that Augustine may have really been on to something with his hermeneutic of love. His interpretive approach demands an actualization of charity in the life of the reader based on the double commandment cited by Jesus to love God and love neighbor. Augustine wrote, "So anyone who thinks that he has understood the divine scriptures or any part of them, but cannot by his understanding build up this double love of God and neighbor, has not yet succeeded in understanding them. Anyone who derives from them an idea which is useful for supporting this love but fails to say what the writer demonstrably meant in the passage has not made a fatal error, and is certainly not a liar."[15]

Fowl has noted that there are several ways of thinking about the relationship between virtue and theological interpretation of the Holy Scriptures. "The first has to do with the ways in which theological interpretation aids in the cultivation of virtue. The second has to do with the ways in which virtue aids in the practice of theological interpretation."[16] By reading the Holy Scriptures as scripture, you will develop virtue. An outgrowth of that will be an expanded ability for you to better interpret those texts in such a manner that will broaden and strengthen your understanding and love of God's Holy Word. "Given that Christians are called to interpret Scripture as part of their ongoing journey into ever-deeper communion with God, it is not surprising that those who have grown and advanced in virtue will tend to be masterful interpreters of Scripture."[17]

---

13. Ibid., 464.

14. Vanhoozer, "Spirit of Understanding," 161.

15. Augustine, *On Christian Teaching*, 1.41.

16. Fowl, "Virtue," 837.

17. Ibid., 838.

The Reader Changes

You, as a developing deep reader of the Holy Scriptures as scripture, will change over time. Indeed, any reader changes over time. Yet, how is it that you will change compared to any other reader who is reading any other book? In a fascinating work on the brain science behind reading, Maryanne Wolf notes that

> The degree to which expert reading changes over the course of our adult lives depends largely on what we read and how we read it. Such changes are best captured, perhaps, not by cognitive studies and images of the brain but by our poets. William Stafford expressed the first element in these changes when he wrote, "A quality of attention has been given you." He may not have been talking about attention networks or expert readers, but this almost ineffable quality in how we attend to a text changes over time as we learn to read—in the German novelist Hermann Hesse's words, "more discriminatingly, more sensitively, more associatively."[18]

I really like her phrase, "the almost ineffable quality of how we attend to a text." Through time, as we read, we change in the way we think about a text in a very enigmatic way. We alter how we read and how we interpret. Yet, this is nothing new. We saw this in the case of Augustine. His first reading of the Bible at eighteen years of age was very different from his reading of the Holy Scriptures at age thirty-four. He was looking for different things in the text at those two stages. At eighteen, he was looking for the artistic literary forms of Cicero in the text. At thirty-four he was looking for God in the text.[19] In Hesse's translated words, the more mature, post-conversion Augustine was reading "more discriminatingly, more sensitively, more associatively." As a result, Augustine aptly noted that "Yesterday you understood a little, today you understand more; tomorrow you will understand still more: the very light of God becomes stronger in you."[20] This is exactly the premise behind this book. It is geared to assist you in changing the way you read the Bible. Yes, that would happen somewhat naturally over time, even without any conscious development. Yet, now you may more purposefully accentuate and accelerate your transformative reading of the

18. Wolf, *Proust and the Squid*, 156.

19. Ibid. She notes that, "This explains how we can read the Bible, *Middlemarch*, or the *The Brothers Karamazov* at ages seventeen, thirty-seven, fifty-seven, and seventy-seven and come away with an entirely new understanding each time."

20. Augustine, *Tractates on the Gospel of John* (*In Johannis evangelium tractatus*), 14.5.

Holy Scriptures. You will read differently because of some of the things you have read in this book.

This ability to change our way of reading through time is a blessing. As Wolf notes, our brain is much like the "open architecture" concept used in computer science "to describe a system that is versatile enough to change—or rearrange—to accommodate the varying demand on it."[21] While Wolf attributes to nature that open architectural structure of the brain, the reader of the Holy Scriptures as scripture attributes it to God.

Elements of Breadth and Depth within the Enterprise

Reading the Bible as one ought in order to read it properly as scripture, necessitates various considerations. This enterprise of reading the Holy Scriptures as scripture would seem, on an intuitive level, to involve a scope of both breadth and depth in one's reading. The church fathers certainly were aware of these two elements, for they understood that the reading of the Holy Scriptures plunges one into a deep part of one's life.

The notion of breadth could set us to thinking of two different aspects of reading. First of all, there is the breadth of the Holy Scriptures themselves. For example, Apponius a very interesting yet somewhat mysterious figure.[22] He "has been variously identified as a fifth-century Syrian, a seventh-century Irishman, or a converted Jew, but recent scholarship identifies him as abbot of a monastery in northern Italy."[23] He wrote of the "wide array of senses and the expansive spaces of the Divine Scriptures."[24] Jerome also hit upon this notion of the breadth of the Bible.[25] He called the Holy Scriptures "an ocean, a labyrinth of the mysteries of God."[26] He was not alone in using the imagery of an ocean in attempting to communicate the vastness of God's Word. Origen, Ambrose and Gregory the Great all used

21. Wolf, *Proust and the Squid*, 5.

22. See Holder, "Patristic Sources." Apponius wrote a commentary on the Song of Solomon sometime between AD 420 and 430. This extensive commentary, written in twelve books was widely read and often cited in the medieval period because it had been used by Bede in his famous commentary on the Song of Solomon.

23. Holder, "Patristic Sources," 372.

24. Apponius, *In Cant.*, Bk 4 (70). *Latissimi sensus, spatial Scripturae divinae.*

25. Perhaps the best book on Jerome is still Kelly, *Jerome*. See also more recently, Rebenich, *Jerome* and Williams, *The Monk*.

26. Jerome, *In Ezk*, bk. 14, *praef.* (PL 25: 448). *Ita et ego istarum Scripturarum ingresus Oceanum, et mysteriorum Dei, ut sic loquar, labyrinthum. . .*

that same picture of an ocean.[27] Yet one image, alone, is clearly not enough to adequately capture the scope of it all. For that reason, the same fellows, at other times, also employed the image of a great, dense forest to describe the daunting breadth of the Bible.[28]

Secondly, there is the breadth of reading required by you and me in order to explore those expansive spaces of the Holy Scriptures. Like ancient monks and fathers of the church who set aside extended periods of time for reading, we ought simply to expand the sphere of our reading time. Of course, there is nothing simple about doing that. Our usual daily schedule is hectic. However, it is within our grasp to manage our time more effectively and to better prioritize our activities. Perhaps it is feasible to collapse time invested in certain activities in order to inflate time spent in other endeavors. Naturally, our culture will fight you every inch of the way on such an endeavor. I suspect that each one of us could sincerely confess a desire to spend more time than we typically do in reading the Holy Scriptures. Yet the reality of a stressful and busy life, so common within our culture, fights against our having a focused and extended time to read God's Word. At this point, I might recommend the highly acclaimed books by Richard Foster in which he articulates, in a reasoned and practical way, for the cultivating of a lifestyle more in tune with how the ancients might have approached the problem.[29] Foster writes, "Stress the quality of life above the quantity of life. Refuse to be seduced into defining life in terms of *having* rather than *being*. Cultivate solitude and silence. Learn to 'listen to God's speech in his wondrous, terrible, gentle, loving, all embracing silence.' . . . If you are too busy to read, you are too busy."[30]

Consider Origen who, if he were not reading, had someone reading to him. One friend of Origen reported that, "He never took a meal in Origen's company without something being read, and that he never fell asleep save to the sound of some brother's voice reciting the Scriptures aloud. Day and night it was their habit to make reading follow upon prayer, and prayer upon reading, without a break."[31]

27. Lubac. *Medieval Exegesis*, 1:75. His notes point to: Origen, *In Gen.*, h. 9, n. 1 where he spoke of the Holy Scriptures as a "vast ocean of mystery." Ambrose (PL 16:738 C) and Gregory also allude to God's Word as an enormous sea (PL 76:834–5).

28. Lubac. See also his *History and Spirit*, 103 where he points to Origen's use of the phrase, *latissimam Scriptuae silvam* (the very broad forest of Scripture).

29. Foster, *Simplicity* and Foster, *Celebration of Discipline*.

30. Foster, *Simplicity*, 123.

31. Jerome, *Letter* 43.

Of course one might think that it was different for the ancients. You may suppose that they did not have the stresses upon time so permanently present in today's modern world against which we constantly strain. I think that argument could well be refuted, and I do not believe it is valid. The lives of the ancients were every bit as stressed and strained as ours, if not considerably more. I certainly would not consider my life as frazzled or frantic as that of the Apostle Paul nor even the simplest farmer in third century. The quantity of our leisure time in twenty-first-century America far surpasses that of nearly anyone living in antiquity. I think all of us can better manage our lives in such a way that we could eek out time for expanding the breadth and depth of our reading of the Holy Scriptures.

The Stunning Conclusion

The modern notion that reading is "an invitation to live temporarily within the thoughts of someone else" is not so modern.[32] Indeed, Augustine, most certainly, would have been in total agreement with this proposition.[33] What is it that this enterprise of deep reading does to you? What actually happens when you are reading the Holy Scriptures as scripture? In a wonderfully insightful statement, John Webster remarked that "Reading is an aspect of our mortification and vivification; to read Holy Scripture is to be gathered into the divine work of reconciliation in which we are slain and made alive."[34] He says that "Reading Scripture involves, first, a 'departure from self.'"[35] So it is that in one fell swoop we move away from the lure of the Ptolemy Factor, and to the contrary, we hear the *viva vox Dei* addressing us. We are newly able to respond because of the relinquishment of self. As Webster notes, this act was for Calvin "one of the chief fruits of the Holy Spirit."[36] Archer has noted that one should always invite the Holy Spirit to be part and parcel of the interpreter's work as the reader comes to the enterprise with a peculiar attitude, one in which the reader is willing to be transformed.[37] And so it is, as a deep reader of the Holy Scriptures as scripture we relinquish ourselves as we hear, really hear, the living voice of

32. Poulet, "Phenomenology of Reading," 53–68.
33. Stock, *Augustine the Reader*, 15.
34. Webster, "Reading Scripture Eschatologically," 251.
35. Ibid.
36. Ibid., 252.
37. Archer, *Pentecostal Hermeneutic*, 183–85.

God. As a result of our act, a gift of the Holy Spirit is bestowed in such a way that we are transformed.

Remember, as a synesthetic reader, a deep reader of the Holy Scriptures as scripture, you will be making connections and observations with a measure of insight and perception that non-synesthetic readers will not make. Your senses will be combining thoughts and ideas in new ways so that connections you did not make in your old way of reading are now popping into your mind and heart as you are cognitively and spiritually processing as a synesthete.

Orange proverbs and purple parables are metaphors for cognitively and spiritually hearing, in a new way, the living voice of God (*viva vox Dei*). "Though Augustine believed that only with the resurrection of the body could a state of ultimate bliss be achieved, something like that state was possible for the earthly traveler, a moment of illumination granted by the act of reading."[38]

With Little More Than Pluck and Belief

As nice and as comforting as it might be to think that we have the matter well in hand when it comes to our personal practice of cultivating a devotional life in which we effectively read the Holy Scriptures as scripture, an unsettling proposition of this book is that you and I do not presently have those things quite so well in hand. Yet, this is a noble enterprise we are considering. Are you game? Do you want to engage this venture of reading the Holy Scriptures as scripture as you never have before? I think that, deep down, you do. I think you realize the power and potency of the Word of God. But what will it take? What will it take for you to read as you ought?

I do not, as a common practice, quote lines from movies for the purpose of inspiring anyone facing a challenge, but I did hear a rather good one the other day. Let me cite Glinda, the beloved good witch who was reading a letter from the wizard in the closing scene of *Oz, the Great and Powerful*. The wizard had written, "With a little more than pluck and belief we made the impossible happen." Now, of course, our motivation for undertaking a serious and spiritual endeavor is not to be rooted in the words of the Wizard of Oz. However, I like the sentiment of his words. So as many preachers are wont to do, let me use these words merely as an illustration, not as any sort of authoritative force. For the Christian, the pluck he speaks of is the

38. Manguel, *Traveler, Tower, Worm*, 73.

courage you have as a Christ follower. The mere fact that you are a follower of Jesus emboldens you. Pluck is that spirit, courage, resolution, and nerve you have to walk the Christian life. Rooted alongside your belief, your faith in Christ as the risen Lord, this pluck enables one to do things that might not, under other conditions, be doable. With little more than pluck and belief, Christians are more capable than they may typically think. Therefore, I encourage you to launch out in this new endeavor. In your belief that God has raised Christ from the dead, believe also that he who has begun a good work in you will carry it on to completion until the day of Christ Jesus (Phil 1:6). Changing your patterns and ways of reading the Holy Scriptures will present you with some challenges. You will not change the way you read overnight. However, with little more than pluck and belief, you can become a reader of the Holy Scriptures in the same way that Augustine, the reader, reinvented himself and became a conspicuous consumer of the *viva vox Dei*.[39]

Best Practices for Reading the Holy Scriptures as Scripture

Finally, as you come to the end, allow me to restate concisely a few of the primary elements of the enterprise that have been addressed in this book. Indeed, there is not a set formula or foolproof method for reading the Holy Scriptures as scripture that will work for everyone in the same way. However, there are some fundamental features that I would suggest you incorporate into your reading. Perhaps these could be labeled as "best practices" within our noble enterprise as we set out to become invigorated readers of the Holy Scriptures.

1. Pray as a pre-reading exercise. Ask the Holy Spirit to empower you as a synesthetic reader to make new connections and glean new insights from the Holy Scriptures.

2. Establish a patterned schedule for your reading, and refine a method in the sense of a personal *lectio divina*. Don't be afraid to experiment in your pattern of reading. Attempt to engage continuous reading of a single book (*lectio continua*).

3. Strive for a diligent and focused period of reading. William of St. Thierry, in the twelfth century noted that, "There is the same gulf between

39. Stock. *Augustine the Reader.*

attentive study and mere reading as there is between friendship and acquaintance with a passing guest, between boon companionship and chance meeting."[40]

4. Embrace the wonders of the fractal nature and the sfumato of the Holy Scriptures.

5. Engage the magic of metaphor as it exists within the Holy Scriptures. Be thoughtful of language as you listen to the *viva vox Dei*.

6. Don't be reticent to consider multiple meanings within the Holy Scriptures. There is room in the believing community for both the lamb and the elephant.

7. Develop the various virtues that will grow within you as a reader of the Holy Scriptures as scripture. Invite the Holy Spirit to be a part of that process as you attempt to cultivate the virtue of humility in your reading.

8. Allow your senses to perceive, as a true synesthete, the majestic Word of God because within the Holy Scriptures there are orange proverbs and purple parables.

Now, go and commence a great and wonderful journey. Read as you have not read before, and hear the voice of God as you have not heard before. The enterprise of reading the Holy Scriptures as scripture is before you.

40. William of Saint Thierry, *Golden Epistle*, 51–52.

Bibliography

Abraham, William. *The Divine Inspiration of Holy Scripture.* Oxford: Oxford University Press, 1981.

Achtemeier, Paul J. *The Inspiration of Scripture.* Philadelphia: Westminster, 1980.

Adam, A. K. M., et al. *Reading Scripture with the Church.* Grand Rapids: Baker, 2006.

Adamson, Donald. *Blaise Pascal: Mathematician, Physicist, and Thinker about God.* New York: St. Martin's, 1995.

Ahem, S. K., and J. Beatty, "Pupillary Responses During Information Processing Vary With Scholastic Aptitude Test Scores." *Science* 205 (1979) 1289–92.

Aland, Kurt, and Barbara Aland. *The Text of the New Testament: An Introduction to the Critical Editions and to the Theory and Practice of Modern Textual Criticism.* Translated by E. F. Rhodes. Grand Rapids: Eerdmans, 1987.

Alexander, Patrick H., et al., eds. *The SBL Handbook of Style.* Peabody, MA: Hendrickson, 1999.

Alster, Bendt *Proverbs of Ancient Sumer.* Bethesda, MD: CDL, 1996.

Anatolios, Khaled. *Athanasius: The Coherence of His Thought.* New York: Routledge, 2005.

Aquinas, Thomas. *Summa Theologiae.* Translated by English Dominicans. New York: Christian Classics, 1981.

Archer, Kenneth J. *A Pentecostal Hermeneutic for the Twenty-First Century: Spirit, Scripture and Community.* JPT Supplement 28. New York: T. & T. Clark, 2004.

Arden, John Boghosian. *Science, Theology, and Consciousness: The Search for Unity.* Westport, CT: Praeger, 1998.

Arlotto, Anthony. *Introduction to Historical Linguistics.* Boston: Houghton Mifflin, 1972.

Arndt, William F., and F. Wilbur Gingrich, eds. *A Greek-English Lexicon of the New Testament and Other Early Christian Literature.* Chicago, University of Chicago Press, 1957.

Ash, Russell, and Brian Lake. *Bizarre Books: A Compendium of Classic Oddities.* New York: Harper Perennial, 2006.

Augustine. *The City of God against the Pagans.* Translated by R. W. Dyson. New York: Cambridge University Press, 1998.

———. *The Confessions.* Translated by Maria Bolding. New York: New City, 2011.

———. *Expositions of the Psalms.* Vol. 1. Translated by Maria Bolding. New York: New City, 2000.

———. *Letters 100–155*. Translated by Edmund Hill and John E. Rotelle. New York: New City, 2003.

———. *On Christian Teaching*. Translated by R. P. H. Green. Oxford: Oxford University Press, 1997.

Bakker, H., P. Van Geest, and H. Van Loon, eds. *Cyprian of Carthage: Studies in His Life, Language and Thought*. Leuven: Peeters, 2010.

Balogh, Josef. "Voces Paginarum." *Philologus* 82 (1927) 84–109, 202–40.

Balthasar, Hans Urs von. *Origen, Spirit and Fire: A Thematic Anthology of His Writings*. Washington, DC: Catholic University of America Press, 1984.

Barth, Karl. *The Word of God and the Word of Man*. Translated by Douglas Horton. New York: Harper Torchbooks, 1957.

———. *The Word of God and Theology*. Translated by Amy Marga. London: T. & T. Clark, 2011.

Bartholomew, Craig, C. Stephen Evans, Mary Healy, and Murray Rae, eds. *"Behind" The Text: History and Biblical Interpretation*. Edited by Craig C. Bartholomew. Scripture and Hermeneutics 4. Grand Rapids: Zondervan, 2003.

Becker, Gary S., and Kevin M. Murphy. "A Theory of Rational Addiction." *The Journal of Political Economy* 96 (1988) 675–700.

Belt, Henk van den. *The Authority of Scripture in Reformed Theology*. Leiden: Brill, 2008.

———. "Scripture as the Voice of God: The Continuing Importance of Autopistia." *International Journal of Systematic Theology* 13/4 (2011) 434–47.

Berkhof, Louis. *Systematic Theology: New Combined Edition*. Grand Rapids: Eerdmans, 1996.

Berkouwer, G. C. *Holy Scripture*. Translated by Jack B. Rogers. Grand Rapids: Eerdmans, 1975.

Blaising, Craig A., and Carment S. Hardin, eds. *Psalms 1–50*. Edited by Thomas C. Oden. Ancient Christian Commentary on Scripture 7. Downers Grove, IL: InterVarsity, 2008.

Bogousslavsky, Julien Hennerici, and M. G. Hennerici, eds. *Neurological Disorders in Famous Artists*. Vol 2. Basel: Karger, 2007.

Boorstin, Daniel. *The Discoverers*. New York: Random House, 1985.

Boroditsky, Lera. "How Language Shapes Thought." *Scientific American* (February 2011) 63–65.

Boroditsky, Lera, and Alice Gaby. "Remembrances of Times East: Absolute Spatial Representations of Time in an Australian Aboriginal Community." *Psychological Science* 21 (2010) 1–5.

Boulding, Maria. *The Confessions*. Hyde Park, NY: New City, 1997.

Bouvy, E. "Saint Augustine Les Enarrations sur les psaumes." *Revue Augustinienne* 3 (1903) 417–24.

Bovon, François. *Exegesis: Problems of Method and Exercizes in Reading*. Pittsburgh: Pickwick, 1978.

Braidwood, Robert J. "Jarmo: A Village of Early Farmers in Iraq." *Antiquity* 24 (1950) 189–95.

Brent, Allen. *Cyprian and Roman Carthage*. Cambridge: Cambridge University Press, 2010.

Briggs, Richard S. *Reading the Bible Wisely: An Introduction to Taking Scripture Seriously*. Eugene, OR: Cascade, 2011.

———. *The Virtuous Reader: Old Testament Narrative and Interpretive Virtue*. Grand Rapids: Baker, 2010.

Brock, Sebastian P. *The Wisdom of St. Isaac of Nineveh*. Piscataway, NJ: Gorgias, 2006.

Brookman, W. R. *Global Scenes of Biblical Injustice*. Lanham, MD: University Press of America, 2012.

Brown, Jeannine K. *Scripture as Communication: Introducing Biblical Hermeneutics*. Grand Rapids: Baker Academic, 2007.

Brown, Peter. "Aspects of the Christianization of the Roman Aristocracy." *JRS* 51 (1961) 7–8.

———. *Augustine of Hippo: A Biography*. Berkeley: University of California Press, 1967.

———. *Poverty and Leadership in the Later Roman Empire*. Waltham, MA: Brandeis University Press, 2002.

———. *Power and Persuasion: Towards a Christian Empire*. Madison: University of Wisconsin Press, 1992.

———. *Religion and Society in the Age of Saint Augustine*. London: Faber & Faber, 1972.

———. *The Rise of Western Christendom*. Oxford: Blackwell, 1996.

———. *Through the Eye of a Needle: Wealth, the Fall of Rome, and the Making of Christianity in the West, 350–550 AD*. Princeton: Princeton University Press, 2012.

———. *The World of Late Antiquity: AD 150–750*. New York: Norton, 1989.

Brown, William P., ed. *Character and Scripture: Moral Formation, Community, and Biblical Interpretation*. Grand Rapids: Eerdmans, 2002.

———. *Seeing the Psalms*. Louisville: Westminster John Knox, 2002.

Bulwer-Lytton, Edward. *Paul Clifford*. Philadelphia: J. P. Lippincott, 1873.

Burgess, John P. *Why Scripture Matters*. Louisville: Westminster John Knox, 1998.

Butcher, Carmen Acevedo. *Man of Blessing: The Life of St. Benedict*. Brewster, MA: Paraclete, 2006.

Cameron, Michael. *Christ Meets Me Everywhere: Augustine's Early Figurative Exegesis*. Oxford: Oxford University Press, 2012.

Camery-Hoggatt, Jerry. *Reading the Good Book Well: A Guide to Biblical Interpretation*. Nashville: Abingdon, 2007.

Campbell, Phillip, ed. *The Complete Works of Saint Cyprian of Carthage*. Merchantville, NJ: Arx, 2013.

Campen, Cretien van. *The Hidden Sense: Synesthesia in Art and Science*. Boston: MIT Press, 2008.

Candler, Peter M. *Theology, Rhetoric, Manuduction, Or Reading Scripture Together On The Path To God*. Grand Rapids: Eerdmans, 2006.

Carruthers, Mary. *The Book of Memory: A Study of Memory in Medieval Culture*. Cambridge: Cambridge University Press, 1993.

Casey, Michael. *Sacred Reading: The Ancient Art of Lectio Divina*. Liguori, MO: Liguori/Triumph, 1995.

Cassian, John. *Conferences*. Translated by Colm Luibheid. New York: Paulist, 1985.

Casson, Lionel. *Libraries in the Ancient World*. New Haven: Yale University Press, 2001.

Chadwick, Owen. *John Cassian*. Cambridge: Cambridge University Press, 1950.

Congressional Record, V. 144, Pt. 19, October 19, 1998 to December 19, 1998, 28013.

Cosgrove, Charles H. "Toward a Postmodern *Hermeneutica Sacra*: Guiding Considerations in Choosing between Competing Plausible Interpretations of Scripture." In *The Meaning We Choose: Hermeneutical Ethics, Indeterminacy and the Conflict of Interpretations*, edited by C. H. Cosgrove, 39–61. London: T. & T. Clark, 2004.

Csikszentmihalyi, Mihaly. *Beyond Boredom and Anxiety: Experiencing Flow in Work and Play*. San Francisco: Jossey-Bass, 1975.

———. *Creativity: Flow and the Psychology of Discovery and Invention*. New York: Harper Perennial, 1996.

———. *Finding Flow: The Psychology of Engagement with Everyday Life*. New York: Basic, 1997.

———. *Flow: The Psychology of Optimal Experience*. New York: Harper & Row, 1990.

———. "Flow, the Secret to Happiness." http://www.ted.com/talks/mihaly_csikszentmihalyi_on_flow.html.

Csikszentmihalyi, M., and I. S. Csikszentmihalyi, eds. *Optimal Experience: Psychological Studies of Flow in Consciousness*. New York: Cambridge University Press, 1988.

Cytowic, Richard E. *Synesthesia: A Union of the Senses*. Boston: MIT Press, 2002.

———. *Wednesday Is Indigo Blue: Discovering the Brain of Synesthesia*. Boston: MIT Press, 2009.

Davidson, Hugh M. *Blaise Pascal*. Boston: Twayne, 1983.

Davies, Paul, and Julian R. Brown, eds. *Superstrings: A Theory of Everything?* Cambridge: Cambridge University Press, 1992.

Davis, Ellen F. *Swallowing the Scroll: Textuality and the Dynamics of Discourse in Ezekiel's Prophecy*. JSOTSup. Sheffield, UK: Almond, 1989.

———. "Teaching the Bible Confessionally in the Church." In *The Art of Reading Scripture*, edited by Ellen F. Davis and Richard B. Hays, 9–26. Grand Rapids: Eerdmans, 2003.

Davis, Ellen F., and Richard B. Hays, eds. *The Art of Reading Scripture*. Grand Rapids: Eerdmans, 2003.

D'Costa, Gavin. *Theology in the Public Square*. Oxford: Blackwell, 2005.

Dickey, Eleanor. *Ancient Greek Scholarship*. Oxford: Oxford University Press, 2007.

Donfried, Karl P. "Alien Hermeneutics and the Misappropriation of Scripture." In *Reclaiming the Bible for the Church*, edited by Carl E. Braaten and Robert W. Jenson, 19–45. Grand Rapids: Eerdmans, 1995.

Drucker, J. P. "Teaching as Pointing in 'The Teacher.'" *AugStud* 28 (1997) 101–34.

Dudden, F. Homes. *The Life and Times of St. Ambrose*. Oxford: Clarendon, 1935.

Duffy, Patricia Lynne. *Blue Cats and Chartreuse Kittens*. New York: Henry Holt, 2001.

Eco, Umberto. *The Role of the Reader: Explorations in the Semiotics of Texts*. Bloomington: Indiana University Press, 1979.

Evans, Gillian R. *Bernard of Clairvaux*. Oxford: Oxford University Press, 2000.

Evans, Gillian R., ed. *Bernard of Clairvaux: Selected Works*. San Francisco: Harper Collins, 2005.

Fackre, Gabriel. *The Doctrine of Revelation: A Narrative Interpretation*. Edinburgh: Edinburgh University Press, 1997.

Fauconnier, Gilles. *Mappings in Thought and Language*. Cambridge: Cambridge University Press, 1997.

Fauconnier, Gilles, and Mark Turner. *The Way We Think: Conceptual Blending and Mind's Hidden Complexities*. New York: Basic, 2002.

Feldman, Jerome. *From Molecule to Metaphor: A Neural Theory of Language*. Boston: MIT Press, 2006.

Firth, J. R. *Papers in Linguistics 1934–1951*. London: Oxford University Press, 1957.

Fortin, Ernest L. "Augustine and the Hermeneutics of Love." In *The Birth of Philosophic Christianity: Studies in Early Christian and Medieval Thought*, edited by J. Brian Benestad, 1–19. Lanham, MD: Rowman & Littlefield, 1996.

Foster, Richard. *Celebration of Discipline*. San Francisco: Harper & Row, 1978.

———. *Freedom of Simplicity*. San Francisco: Harper & Row, 1981.

Fowl, Stephen E. *Engaging Scripture: A Model for Theological Interpretation*. Eugene, OR: Wipf & Stock, 1998.

———. *Theological Interpretation of Scripture*. Eugene, OR: Cascade, 2009.

———. "Virtue." In *Dictionary for Theological Interpretation of the Bible*, edited by Kevin J. Vanhoozer, 837–39. Grand Rapids: Baker Academic, 2005.

Fowl, Stephen E., and L. Gregory Jones. *Reading in Communion: Scripture and Ethics in Christian Life*. Grand Rapids: Eerdmans, 1991.

Fox, Michael V. *Proverbs 1–9*. The Anchor Bible 181A. New Haven: Yale University, 2000.

Frascolla, Pasquale. *Understanding Wittgenstein's Tractatus*. New York: Routledge, 2007.

Fromkin, Victoria, and Robert Rodman, eds. *An Introduction to Language*. New York: Holt, Rinehart and Winston, 1978.

Fulghum, Robert. *All I Really Need to Know I Learned in Kindergarten*. New York: Random House, 1985.

Gadamer, Hans Georg. *Truth and Method*. Translated by Joel Weinsheimer and Donald G. Marshall. New York: Continuum, 2004.

Gadd, C. J., and S. N. Kramer. *Ur Excavation Texts: Religious and Literary Texts, 6/2*. London: Trustees of the British Museum, 1963.

Gallup, George, Jr. *The Role of the Bible in American Society*. Princeton: Princeton Religion Research Center, 1990.

Gelb, Michael J. *How to Think Like Leonardo da Vinci*. New York: Dell, 1998.

Glidden, David. "Augustine's Hermeneutics and the Principle of Charity." *Ancient Philosophy* 17 (1997) 135–57.

Goldsworthy, Graeme. *Gospel-Centered Hermeneutics*. Downers Grove, IL: InterVarsity, 2006.

Gracia, Jorge J. E. "Meaning." In *Dictionary for Theological Interpretation of the Bible*, edited by Kevin J. Vanhoozer, 492–99. Grand Rapids: Baker Academic, 2005.

Graffin, F. "La Lettre de Philoxène de Mabboug à un supèreur de monastère sur la vie monastique." *L'Orient Syrien* 6 (1961) 442–65.

Graybiel, Ann M. "Guide to the Anatomy of the Brain: The Basal Ganglia." In *Encyclopedia of Learning and Memory*, edited by J. H. Byrne, 204–6. New York: MacMillan, 2002.

Graybiel, Ann M., and S. Grillner, eds. *Microcircuits: The Interface between Neurons and Global Brain Function*. Cambridge, MA: MIT Press, 2006.

Graybiel, Ann M., and E. Saka. "The Basal Ganglia and the Control of Action." In *The New Cognitive Neurosciences*, edited by M. S. Gazzaniga, 495–510. Cambridge, MA: MIT Press, 2003.

Green, Joel B. *Practicing Theological Interpretation*. Grand Rapids: Baker, 2011.

———. *Seized by Truth: Reading the Bible as Scripture*. Nashville: Abingdon, 2007.

Greene, Brian. *The Fabric of the Cosmos: Space, Time, and the Texture of Reality*. New York: Knopf, 2004.

Greene-McCreight, Kathryn. *Ad Litteram: How Augustine, Calvin, and Barth Read the "Plain Sense" of Genesis 1–3*. New York: Peter Lang, 1999.

———. "Literal Sense." In *Dictionary for Theological Interpretation of the Bible*, edited by Kevin J. Vanhoozer, 455–56. Grand Rapids: Baker Academic, 2005.

Griffiths, Paul. *Religious Reading: The Place of Reading in the Practice of Religion*. New York: Oxford University Press, 1999.

Guigo II. *The Ladder of Monks*. Translated by E. Colledge and J. Walsh. Kalamazoo, MI: Cistercian, 1979.

Gwynn, David M. *Athanasius of Alexandria: Bishop, Theologian, Ascetic, Father*. Oxford: Oxford University Press, 2012.

Hanson, N. R. *Patterns of Discovery*. London: Cambridge University Press, 1958.

Hanson, R. P. C. *Allegory and Event: A Study of the Sources and Significance of Origen's Interpretation of Scripture*. Louisville: Westminster John Knox, 2003.

Hardison, O. B., Jr. *Disappearing Through the Skylight: Culture and Technology in the Twentieth Century*. New York: Penguin, 1989.

Heather, Peter. *The Goths*. Cambridge, MA: Blackwell, 1996.

———. *Goths and Romans*. Oxford: Oxford University Press, 1991.

Hecke, P. van. *Metaphor in the Hebrew Bible*. Leuven: Leuven University Press, 2005.

Hecker, Joel. *Mystical Bodies, Mystical Meals: Eating and Embodiment in Jewish Kabbalah*. Detroit: Wayne State University Press, 2005.

Heine, Ronald E. *Origen: Scholarship in the Service of the Church*. Oxford: Oxford University Press, 2010.

Hendrickson, G. L. "Ancient Reading." *CJ* 25 (1929) 182–96.

Hess, Eckhard H. *The Tell-Tale Eye*. New York: Van Nostrand Reinhold, 1975.

Hess, Eckhard H., and J. M. Polt. "Pupil Size in Relation to Mental Activity During Simple Problem Solving." *Science* 43 (1964) 1190–92.

Hildebrandt, Ted A. "Genre of Proverbs." In *Dictionary of the Old Testament: Wisdom, Poetry, and Writings*, edited by Tremper Longman III and Peter Enns, 528–39. Downers Grove, IL: InterVarsity, 2008.

Hirsch, E. D. *The Aim of Interpretation*. Chicago: University of Chicago Press, 1978.

———. *Validity in Interpretation*. New Haven: Yale University Press, 1967.

Holder, A. G. "The Patristic Sources of Bede's Commentary on the Song of Songs." In *StPat*, edited by M. F. Wiles and E. J. Yarndo, 370–75. Leuven: Peeters, 2001.

Hoover, Eric. "The Millennial Muddle: How Stereotyping Students Became a Thriving Industry and a Bundle of Contradictions." *The Chronicle of Higher Education*. October 11, 2009.

Hugh of St. Victor. *The Didascalicon of Hugh of Saint Victor*. Translated by Jerome Taylor. New York: Columbia University Press, 1991.

Illich, Ivan. *In the Vineyard of the Text: A Commentary to Hugh's Didascalicon*. Chicago: University of Chicago, 1993.

Isaac of Nineveh. *Mystic Treatises*. Translated by A. J. Wensick. Piscataway, NJ: Gorgias, 2010.

Jacobs, Alan. *A Theology of Reading: The Hermeneutics of Love*. Boulder, CO: Westview, 2001.

Jasper, David. *A Short Introduction to Hermeneutics*. Louisville: Westminster John Knox, 2004.

Jerome. *Commentariorum In Ezechielem Prophetam Libri Quatuordecim*, PL 25.

———. *Isaiam prophetam*, PL 24.

———. *Selected Letters*. Translated by F. A. Wright. Loeb Classical Library 262. Cambridge, MA: Harvard University Press, 1933.

Johnson, Clifford. *D-branes*. Cambridge: Cambridge University Press, 2003.

Jones, L. Gregory. "Formed and Transformed by Scripture: Character, Community, and Authority in Biblical Interpretation." In *Character and Scripture: Moral Formation,*

Community, and Biblical Interpretation, edited by William P. Brown, 18–33. Grand Rapids: Eerdmans, 2002.

Jungman, Robert. "Mining for Augustinian Gold in John Donne's Meditation 17." *American Notes and Queries* 20 (2007) 16–20.

Kahneman, Daniel. *Attention and Effort*. Englewood Cliffs, NJ: Prentice Hall, 1973.

———. *Thinking, Fast and Slow*. New York: Farrar, Straus and Giroux, 2011.

Kahneman, Daniel, and W. S. Peavler, "Incentive Effects and Pupillary Changes in Association Learning." *Journal of Experimental Psychology* 79 (1969) 312–18.

Kahneman, Daniel, and P. Wright, "Changes of Pupil Size and Rehearsal Strategies in a Short-term Memory Task." *Quarterly Journal of Experimental Psychology* 23 (1971) 187–96.

Kang, Joshua Choonmin. *Scripture by Heart*. Downers Grove, IL: InterVarsity, 2010.

Kardong, Terrence G. *The Life of Saint Benedict by Gregory the Great: Translation and Commentary*. Collegeville, MN: Order of Saint Benedict, 2006.

Katz, Jerrold. J. "Analyticity and Contradiction in Natural Language." In *The Structure of Language*, edited by Jerry A. Foder and Jerrold J. Katz, 519–43. Englewood Cliffs, NJ: Prentice Hall, 1964.

Kearney, R. *On Paul Recoeur*. Brookfield, VT: Ashgate, 2004.

Kelly, J. N. D. *Jerome: His Life, Writings, and Controversies*. New York: Harper & Row, 1975.

Kierkegaard, Søren. *For Self Examination*. Translated by Edna Hong and Howard Hong. Minneapolis: Augsburg, 1940.

Kilgallen, John J. "The Plan of the 'NOMIKOS' (Luke 10:25–37)." *NTS* 42 (1996) 615–19.

Knox, Bernard M. W. "Silent Reading in Antiquity." *GRBS* 9/4 (1968) 421–35.

Kort, Wesley A. "Reading Places/Reading Scriptures." In *Theorizing Scriptures*, edited by Vincent Wimbush, 220–26.. Piscataway, NJ: Rutgers University Press, 2008.

———. *Take, Read*. University Park: Pennsylvania State University Press, 1996.

Kramer, Samuel N. *History Begins at Sumer*. Philadelphia: University of Pennsylvania Press, 1985.

Krey, Philip D. W., and Lesley Smith, eds. *Nicholas of Lyra: The Senses of Scripture*. Leiden: Brill, 2000.

Kuhn, Thomas. *The Structure of Scientific Revolutions*. Chicago: University of Chicago Press, 1996.

Kulikowski, Michael. *Rome's Gothic Wars: From the Third Century to Alaric*. Cambridge: Cambridge University Press, 2007.

Kushner, Harold S. *When Bad Things Happen to Good People*. New York: Random House, 1981.

Kysar, Robert. *Stumbling in the Light: New Testament Images for a Changing Church*. St. Louis: Chalice, 1999.

Lakoff, George, and Mark Johnson. *Metaphors We Live By*. Chicago: University of Chicago Press, 1980.

———. *Philosophy in the Flesh*. New York: Basic, 1999.

Lambert, W. G. *Babylonian Wisdom Literature*. Winona Lake, IN: Eisenbrauns, 1996.

Lane, Anthony N. S. *Bernard of Clairvaux: Theologian of the Cross*. Collegeville, MN: Liturgical, 2013.

Law, David. *Inspiration*. London: Continuum, 2001.

Leclercq, Jean. *The Love of Learning and the Desire for God*. Translated by Catharine Misrahi. New York: Fordham University Press, 1982.

Leithart, Peter J. *Athanasius*. Grand Rapids: Baker, 2011.

———. *Deep Exegesis: The Mystery of Reading Scripture*. Waco, TX: Baylor University Press, 2009.

LeMoine, Fannie J. "Jerome's Gift to Women Readers." In *Shifting Frontiers in Late Antiquity*, edited by Ralph W. Mathisen and Hagith S. Sivan, 230–41. Brookfield, VT: Ashgate, 1996.

Levering, Matthew. *The Theology of Augustine: An Introductory Guide to His Most Important Works*. Grand Rapids: Baker, 2013.

Longman, Tremper, III. "Book of Proverbs." In *Dictionary of the Old Testament: Wisdom, Poetry, and Writings*, edited by Tremper Longman III and Peter Enns, 539–52. Downers Grove, IL: InterVarsity, 2008.

Lubac, Henri de. *History and Spirit: The Understanding of Scripture According to Origen*. Translated by Anne Englund Nash. San Francisco: Ignatius, 2007.

———. *Medieval Exegesis*. 2 vols. Grand Rapids: Eerdmans, 1998, 2000.

———. "Spiritual Understanding." In *The Theological Interpretation of Scripture*, edited by Stephen E. Fowl, 3–25. Oxford: Blackwell, 1997.

Mach, Ernst. *The Analysis of Sensations*. Chicago: Open Court, 1914.

Magrassi, Mariano. *Praying the Bible: An Introduction to Lectio Divina*. Translated by E. Hagman. Collegeville, MN: Liturgical, 1998.

Mandelbrot, Benoit B. *The Fractal Geometry of Nature*. New York: Freeman, 1977.

Mangina, Joseph L. *Karl Barth: Theologian of Christian Witness*. Louisville: Westminster, 2004.

Manguel, Alberto. *A History of Reading*. New York: Penguin, 1996.

———. *The Traveler, the Tower, and the Worm: The Reader as Metaphor*. Philadelphia: University of Pennsylvania Press, 2013.

Marshall, I. Howard. *Beyond the Bible: Moving From Scripture to Theology*. Grand Rapids: Baker Academic, 2004.

Martens, Peter. *Origen and Scripture: The Contours of the Exegetical Life*. Oxford: Oxford University Press, 2012.

Martin, Francis. "Spiritual Sense." In *Dictionary for Theological Interpretation of the Bible*, edited by Kevin J. Vanhoozer, 769–72. Grand Rapids: Baker Academic, 2005.

Massimini, F., and M. Carli. "The Systematic Assessment of Flow in Daily Experience." In *Optimal Experience: Psychological Studies of Flow in Consciousness*, edited by M. Csikszentmihalyi and I. S. Csikszentmihalyi, 288–306. New York: Cambridge University Press, 1988.

McGinn, Bernard. *The Growth of Mysticism: Gregory the Great through the 12th Century*. New York: Crossroad, 1996.

McGuckin, John Anthony, ed. *The Westminster Handbook to Origen*. Louisville: Westminster John Knox, 2004.

Mellaart, James. *The Neolithic of the Near East*. New York: Scribner's, 1975.

Merton, Thomas. *Opening the Bible*. Collegeville, MN: Liturgical, 1970.

Metzger, Bruce M. *The Canon of the New Testament: Its Origin, Development, and Significance*. Oxford: Oxford University Press, 1987.

———. *The Text of the New Testament*. New York: Oxford University Press, 1992.

Migne, J.-P., ed. *Patrologia graeca*. 162 vols. Paris, 1857–1886.

———. *Patrologia latina*. 217 vols. Paris, 1844–1864.

Miller, Donald. *Blue Like Jazz*. Nashville: Thomas Nelson, 2003.

Misch, Georg. *A History of Autobiography in Antiquity*. Translated by E. W. Dickes. Cambridge, MA: Harvard University Press, 1951.

Möller, Karl. "Renewing Historical Criticism." In *Renewing Biblical Interpretation*, edited by Craig G. Bartholomew, Colin J. D. Greene, Karl Möller, 145–71. Grand Rapids: Zondervan, 2000.

Mulholland, M. Robert, Jr. *Shaped By The Word: The Power of Scripture in Spiritual Formation*. Nashville: Upper Room, 1985.

Mulvenna, Catherine M. "Synaesthesia, the Arts and Creativity: A Neurological Connection." In *Neurological Disorders in Famous Artists*, edited by Julien Bogousslavsky and M. G. Hennerici, 202–21. Basel: Karger, 2007.

Musser, George. *The Complete Idiot's Guide to String Theory*. Indianapolis: Alpha, 2008.

Nachmanson, Ernst. *Der griechische Buchtitel*. Darmstadt, Ger.: Wissenschaftliche Buchges, 1969.

Nakamura, J., and M. Csikszentmihalyi. "Flow Theory and Research." In *Handbook of Positive Psychology*, edited by C. R. Snyder and S. J. Lopez, 195–206. Oxford: Oxford University Press, 2009.

Newton, Francis. *The Scriptorium and Library at Monte Cassino, 1058–1105*. Cambridge: Cambridge University Press, 1999.

Norman, D. A. *Memory and Attention*. New York: Wiley, 1976.

O'Connell, Marvin R. *Blaise Pascal: Reasons of the Heart*. Grand Rapids: Eerdmans, 1997.

O'Keefe, John J., and R. R. Reno. *Sanctified Vision: An Introduction to Early Christian Interpretation of the Bible*. Baltimore: Johns Hopkins University Press, 2005.

Oliverio, L. William. *Theological Hermeneutics in the Classical Pentecostal Tradition*. Boston: Brill, 2012.

Origen. *On First Principles*. Translated by G. W. Butterworth. Gloucester, MA: Peter Smith, 1973.

———. "Letter of Origen to Gregory." Translated by M. Slusser. FC 98:192.

Osborne, Grant R. *The Hermeneutical Spiral: A Comprehensive Introduction to Biblical Interpretation*. Downers Grove, IL: InterVarsity, 2006.

Ouellette, J. A., and Wendy Wood. "Habit and Intention in Everyday Life: The Multiple Processes by Which Past Behavior Predicts Future Behavior." *Psychological Bulletin* 124 (1998) 54–74.

Paddison, Angus. *Scripture: A Very Theological Proposal*. London: T. & T. Clark, 2009.

Paredi, Angelo. *Saint Ambrose: His Life and Times*. Translated by Joseph Costelloe. Notre Dame: University of Notre Dame Press, 1964.

Pauw, Amy Plantinga. "Attending to the Gaps between Beliefs and Practices." In *Practicing Theology*, edited by Miroslav Volf and Dorothy C. Bass, 33–48. Grand Rapids: Eerdmans, 2002.

Pennington, M. Basil. *Bernard of Clairvaux: Lover Teaching the Way of Love*. Hyde Park, NY: New City, 1997.

Peterson, Eugene H. *Christ Plays in Ten Thousand Places: A Conversation in Spiritual Theology* Grand Rapids: Eerdmans, 2005.

———. *Eat This Book*. Grand Rapids: Eerdmans, 2006.

Pinnock, Clark H., and Barry L. Callen. *The Scripture Principle*. Grand Rapids: Baker, 2006.

Porter, Stanley E., and Jason C. Robinson. *Hermeneutics: An Introduction to Interpretive Theory*. Grand Rapids: Eerdmans, 2011.

Poulet, Georges. "Phenomenology of Reading." *New Literary History* 1 (1969–70) 53–68.

Preus, James Samuel. *From Shadow to Promise: Old Testament Interpretation from Augustine to the Young Luther*. Cambridge, MA: Harvard University Press, 1969.

Rae, Murray A. *History and Hermeneutics*. London: T. & T. Clark, 2005.

Rebenich, Stefan. *Jerome*. New York: Routledge, 2002.

Robertson, Duncan. *Lectio Divina: The Medieval Experience of Reading*. Collegeville, MN: Liturgical, 2011.

Rusconi, Robert. *Francis of Assisi in the Sources and Writings*. Translated by Nancy Celaschi. St. Bonaventure, NY: Franciscan Institute, 2008.

Saenger, Paul. *Space Between Words: The Origins of Silent Reading*. Stanford: Stanford University Press, 1997.

Sandor, Monica. "Lectio Divina and the Monastic Spirituality of Reading." *American Benedictine Review* 40 (1989) 82–114.

Schröder, Bianca-Jeanette. *Titel und Text*. Berlin: de Gruyter, 1999.

Schubart, Wilhelm. *Das Buch bei den Griechen und Römern*. Leipzig: de Gruyter, 1921.

Schwarcz, Andreas. "Cult and Religion Among the Tervingi and the Visigoths and their Conversion to Christianity." In *The Visigoths: From the Migration Period to the Seventh Century*, edited by Peter Heather, 447–58. Woolbridge, UK: Boydell, 1999.

Seitz, Christopher R. *Word Without End*. Waco, TX: Baylor University Press, 2004.

Sheppard, Gerald T. "Biblical Interpretation after Gadamer." *PNEUMA* 16 (1994) 121–41.

Simner, J., et. al. "Synaesthesia: The Prevalence of Atypical Cross-Modal Experiences." *Perception* 35 (2006) 1024–33.

Simpson, Evelyn M., and George R. Potter, eds. *The Sermons of John Donne*. Oxford: Clarendon, 1948.

Smith, Frank. *Understanding Reading: A Psycholinguistic Analysis of Reading and Learning to Read*. New York: Routledge, 2012.

Smith, James K. A. *The Fall of Interpretation: Philosophical Foundations for a Creational Hermeneutic*. Downers Grove, IL: InterVarsity, 2000.

Soccio, Douglas J. *Archetypes of Wisdom: Introduction to Philosophy*. Boston: Wadsworth, 2013.

Sommerfeldt, John R. *Bernard of Clairvaux on the Life of the Mind*. Mahwah, NJ: Neuman, 2004.

Soskice, Janet. *Metaphor and Religious Language*. Oxford: Cambridge University Press, 1985.

Steinmetz, David. "The Superiority of Pre-Critical Exegesis." In *The Theological Interpretation of Scripture*, edited by Stephen E. Fowl, 26–38. Oxford: Blackwell, 1997.

———. "Uncovering a Second Narrative: Detective Fiction and the Construction of Historical Method." In *The Art of Reading Scripture*, edited by E. F. Davis and R. B. Hays, 54–65. Grand Rapids: Eerdmans, 2003.

Stemberger, Gunter. *Jews and Christians in the Holy Land: Palestine in the Fourth Century*. Edinburgh: T. & T. Clark, 2000.

Stendahl, Krister. "Biblical Theology, Contemporary." In *The Interpreter's Dictionary of the Bible*, edited by George A. Buttrick, 1:418–32. Nashville: Abingdon, 1962.

Stewart, Columba. *Cassian the Monk*. New York: Oxford University Press, 1998.

Stiver, Dan. *Theology after Ricoeur: New Directions in Hermeneutical Theology*. Louisville: Westminster John Knox, 2001.

Strack, H. L., and Gunter Stemberger. *Introduction to the Talmud and Midrash*. Translated by Markus Bockmuehl. Minneapolis: Fortress, 1992.

Strauss, William, and Neil Howe. *Generations: The History of America's Future, 1584 to 2069*. New York: William Morrow, 1992.

———. *Millennials Rising: The Next Great Generation*. New York: Vintage, 2000.

Stock, Brian. *After Augustine: The Meditative Reader and the Text*. Philadelphia: University of Pennsylvania Press, 2001.

———. *Augustine's Inner Dialogue*. Cambridge: Cambridge University Press, 2010.

———. *Augustine the Reader: Meditation, Self-Knowledge, and the Ethics of Interpretation*. Cambridge, MA: Harvard University Press, 1996.

Studzinski, Raymond. *Reading to Live: The Evolving Practice of Lectio Divina*. Collegeville, MN: Liturgical, 2009.

Taylor, Jerome. *The Didascalicon of Hugh of Saint Victor*. New York: Columbia University Press, 1991.

Taylor, John Hammand. "St. Augustine and the *Hortensius* of Cicero." *Studies in Philology* 60 (1963) 487–98.

Teske, Roland. *Augustine's Letters 156–210*. New York: New City, 2000.

Thiselton, Anthony C. *Hermeneutics: An Introduction*. Grand Rapids: Eerdmans, 2009.

———. *New Horizons in Hermeneutics*. Grand Rapids: Zondervan, 1992.

———. "Semantics and New Testament Interpretation." In *New Testament Interpretation*, edited by I. Howard Marshall, 75–104. Grand Rapids: Eerdmans, 1977.

Thompson, Augustine. *Francis of Assisi: A New Biography*. Ithaca, NY: Cornell University Press, 2012.

Thompson, E. A. *The Visigoths in the Time of Ulfila*. London: Duckworth, 2008.

Thornton, John F., and Susan B. Varenne, eds. *Honey and Salt: Selected Spiritual Writings of Saint Bernard of Clairvaux*. New York: Vintage, 2007.

Thurneysen, Eduard. *A Theology of Pastoral Care*. Eugene, OR: Wipf & Stock, 2010.

Treat, Jay Curry. "The Epistle of Barnabas." In *The Anchor Bible Dictionary*, edited by David N. Freedman, 1:611–14. New York: Doubleday, 1992.

Treier, Daniel J. *Introducing Theological Interpretation of Scripture: Recovering a Christian Practice*. Grand Rapids: Baker, 2008.

Triandis, Harry C. *Interpersonal Behavior*. Monterey, CA: Brooks/Cole, 1977.

Trigg, Joseph W. *Origen*. New York: Routledge, 1998.

Turner, Eric G. *Greek Manuscripts of the Ancient World* Princeton, N.J.: Princeton University Press, 1968.

Twenge, Jean M. *Generation Me: Why Today's Young American Are More Confident, Assertive, Entitled—and More Miserable than Ever Before*. New York: Free Press, 2006.

Twenge, Jean M., and W. Keith Campbell. *The Narcissism Epidemic*. New York: Atria, 2013.

Vaccaro, Jody L. "Digging for Buried Treasure: Origen's Spiritual Interpretation of Scripture." *Communio* 25 (1998) 757–75.

Valdes, M. J., ed. *A Ricoeur Reader*. Toronto: University of Toronto Press, 1991.

Van Buren, Paul. *According to the Scriptures: The Origins of the Gospel and the Church's Old Testament*. Grand Rapids: Eerdmans, 1998.

———. "On Reading Someone Else's Mail: The Church and Israel's Scriptures." In *Die Hebräische Bibel und ihre zweifache Nachgeschichte*, edited by Ehrard Blum et al., 595–606. Neukirchen-Vluyn: Neukirchener, 1990.

Van Fleteren, Frederick. "The Principles of Augustine's Hermeneutic: An Overview." In *Augustine: Biblical Exegete*, edited by Frederick Van Fleteren and Joseph C. Schnaubelt, 1–32. New York: Peter Lang, 2001.

Vanhoozer, Kevin J. *Biblical Narrative in the Philosophy of Paul Ricoeur*. Cambridge: Cambridge University Press, 1990.

———. *The Drama of Doctrine A Canonical-Linguistic Approach To Christian Theology*. Louisville: Westminster John Knox, 2005.

———. *First Theology: God, Scripture, and Hermeneutics*. Downers Grove, IL: InterVarsity, 2002.

———. *Is There Meaning in This Text? The Bible, the Reader, and the Morality of Literary Knowledge*. Grand Rapids: Zondervan, 1998

———. "The Spirit of Understanding: Special Revelation and General Hermeneutics." In *Disciplining Hermeneutics: Interpretation in Christian Perspective*, edited by Roger Lundin, 131–66. Grand Rapids: Eerdmans, 1997.

Vauchez, Andre. *Francis of Assisi: The Life and Afterlife of a Medieval Saint*. New Haven: Yale University Press, 2013.

Verplanken, Bas, and Wendy Wood. "Interventions to Break and Create Consumer Habits." *Journal of Public Policy and Marketing* 25 (2006) 90–103.

Virkler, Henry A. *Hermeneutics: Principles and Processes of Biblical Interpretation*. Grand Rapids: Baker, 2007.

Visotzky, Burton L. *The Midrash on Proverbs*. New Haven: Yale University Press, 1992.

Vogüé, Adalbert de. *The Rule of Saint Benedict: A Doctrinal and Spiritual Commentary*. Translated by J. B. Hasbrouck. Kalamazoo, MI: Cistercian, 1983.

Ward, Graham. "Allegoria: Reading as a Spiritual Exercise." *Modern Theology* 15/3 (1999) 271–95.

Ward, Timothy. *Words of Life: Scripture as the Living and Active Word of God*. Downers Grove, IL: InterVarsity, 2009.

Watson, Francis. "Authors, Readers Hermeneutics." In *Reading Scripture With The Church*, edited by K. M. Adam et al., 119-23. Grand Rapids: Baker Academic, 2006.

Weber, Ronald J. "Albinus: The Living Memory of a Fifth Century Personality." *Historia: Zeitschrift für Alte Geschichte* 38 (1989) 472–97.

Webster, John. *Holy Scripture: A Dogmatic Approach*. Cambridge: Cambridge University Press, 2003.

———. "Reading Scripture Eschatologically." In *Reading Texts, Seeking Wisdom*, edited by David F. Ford and Graham Stranton, 245–56. London: SCM, 2003.

———. *Word and Church: Essays in Church Dogmatics*. New York: T. & T. Clark, 2001.

Wegner, Paul D. *The Journey from Texts to Translations*. Grand Rapids: Baker, 1999.

Weinandy, Thomas G. *Athanasius: A Theological Introduction*. Burlington, VT: Ashgate, 2007.

Weiss, Meir. *The Bible from Within*. Jerusalem: Magnes, 1984.

West, Norvene. *No Moment Too Small: Rhythms of Silence, Prayer, and Holy Reading*. Kalamazoo, MI: Cistercian, 1994.

White, G. I., and L. Maltzman. "Pupillary Activity While Listening to Verbal Passages." *Journal of Research in Personality* 12 (1977) 361–69.

William of Saint Thierry. *The Golden Epistle: A Letter to the Brethren at Mont Dieu*. Translated by Theodore Berkeley. Spencer, MA: Cistercian, 1971.

Williams, Megan Hale. *The Monk and the Book: Jerome and the Making of Christian Scholarship*. Chicago: University of Chicago Press, 2006.

Williams, Peter J. "The Bible, the Septuagint, and the Apocrypha: A Consideration of Their Singularity." In *Studies on the Text and Versions of the Hebrew Bible in Honour of Robert Gordon*, edited by Geoffry Kahn and Diana Lipton, 169–90. Leiden: Brill, 2012.

Wirt, Sherwood E., ed. *The Confessions of Augustine in Modern English*. Grand Rapids: Zondervan, 1971.

Wittgenstein, Ludwig. *Culture and Value*. Translated by Peter Winch. Oxford: Blackwell, 1980.

———. *Zettel*. Translated by G. E. M. Anscombe. Oxford: Blackwell, 1967.

Wolf, Maryanne. *Proust and the Squid: The Story and Science of the Reading Brain*. New York: Harper Perennial, 2008.

Wolterstorff, Nicholas. *Divine Discourse*. Cambridge: Cambridge University Press, 1997.

Wood, Wendy, et al. "Changing Circumstances, Disrupting Habits." *Journal of Personality and Social Psychology* 88 (2005) 918–33.

Wright, N. T. *The New Testament and the People of God*. London: SPCK, 1992.

———. *Scripture and the Authority of God*. New York: HarperCollins, 2011.

Wright, William. *A Short History of Syriac Literature*. London: Adam and Charles Black, 1894.

Yankah, Kwesi. "Do Proverbs Contradict?" In *Wise Words*, edited by Wolfgang Mieder, 127–41. New York: Garland, 1994.

Yong, Amos. *Beyond the Impasse: Toward a Pneumatological Theology of Religions*. Grand Rapids: Baker Academic, 2003.

———. *Spirit-Word-Community: Theological Hermeneutics in Trinitarian Perspective*. Eugene, OR: Wipf & Stock, 2002.

Zinn, Grover A., Jr. "Hugh of Saint Victor and the Art of Memory." *Viator* 5 (1974) 211–34.

Subject Index

Abraham, William, 50n44
Achtemeier, Paul J., 50n44
Adam, A. K. M., 154n33
Adamson, Donald, 107n5
Adele, 22–23
Adversus Haereses, 3n3
Aeneid, The, 139, 139n61
Aesop, 59–60
Aland, Kurt and Barbara, 8n9
Alaric, 112n23, 113, 113n28
Alexander the Great, 4n5
Alexander, Patrick, H., 23
All I Really Need to Know I Learned in Kindergartern, 123, 124n19
allegory/allegorical, 91, 135–39. 141–43
Allen, Woody, 24
Alster, Bendt, 159n39
Alypius, 43–44
Ambrose, 80n2, 86, 86n20, 87, 94, 108, 140, 140n65, 141, 171, 172n27
anagogic, 137
analogy, 30, 35, 37, 128, 141
  synesthetic, 29
  thematic, 29
anthropology, 37
Apponius, 171n24
Aquinas, Thomas, Saint, 138, 139n58
Aramaic, 4n4
Archer, Kenneth J., 133n31, 173, 173n37
Arden, John Boghosian, 85n15
Aristotle, 3n3, 28, 60, 130
Arithmoi, 6

Arlotto, Anthony, 177n3
assiduity/assiduously, 73–74, 74n28, 75
Athanasius, 113, 113n26
Augustine, Saint, 7, 42, 42n19, 43, 43n21, 44–45, 55, 55n4, 58, 61–62, 73, 73n26, 80n2, 82–83, 86–87, 87n22, 90n28, 94, 99, 106–107, 107n8–9, 108, 108n11, 109, 109n14, 110-12, 112n22–23, 113–15, 115n36, 119, 119n8, 124, 127, 137–39, 139n61, 140, 140n62–64, 141, 143–144, 144n77, 145–46, 146n90, 147, 147n91, 149, 149n4, 150, 150n6–7, 151, 156, 160, 160n42–43, 161, 169–70, 173, 173n33, 174–75, 175n39
autopistia, 48, 48n37, 49, 51
autotelic, 70, 72–73

Balogh, Josef, 86n19
Balthasar, Hans Urs von, 74n30
Barth, Karl, 38–39, 39n9,11, 40, 40n12, 41, 44, 44n24, 4b
basal ganglia, 58, 58n13, 59
Basil the Great, 155
Belt, Henk van den, 47, 47n33, 48n38, 49, 49n41
Benedict, Saint, 84, 84n14
Berkhof, Louis, 45n29
Berkouwer, G. C., 45n29
Bernard of Clairvaux, 128, 128n13, 129, 129n14, 139

Ancient Document Index

Old Testament/Hebrew Bible

Greco-Roman Writings

Early Christian Writings

Later Christian Writings